Yale Publications in History

Miscellany, 97

THE SEPARATION OF
COLLEGE AND STATE

Columbia, Dartmouth, Harvard, and Yale, 1776-1876

by John S. Whitehead

New Haven and London, Yale University Press, 1973

Designed by John O. C. McCrillis
and set in Baskerville type.
Printed in the United States of America by
The Colonial Press Inc., Clinton, Massachusetts.

Published in Great Britain, Europe, and Africa by
Yale University Press, Ltd., London.
Distributed in Latin America by Kaiman & Polon,
Inc., New York City; in Australasia and Southeast
Asia by John Wiley & Sons Australasia Pty. Ltd.,
Sydney; in India by UBS Publishers' Distributors Pvt.,
Ltd., Delhi; in Japan by John Weatherhill, Inc., Tokyo.

For
George Wilson Pierson

Contents

Editorial Note

Unless otherwise specified, a year in parentheses following a man's name indicates the year of his graduation from college. When the college is obvious from the text, only the year is given. When, on the other hand, the college is not mentioned in the text, the name of the college precedes the year he received his B.A. degree, unless another degree is specified. The letter *e* indicates that the person entered college in that year but never graduated.

A year in parentheses following the name of a college is the year in which the college was chartered.

The following is a brief list of abbreviations frequently used in the footnotes:

CCT	Columbia College Trustees
DCT	Dartmouth College Trustees
HC	Harvard Corporation
YC	Yale Corporation
HUA	Harvard University Archives
DCA	Dartmouth College Archives

When a pamphlet—even though printed—in an archives collection did not appear to be readily available in other libraries, I have indicated the archives in which I found it.

Acknowledgments

In searching for the meaning of the terms *public* and *private,* I have asked for and received the time and patience of many people. Gratefully, I am in their debt.

While this work first took form as a dissertation in the Yale Graduate School, I was guided by George W. Pierson and Robert R. Palmer. Both men gave vast amounts of their time to reading my drafts and, more importantly, warned me of the dangers of vigorous iconoclasm. Brooks M. Kelley read the final manuscript and suggested several alternative interpretations of Yale history.

Men at universities other than Yale and in fields other than history have aided me. W. H. Cowley of Stanford has offered many suggestions on the development of academic government. In a conversation with Dwight C. Miner of Columbia I first learned of that college's early quest for "identity." Both E. Merton Coulter of the University of Georgia and Henry Nash Smith of the University of California, Berkeley, have shared their thoughts on state universities. And Robert M. Hutchins of the Center for the Study of Democratic Institutions told me of his experience as the president of a private university, the University of Chicago.

I would also like to thank the archivists and their staffs at the Harvard University Archives; Columbiana Library and Butler Library, Columbia; Dartmouth College Archives; Yale University Archives and Beinecke Library, Yale, for their help in locating materials and for allowing me to make copies.

During the year I spent revising the manuscript for publication, the Institution for Social and Policy Studies at Yale University kindly provided financial support.

Finally, my appreciation goes to Kirke M. Hasson for typing and, in many instances, editing the manuscript.

J.W.

Selwyn College
Cambridge
April, 1973

Introduction

Although Alexis de Tocqueville made little mention of American institutions of higher education in his *Democracy in America* (1835), James Bryce, an Englishman who used Tocqueville's work as a model for his *American Commonwealth* (1888), devoted an entire chapter to "The Universities." Having no historical perspective from the Frenchman to guide him, Bryce had to categorize the bevy of institutions confronting him by the criteria that seemed evident in the 1880s. Thus he observed, "Most of the American universities are referable to one of two types, which may be described as the older and the newer, or the Private and the Public type." [1] The former type, "usually of private foundation," was controlled by "a body of governors or trustees in whom the property and general control of the institution is vested"; the public type included institutions "established, endowed, and governed by a state, usually through a body of persons called Regents." Bryce's categories probably sound familiar to most readers of today.

The Englishman attempted to expand his definition of the two types beyond a simple description of control and foundation by noting that the private institutions or "colleges" usually followed a prescribed curriculum and housed their students in dormitories, while the public "universities" offered freedom of choice in the curriculum and allowed students to live anywhere they pleased.

After defining these two categories, Bryce went on to note that a number of institutions did not fit neatly into either class. "Some of these," he pointed out, "began as private foundations with a collegiate and quasi-domestic character but have now developed into true universities, generally resem-

---

1. James Bryce, *American Commonwealth*, 2 vols. (London, 1888), 2:527.

bling those of Germany or Scotland. Harvard in Massachusetts and Yale in Connecticut are instances." [2] Bryce found
still other institutions that seemed to resist being categorized:
"Some have been founded by public authority yet have been
practically left to be controlled by a body of self-renewing
trustees. Columbia College in New York City is an instance." [3]

So three of the five oldest institutions in America did not
really fit either the private or the public type.[4] It did not
occur to Bryce to question the historical base of these two
categories, as the present work will try to do, but at least he
noticed that the categories were not fast and solid. Were
Harvard, Yale, and Columbia maverick institutions or had
they developed during a time when it did not occur to anyone to type institutions as private or public? That question
Bryce did not choose to pursue.

Ten years later, in 1898, many Americans had forgotten
the exceptions to the rule Bryce had emphasized and simply
assumed that two distinct categories existed. The private institutions, which supported themselves through tuitions and
endowments, were thought to represent the older, traditional
American way of higher education; the public or state universities, which received legislative appropriations, were radical innovations.

This view seemed so entrenched that a number of educators, including the presidents of some of the "new" state
universities, held a conference on State Aid to Higher Education at the even newer Johns Hopkins University to offer
some historical insight into the origins of the private and
public types. Charles K. Adams, president of the University
of Wisconsin, opened the session by saying:

> It has sometimes been asserted and at other times as-
> sumed that the policy of supporting higher education by
> the State is in this country practically a new policy, or

2. Ibid.
3. Ibid., p. 528.
4. Harvard, 1636; William and Mary, 1693; Yale, 1701; Princeton, 1746;
Columbia (Kings), 1754.

one which does not rest upon a traditional or historical
foundation . . . very few seem to be aware of the fact
that State assistance to education, in all its branches, has
been the traditional policy of the country.[5]

Adams went on to explain that in the last seventy-five years
the oldest colleges, "which, during their infancy had been
nursed into vigor and efficiency by public support, had been
turned over to the care of their wealthy children and had
ceased to be dependent upon their parents." He added that
these older colleges were later joined by newer institutions
established through denominational zeal and private benevolence. "It is nevertheless true," he concluded, "that beneath
and back of these specious appearances is the great fact that
during the whole of the first two hundred years of our history
education in all of its grades was chiefly supported by the
taxation of all the people." [6]

Adams exaggerated the case somewhat. Taxation had rarely
been used to support colleges, but for nearly fifty years after
the American Revolution state governments had made land
grants and cash grants resulting from "windfalls" such as
bonuses for bank charters or federal refunds for wartime expenses to such colleges as Yale, Harvard, Columbia, and Dartmouth—all institutions that would certainly have been called
"private" by the standards of 1898. Also, these four private
colleges had at one time been connected with their respective
states in matters of supervision and control. The Massachusetts General Court had elected Harvard's board of overseers
until 1865; in Connecticut the governor, lieutenant governor,
and six state senators had sat on the Yale Corporation until
1872; and the governor of New Hampshire still sat on the
Dartmouth Board of Trustees in 1898, just as he had done
in 1769 when the college was founded. Though state officials
had been represented on Columbia's board of trustees only

5. Herbert B. Adams, ed., *State Aid to Higher Education* (Baltimore, 1898),
p. 1.
6. Ibid., p. 2.

for a brief period in the 1780s, the college was technically under the supervision of the University of the State of New York even when Bryce made his visit.

Despite his exaggerations, Charles K. Adams offered a clue in his 1898 speech at Johns Hopkins which might explain why Bryce could not easily fit some of the older institutions into his categories: the institutions had changed; for some reason there had been a separation of college and state and a consequent transformation of the colleges from quasi-public to private institutions. Also, had Adams talked with Bryce, he might have explained that the two categories the Englishman thought were clear had really been distinct for a very short time—in fact, less than two decades before Bryce's 1884 visit.[7] Before that time the connections, and lack of connections, between colleges and states were so varied and changing that it would have been difficult, if not impossible, to perceive two clear categories. Had Tocqueville bothered to describe higher education in 1835, he probably would not have made a distinction between private and public at all.

Though Adams offered a clue to the background of Bryce's public and private categories, he did not give the complete history. This book will attempt to paint the picture that Adams only sketched. To do this, four colleges will be studied in detail—the three Bryce mentioned, Yale, Harvard, and Columbia; and Dartmouth, the college which, with the aid of Daniel Webster, seemingly asserted its independence from the state in the famous Dartmouth College case of 1816–19.

My history will trace the development of these four institutions from the time of the American Revolution, when all four maintained some connection with a state government, until 1876, when that previous alliance seemed to have disappeared.

In tracing the separation of college and state an argument will be made that a distinction between private and public

7. Though Bryce did not talk with Charles K. Adams, he met James B. Angell, president of the University of Michigan, and Andrew D. White, president of Cornell. Both men shared Adams's view of the origins of state support for higher education.

or state institutions was not commonly recognized before the Civil War. Hence, references will be made to the antebellum state universities to show in what way they differed or did not differ from our four colleges.

One might ask at this point why I have not chosen to study the fate of the other colonial colleges (Princeton, Rutgers, Brown, Pennsylvania, and William and Mary) from 1776 to 1876. And if the state universities will be examined, why not investigate the scores of denominational colleges that were founded in the nineteenth century without state control or support?

I have omitted a detailed study of the other five colonial colleges, frankly, so that I could provide a thorough history of four colleges which, I think, underwent the most interesting transformation over the course of the century—and which did not collapse in the process, as did William and Mary. Still, does the omission of these colleges affect the assertion that no clear distinction between private and public emerged before the Civil War? I think not. It is true that at Princeton, Rutgers, and Pennsylvania (except for a brief period after the Revolution) connections of state support and control were minimal. And such connections were nonexistent at Brown. But none of these institutions, to my knowledge, asserted itself to be independent of the state in the way that Charles Eliot proclaimed Harvard's freedom in the 1870s (see chapter 5). Even William and Mary, the college that had been as closely allied to Virginia in the colonial and revolutionary periods as Harvard had been to Massachusetts, did not call itself "private" after Jefferson created his University of Virginia in 1819.

Historians such as Willard Smith and Elmer E. Brown have indicated that in the colonial period the interests of college and state were allied in all the colleges—including Brown where no state support or control was ever present.[8]

8. Willard Wallace Smith, "The Relations of College and State in Colonial America," (Ph.D. diss., Columbia University, 1950), and Elmer E. Brown, *The Origin of American State Universities* (Berkeley, 1903). See chapter 2 for more on Brown.

Thus, the "private" college was not a colonial creation. But these same historians and others do claim that a distinction between private and public arose before the Civil War. They base this, however, not on any assertion of "privateness" by institutions such as Princeton or Brown, which seemed to have little interaction with their states in the first half of the nineteenth century, but on the actions of state governments in creating distinctly different and new institutions after the Dartmouth College decision. It is this latter claim that I will try to refute by arguing that no clear distinction existed before the Civil War (see chapter 2).

As for the denominational colleges founded in the nineteenth century, I refer the reader to my comments in chapter 5 on the attempts of some of these colleges to obtain state aid. Even the church colleges of the antebellum period did not actively declare themselves independent of the state.

If it is remembered that this is a study of the transformation of four colleges, but nonetheless a study with broader implications, I think the omission of some of the colonial colleges and of the nineteenth-century denominational colleges is justified. Of course, every reader may think of certain instances that would curtail the limits of the generalizations.

For the most part the college-state relationship will be viewed from the rather legalistic perspective of financial support and of control either through state representation on a board of trustees or through visitorial power exercised by an external state body such as the University of the State of New York. This will be a story of the external interactions between the institutions and state governments rather than of curricular development or of student life. However, these internal components often affected external relations. They will be touched upon when relevant.

Although "facts" are obviously the most crucial and persuasive part of any history, the connection between campus and state house was often more subtle than the legal connections might have indicated. It was frequently influenced by the college's view of itself and the state's view of the college, regardless of support or control. To some extent Bryce was correct in calling "colleges" private and "universities" public. At different times our four institutions used both labels. In changing titles they often changed their self-image. For example, Dartmouth, which had proudly called itself a "university" in the first fifteen years of the nineteenth century, suddenly became a "college" to defend itself against the state in 1816. So images as well as facts enter into the history. With these indications of what is to come, let us begin our story and see in what manner our "private" colleges were once allied with their respective states.

1 A Variety of Alliances Between College and State, 1776–1820

Much of all universities consist of endowments by individual persons and public communities or States or Princes.

Ezra Stiles, 1777

By 1776 the respective alliances between Columbia, Dartmouth, Harvard, and Yale and the newly emerging states of New York, New Hampshire, Massachusetts, and Connecticut were not uniform; they varied from college to college in regard to supervision, support, and founding. At Harvard and Columbia a substantial number of state officials held supervisory power ex officio over the institutions, at Dartmouth only the governor was allied with the college, and at Yale state officials were not represented in the governing structure at all. While no college ever received all of its funds from a legislature, the proportion of public aid in relation to student fees and private philanthropy differed from institution to institution. Finally, although all of the institutions based their legal existence on a charter issued by a civil authority, two of our colleges, Harvard and Yale, had received their charters from colonial assemblies, while Columbia and Dartmouth had been chartered by the king of Great Britain.

Despite the diversity among these alliances, two commonly held beliefs underlay, and to some extent allowed, the variations. It was assumed by many people that the states should necessarily take an interest in and feel some responsibility for the life of institutions which admittedly trained civil leaders. Also, it was thought that by training these leaders the colleges obviously expressed concern for the welfare of the state. College and state, at least our colleges and our states, were implicated with each other. So entwined were the two

that public financial support was often thought to be a duty
of the legislature rather than a charitable gift. Professor
Dwight C. Miner of Columbia has observed that, as a seminary for future government officials, Columbia felt "entitled"
to state support in the colonial and early national periods.[1]

Now and then an individual such as Yale's Thomas Clap
(rector, then president, 1740–66) had challenged the notion
that college and state were intimately connected and had
announced the independence of the institution from the
legislature. But the belief in a connection between college
and state survived his attack, and by 1776 it still remained
a part of Yale's colonial legacy.

As long as the necessity of a college-state alliance was held
almost as an article of faith, the precise form that alliance
took was not really crucial. Often the stronger the trust between college and state, the less need for complicated legal
connections of supervision was felt; the converse was also
true. Also, the precise proportions of public and private support, from both individuals and churches, was rarely a subject of controversy. Individuals, churches, and legislatures
did not hesitate to combine their resources for the good of
an institution. Since these parties rarely became jealous or
fearful of the contribution made by each other, the proportions of financial support from different sources could fluc-
tuate depending on local circumstances.

To illustrate the variety of alliances that had developed
by the year of independence, a brief review of the founding
and colonial history of our institutions will help.[2] After all,

1. Conversation between J. S. W. and Dwight C. Miner, March 17, 1971.
2. An introductory comment is needed here. In the course of this book,
reviews and sketches of the background leading to certain alliances and de-
velopments will be given. Often these vignettes will describe only selected
aspects, say, of the colonial history of our colleges, which seem particularly
relevant to the college-state alliance. They are in no sense intended to be
complete digests or résumés of the past. Hopefully, these sketches will not
seem too superficial or appear to omit important aspects of a college's history
that may not be absolutely necessary to an understanding of the college-state
alliance. At all times, all of our colleges professed functions other than the
training of civil leaders—scholarship, the preservation of morals, and in some

to describe the alliances as they existed in 1776 is really to describe the colonial heritage. Later, the changes in these alliances brought about by the Revolution will be treated.

Harvard had been founded by the General Court of Massachusetts in 1636 with a grant of £400. From the first years of Harvard's existence no one thought this gift of the state constituted a sufficient endowment. In 1638 John Harvard bequeathed £779, and by 1650 other individuals had given the college over £1,056. Although the state allotted the revenue of the Charles River Ferry to Harvard in 1640, private individuals had given more than three times as much money as the state by 1650.

Originally, the affairs and funds of the college were managed by a committee of the assembly, but only six years after founding the college the General Court delegated its supervisory function to a board of overseers consisting of the governor, deputy governor, president of the college, and the magistrates and teaching elders of Cambridge, Watertown, Charlestown, Boston, Roxbury, and Dorchester. By 1650 the private munificence that had been bestowed on the college needed careful management and closer attention than the General Court or the overseers could give. So in that year the assembly chartered the college and created the Harvard Corporation, consisting of five fellows, the president, and the treasurer.[3]

The wording of the charter is instructive for an understanding of its purpose:

---

cases the advocacy of particular theologies. Some people might say these objectives were more important than any civil function. Still, space and time really permit mention only of the events directly affecting the relation to the state. Though my choice of these events out of the web of the past may seem arbitrarily selective, I hope it does not distort the history either of the college in question or of its relation to the state.

3. A good sketch of early Harvard history was reported to the legislature in 1821 as "Report Upon the Constitutional Rights and Privileges of Harvard College and Upon the Donations made by this Commonwealth." A modern account can be found in Samuel Eliot Morison, *Three Centuries of Harvard* (Cambridge, 1936), pp. 3–19, and Margery Somers Foster, *Out of Small Beginnings* (Cambridge, 1962).

> Whereas through the good hand of God many well-
> devoted persons have been and daily are moved and
> stirred up to give and bestow sundry gifts, legacies, lands
> and revenues for the advancement of all good literature,
> arts and sciences in Harvard college. . . . It is therefore
> ordered that for the furthering of so good a work . . .
> that the said College in Cambridge in Middlesex in New
> England shall be a Corporation consisting of seven per-
> sons.

The corporation was given full power to govern the college
with the consent of the overseers. Seven years later (1657) the
power of the corporation was increased so that all of its acts
were immediately operational unless reversed by the overseers.

The Harvard Corporation was the response of the legislature to private munificence. The necessity of holding funds
in perpetuity and managing an increasingly complicated
organization had led the General Court to delegate some of
its authority to a self-perpetuating board of trustees under
the supervision of a public body. But this delegation of
power was not a separation of college and state. The state
had not delegated the college away to private individuals;
the college still needed its guidance. As the donations of
philanthropists were often made in an erratic and uneven
fashion that did not always correspond to the needs of the
college, it was still necessary for the state to finance those
expenses which philanthropy ignored or only partially endowed. The General Court paid the salary of the president
annually until 1781, and when Harvard found, even in the
colonial period, that the income from endowed professorships
rarely paid the full salary necessary to secure a professor for
the chair, the state usually subscribed the difference. Massachusetts also provided funds for the construction of three
buildings at Harvard: Massachusetts Hall (1723), Hollis Hall
(1763), and Harvard Hall (1765).

The public contribution to Harvard took the form of

founding grants, operational funds, and building expenses. This money was spent immediately rather than put into an accumulating fund. Thus the combination of private and public aid at Harvard in the colonial period was complementary. The exuberance of individuals caused the college to expand and grow much faster than if it had depended solely on public support. The state guarded and smoothed this growth. If there was, for instance, money from private sources for professors but no buildings in which they could teach, the state would fill in the missing gap.

Yale had been founded in a somewhat different manner. The college had been organized in 1701 by ten Congregational ministers who had supposedly met at Branford to donate their books for a college.[4] The clerics next secured a charter from the colony to form themselves into a self-perpetuating corporation. Although the state imposed no visitorial board, it did not consider its responsibility fulfilled after merely granting a charter. Connecticut made an annual financial grant to Yale from 1710 to 1754 and numerous special grants for buildings or specific needs, all of which totaled around $21,567. In addition to cash, the state gave the college 1,500 acres of land valued at $600 in 1732.[5]

The charter of 1701 was revised in 1723 and again in 1745, the form which has lasted to the present day. The 1745 charter itemized the financial privileges and encouragements granted by the state. Land and property owned both by the college and by its instructors up to a yearly value of £500 were tax exempt, and an annual appropriation of £100 was to continue at the pleasure of the assembly. Though no mention of public representation on the corporation or of a visitorial committee was made in this document, the colony asserted

4. A number of scholars, including W. H. Cowley of Stanford and Richard Warch of Yale, believe that the meeting of the ministers at Branford was a fictitious story created by Yale President Thomas Clap in 1763 to justify his stand against visitation by the colony. See p. 37 for more on this.

5. All gifts made to Yale by the state and individuals are listed in Ebenezer Baldwin, *Annals of Yale College,* 2d ed. (New Haven, 1838), pp. 306–43.

some control over the college by stating in the charter that the "laws, rules, and ordinances" established by the president and fellows "shall be laid before this Assembly as often as required and may also be repealed or disallowed by this Assembly when they shall think proper." Evidently, the assembly felt that it could maintain some influence over Yale without its physical presence on the corporation. Later that assumption changed.

State connections in the founding of King's College (Columbia) and Dartmouth differed from those at either Harvard or Yale. As previously noted, the king of Great Britain, rather than a colonial assembly, chartered King's and Dartmouth. While the legislature formally allied with or recognized a particular religious denomination in the governing structure of Yale and Harvard, such was not the case in New York or New Hampshire. The 1754 charter of King's College did not place the institution in the hands of the Anglicans, which many people feared would happen because of a proposed gift of land to the college from Trinity Church. Instead, a broadly representative governing board was created through an alliance of public officials with representatives of every religious denomination. Only the president of the college was by charter right an Anglican. As in Connecticut and Massachusetts, the colonial assembly of New York accepted responsibility for the financial well-being of a college chartered within its boundaries, even if by the king, and supported King's College with grants and lotteries totaling $17,358 by the time of the Revolution.[6]

6. The following were ex officio members of the Governors of the College of the Province of New York: Lord Commissioner for Trade and Plantations; governor; lieutenant governor; eldest councilor; judges of the superior court; secretary; attorney-general; Speaker of the General Assembly; treasurer; mayor of New York City; archbishop of Canterbury; rector of Trinity Church; and the ministers of the Reformed Protestant Dutch Church, Ancient Lutheran Church, French Church, Presbyterian Church. In addition, twenty-four men were named to the Governors. A summary of the financial history of King's College can be found in F. B. Hough, *Historical and Statistical Record of the University of the State of New York* (Albany, 1885), p. 17.

Dartmouth differed even from King's. The college began not in New Hampshire but in Connecticut as Moor's Charity School, a school for Indians. The founder of the college, Eleazar Wheelock, raised money for the school in Scotland and England, where resident boards of trustees continued to manage the funds. Being a sort of educational entrepreneur, Wheelock wanted to raise his school to the level of a chartered college and himself to the level of a college president. After Connecticut indicated that it was uninterested in aiding Wheelock with either a charter or financial support, he set out with his school in his satchel to find a buyer. Before long he discovered a client, John Wentworth, royal governor of New Hampshire. The governor offered Wheelock a charter to be obtained from the king and, as was customary, some form of financial support — a land grant. Though the title to the property known as Landraff was in doubt, Wheelock accepted the offer, and in December, 1769 Dartmouth was chartered with a board of twelve trustees, including a good number of Wheelock's family. The governor and college president were ex officio members of the board; other charter stipulations specified that eight trustees must be from New Hampshire and seven must be laymen.

The chartering of our four colleges thus exhibited four different alliances with a state: the delegation of authority by a legislature to a corporation overseen by public and clerical officials, the public confirmation of an act by a group of ministers, the creation of a broadly representative corporation, and the sanctioning of an arrangement made by a governor and a private individual. In all four cases, however, the granting of a charter signified the establishment of a self-perpetuating body of men, in some cases allied with or supervised by public officials, who could receive and hold endowments made by individuals and act as agents of the state in awarding degrees. If our colleges had been mere extensions of the legislature receiving annual appropriations, no charter would have been necessary. Also, had a band of educators not wanted the privilege of granting degrees which only the state could give, they could also have existed without a charter. In a symbolic way, the granting of a charter signified the mixed public-private nature of our colleges. And in each case, different circumstances of men, of churches, and of time had affected the proportions of the mixture, and consequently the nature of the college-state alliance.

This mixed nature of our four chartered colleges was a colonial legacy to our states during and after the Revolution. Of course, they did not have to accept this inheritance; they certainly renounced other aspects of the past. But for the next forty-five years, our colleges and states maintained the alliances they had earlier forged. The colleges continued to look to the legislatures for aid, and the legislatures in some cases increased their interest in these institutions by trying to pull them into a closer alliance with the state. And as some of the alliances became more intimate, our colleges often found themselves called "universities."

In Massachusetts, as in most of the other former colonies, independence from Great Britain created the need to plan for statehood in America. When the "Revolutionary worthies," as Edward Everett would later call them, met in 1779 to draft a constitution for a proposed "Commonwealth," Harvard College was much on their minds. The 1780 document that emerged from this convention greatly strengthened the bond between Harvard and Massachusetts. Chapter 5 of the constitution, "The University at Cambridge and Encouragement of Literature," confirmed the 1650 charter of Harvard, made it the duty of the legislature to cherish the interests of the University at Cambridge, and increased state representation on the board of overseers by composing a new body that included the governor, the lieutenant governor, the council, the senate, the president of the college, and the Congregational ministers in Cambridge, Watertown, Charlestown, Boston, Roxbury, and Dorchester.

The constitution even intimated that college officials (i.e. president, professors, and instructors) were viewed as officers of the state. Like civil officials (e.g. sheriffs, justices of the peace, etc.) the college officers were prohibited from holding a seat in the house of representatives or in the senate.

So Harvard was a favored institution of the state. The inclusion of Harvard in the Massachusetts constitution seems to have arisen from a broad-based satisfaction with the college in Massachusetts. Harvard historian Samuel Eliot Morison has noted, "Apparently the College had won golden opinions for the services of her sons in war and peace; and there was no serious objection to her ancient rights and privileges being confirmed by the new regime." [7]

Naturally, the president and fellows thought that this favored status would include financial support. In January, 1781 the corporation petitioned the General Court to establish a permanent salary for the president that would "characterize the General Court as the encourager of literature and be for the honor and reputation of the new constitution." [8] The college was without a president at this time, but when Joseph Willard was inaugurated in December, 1781, the General Court voted him a salary of £300 for one year. Much to the distress of the trustees, the state failed to renew the grant in 1782 or 1783. Fortunately, the lapse was only temporary. A petition to the assembly in June, 1783, noting that Harvard was founded by the "General Assembly of the Ancient Colony of Massachusetts Bay," secured £150 for the president and £100 each for three professors; this gift was repeated in July, 1784. Although these grants were not sufficient to pay the salary of the president, the trustees lent him the remainder in anticipation of a refund from the state. After no refund had come in 1784, 1785, or early 1786, the corporation petitioned the General Court in April, 1786. This time the state granted £480 to the president and £240 to each professor, which it considered to be a full back-payment of all the demands of the college up to August 31, 1786.

The grant of 1786 was the last state financial subsidy until

7. Morison, *Three Centuries of Harvard*, p. 161.
8. HC Minutes, Jan. 31, 1781.

1814. Of course, the trustees did not realize this at the time and repeated their requests for aid from 1786 to 1793. Eventually they concluded that their best chance would be to ask for a lottery authorization; this request was granted in 1793.

Shortly after the financial alliance between Harvard and Massachusetts began to falter, changes both at Harvard and in the General Court brought uncertainty to the link forged between the two in the board of overseers. The drama began at Harvard in 1805 with the election of Henry Ware (1785), a Unitarian, to the Hollis Professorship of Divinity. When Samuel Webber (1784) became president the following year, two of the most important positions in the college were in the hands of Unitarians. At the same time the addition of Chief Justice Theophilus Parsons to the corporation made that body a Federalist stronghold. The college had taken sides — Federalist in politics and Unitarian in religion. In the coming years of denominational and political zeal it would be difficult for Harvard to secure that broad-based support it had enjoyed immediately after the Revolution.

For a while the association of the college along party lines yielded substantial gains. In 1810 a Federalist legislature reduced the size of the board of overseers by removing the state senate and reconstituting the board with the governor, lieutenant governor, counselors, president of the senate, speaker of the house, president of the college, fifteen Congregational ministers, and fifteen laymen to be chosen by the new board rather than the legislature. The preamble to "An Act to Alter and Amend the Constitution of the Board of Overseers of Harvard College" justified the move by claiming, "The Board of Overseers of Harvard College as heretofore constituted cannot conveniently or constantly attend to the diligent discharge of the duties enjoined on it."

Undoubtedly, the presence of the senate on the board of overseers made for an unwieldy body, but Morison has suggested that more than administrative efficiency was at stake in the change of 1810. According to him, the Federalists removed the senate and ended the legislative election of laymen members because they feared a Republican assembly would soon come to power and dominate the overseers, thus exerting an influence over the college.[9]

Two years later, in 1812, that Republican assembly came to power and ordered the corporation to present all documents relating to Harvard and the state. The trustees readily complied, noting that the legislature would certainly see the prosperous condition of the college and want to make a generous monetary contribution.[10] The assembly responded by passing an act that repealed the Act of 1810, thereby restoring the senate to the overseers. The Act of 1812 contained no clause which would require the approval of the corporation and overseers for its implementation.

The president and fellows were outraged at what seemed to be an invasion of their privileges, and protested the altering of the charter without their consent. Although the board of overseers organized by the Act of 1810 was decidedly Federalist, the Federalist trustees disclaimed any partisan position and announced to the legislature, "In regard to the political divisions of the times they believe that persons best acquainted with the course of instruction and discipline in that place will acquit the College of any attempts to prejudice or unduly excite the youthful mind." [11] The corporation went on to say that the Republican legislature should not construe the Act of 1810, written by Harvard's Federalist friends, as an attempt to exclude the General Court from "its just participation in the University."

Yet after protesting the Act of 1812, what more could Harvard do? The fellows admitted that a legislature could properly alter a corporate body with the consent of the trustees, but they did not know if the legislature could take action solely of its own accord. They hoped the Republicans would reconsider and ask for the consent of the college, but the legislature held fast. As it was the board of overseers, not

9. Morison, p. 212.
10. HC Minutes, Jan. 27, 1812.
11. HC Minutes, Feb. 24, 1812.

the corporation, which had been altered by the act, the fellows decided not to challenge the change unless the overseers chose to do so. At first that body wanted to test the validity of the act in court, but on second thought decided not to seek a judicial ruling. Finally, they announced that the legislature had no right to pass the act but turned over their records to the new board. The corporation then voted that as long as the overseers had not challenged the act, they would accept the new board too.[12]

The drama was not over. In 1814 the legislature returned to the Federalists, who promptly passed an act repealing the Act of 1812 and adding the senate to the overseers as constituted in the Act of 1810. The 1814 legislation included a clause calling for the consent of the corporation and overseers, which was quickly given. Now the board of overseers was an even more unwieldy body than it had been before 1810 because the fifteen laymen added in 1810 remained; it contained seventy-seven men, forty-six of whom were annually chosen by the people.

After thrusting the college into a sea of uncertainty for four years, supposedly to protect it from the Republicans, the Federalists at last compensated Harvard financially, along with Williams and Bowdoin, by passing an act in 1814 that distributed the proceeds of a bank tax to these institutions. Harvard received $10,000 annually over the next ten years. Of this grant, one-fourth was to be allotted for scholarships.

The maneuvering and changes in the board of overseers during the 1810–14 period were in many ways a rehearsal for the Dartmouth College case (1816–19). The Federalists, concerned at the prospect of a Republican legislature altering the policy of a college over which they exerted dominant influence, attempted to remove the potentially Republican source of control from the board of overseers. I call this attempt to remove a political body from college government the "Federalist innovation." After seeing that the Republi-

12. HC Minutes, Apr. 15 and June 17, 1812.

cans could change the charter too, the Massachusetts Federalists tried to stabilize the situation with a return to the status quo. In New Hampshire the Federalists tried to "innovate" the college completely out of the realm of legislative action. But that is running ahead of the story. Innovations and changes occurred at other colleges soon after the Revolution.

King's College was virtually immobilized by the Revolution. Myles Cooper, president of the college and a staunch loyalist, had fled New York as early as 1775 in the face of an angry mob of patriots. Academic activities were mostly suspended throughout the Revolutionary period, and the trustees who had often met weekly convened less than ten times between 1776 and 1784. Both the distressed condition of the college and the anticipation that the New York assembly would eventually make some change in a charter that named a college "King's" and placed the archbishop of Canterbury on the board of trustees put the institution in a precarious condition. When the remaining trustees heard that the assembly was thinking of creating a new state university, they petitioned the legislature in 1784 to reorganize the college.

The legislature did far more than merely reorganize King's College. Under the influence of James Duane, mayor of New York, and John Jay (King's, 1764) it passed an act in May, 1784 that created a grand public organization known as the University of the State of New York. King's College, renamed Columbia, was to be a division of the university, and in 1784 the only division. With a governing body called the Regents consisting of state officials, denominational delegates, and representatives from every New York county, the "state university" would govern all academies and "colleges" in New York.[13]

13. The influence of Columbia was evident in the full title of the Act of 1784: "An Act for the Granting Certain Privileges to the College heretofore called King's College, for altering the Name and Charter thereof and Erecting a University in this State." The governor, lieutenant governor, president

The state legislation contained no provision for financial support of the university; this task was left to the regents. They thought the best source of funds could be found among benefactors in France and the Netherlands. To secure this aid they appropriated £410 to send an agent overseas; the following year the regents appointed agents in each New York county to solicit private subscriptions. And the board did not forget the legislature; it suggested that the state might make a grant using a tax on marriage licenses as the source.[14]

Supervision and control rather than financial support appeared to be uppermost in the minds of the assembly. Although it failed to appropriate any money for the university, in 1787 it passed an act to reorganize both the university and its lone division, Columbia College. By this act the college was returned to a self-perpetuating board of trustees who were named; no posts were ex officio. The University of the State of New York became a supervisory body over all colleges and academies in the state and acquired from the legislature the right to incorporate new institutions at these levels.

But why the change? Had Columbia become fearful of state control? The reason lay not so much in any fear of state control as in the stubborn independence expressed both by supporters of Columbia and by those who did not care for the college. This division also reflected the city-country rivalry in New York.

When Columbia agreed — even petitioned — to become part of the state university, both its trustees and other friends saw the college as the dominant force in the university.

---

of the senate, Speaker of the assembly, mayor of New York, mayor of Albany, attorney general and secretary of state were ex officio members of the Regents of the University of the State of New York. The board also included two men from each of New York's twelve counties, a representative from each religious denomination, and potential members to be added when anyone contributed the equivalent of 1,000 bushels of wheat. The officers of each college would sit with the regents when they discussed the affairs of the particular college.

14. Minutes of the Regents of the USNY, June 4 and Apr. 4, 1785.

Through an amendment to the Act of 1784 passed in November of that year, Columbia men secured control of the university by adding thirty-three new regents, twenty of whom must be from New York City, to the board. As long as they held the reins, Columbia could only gain by being a state institution. Its influence and prestige in New York would be enhanced, as the guiding wisdom from the city institution radiated into the provinces of the state. However, in 1785 a group of men from Suffolk County requested the legislature to charter an academy in East Hampton independent of the university. The sponsors claimed they did not want to be under the control of a body dominated by Columbia. The college would not compromise; it refused to be part of a system it did not control. Thus, to pacify all parties, Columbia relinquished its dominant position and the assembly lessened the power of the university.[15]

The city-country, Columbia–non-Columbia split was personified in the two men who were most active in drafting the 1787 bill. Ezra L'Hommedieu, a 1754 graduate of Yale and regent from Suffolk County, wanted the trustees of each college appointed by the state. Alexander Hamilton (King's, 1774e) would not entertain the thought that a country-dominated assembly would ever have a voice in selecting the trustees of Columbia College and succeeded in making the trustees self-perpetuating.

In some ways the 1784–87 change at Columbia was a precursor to the 1810–14 events at Harvard. In both cases the colleges agreed to or acquiesced to the supervision or control of a state body as long as the officials on that body represented the college or the political party associated with the institution. When it looked as if the state board would not be a college board, the Columbia and Harvard interests in the assemblies tried to remove the state body from any control over the college. Rightly or wrongly, these two colleges

15. A full account of the 1784–87 changes in the University of the State of New York can be found in Sidney Sherwood, *The University of the State of New York* (Washington, D.C., 1900), pp. 44–81.

seemed to champion their own particular interests rather than the general diffusion of learning in the state.

Even though Columbia retreated from direct state control in 1787, the new trustees decided that the legislature was still a natural source of funds. It was not assumed that financial support was necessarily tied to control. In 1792 the trustees petitioned for aid. With the support of Governor George Clinton, a Columbia trustee, the assembly granted £6,900 for buildings and £750 annually for five years for the salary of three professors — those of French, Oriental languages, and law. The legislature extended this grant for two additional years, but in 1799 the failure to continue the funds led to an abolition of the new professorships. To counteract the state parsimony, the trustees gave the president and remaining professors the right to charge every student in their classes a fee of eight dollars.[16]

The five-year grant Columbia received in 1792 was a popular form of appropriation in New York. In addition to such a grant for higher education, the legislature had made a five-year appropriation totaling $100,000 to common schools in 1795. By 1800 the common schools, Columbia, and newly chartered Union College (1795) were clamoring for state support. Though Columbia's claim was supported by the regents and Governor John Jay (King's, 1764), only Union won the favor of the assembly, with a grant of $10,000. Both Columbia and the common schools failed to get an appropriation.

The question of state support for education arose again in 1805. Governor Morgan Lewis, a 1773 graduate of Princeton but a trustee of Columbia, concluded that appropriations from the annual revenue of the state would not work. Not only was it cumbersome to make continual grants, but some men, Lewis included, did not want the legislature to have access to money that could be appropriated. "A rich treasury," noted the governor in his address to the assembly, "is frequently an evil. It too often becomes the parent of specula-

16. CCT Minutes, Feb. 22 and Mar. 19, 1799.

tion, and the corruptor of the administrators of the government." Lewis suggested the establishment of an "adequate, permanent and certain fund" to be realized from the sale of unappropriated state lands. The fund would have a capital of $1 million yielding $60,000 a year, and would be under the control of the regents.

As to its disposition, Lewis advised, "A competent sum being first appropriated for the support of colleges, the residue should be applied to the support of, perhaps academies, but certainly of common schools." The governor placed the colleges before the common schools because the latter could receive funds from local authorities whereas the state was the only source of public support for the higher institutions, if they were to be supported at all. Lewis believed such aid was necessary, explaining, "For if seminaries of learning are not patronized by the state and for want of this patronage, a liberal education is very expensive, the consequence will be that the rich alone can afford to educate their children; a consequence not desireable in any government, and highly dangerous in our own." [17]

The legislature followed part of Lewis's advice. It passed a bill in 1805 creating a perpetual fund, but granted the proceeds to the common schools. The two colleges were omitted from the fund but jointly given a grant of land near Lake Ticonderoga. If colleges with self-perpetuating boards of trustees were to receive state aid, they would have to make continual applications to the legislature rather than expect automatic revenue from a permanent fund. The assembly was probably wary of granting a perpetual fund to colleges over which it had no direct control.

In this 1805 act of the New York assembly a trend appeared that would later become crucial in the separation of college and state. Confronted by the claims of both common schools and colleges, the legislature gave most of its support

17. Charles Z. Lincoln, *Messages from the Governor of New York*, 11 vols. (Albany, 1909), 2:559.

to the lower schools. Though it still tried to aid both levels of education, the proportion of aid to common schools was greater in 1805 than it had been in the 1790s. In later chapters it will be seen that the competition between "democratic education" and the "aristocratic" colleges recurred and increased in intensity.

Still, in 1805, and for the next decade, state support for higher education was a concern of the legislature despite the rising claims of the common schools. By 1812 there were three colleges in the state: Hamilton College joined Columbia and Union in that year. Rather than compete for the favor of the assembly, the three thought it logical to petition for one legislative act granting aid to all of them. Such a bill was enacted in 1814, which authorized Union to conduct a lottery for $200,000 and gave Hamilton the same privilege at $40,000. Columbia received no lottery grant but was handed a plot of land in New York City known as Hosack's Botanical Garden.

The history of this garden is instructive in understanding the thinking of the state in regard to public institutions. The story began in 1801 when a Dr. David Hosack, professor of Botany and Materia Medica at Columbia, purchased a plot of land near present-day 48th Street and Fifth Avenue which he hoped to turn into a public garden similar to the Jardin des Plantes in Paris. After spending $100,000 of his own money to plant this garden, he petitioned the legislature unsuccessfully in 1805 and again in 1808 to purchase it. In 1810 the assembly responded favorably to Hosack's scheme and paid him the proceeds of a state lottery realizing $74,268. The doctor was delighted; he thought that an enlightened assembly was finally patronizing a significant enterprise.

Hosack's enthusiasm was premature. The state turned the garden over to the regents who placed it under the management of the College of Physicians and Surgeons. As the medical college had never supported the purchase of the garden, it took little interest in its care and did not object when the assembly decided to transfer the land to Columbia. Probably to enhance the usefulness of the garden, the assembly stipulated in making the grant that the college keep the garden in good repair and move there within ten years.[18]

Columbia accepted the gift with these provisos but quickly decided it had no intention of moving from its downtown location. A move to the garden, according to the trustees, would be the equivalent of changing Columbia from a city to a country college. Also, Columbia had no funds to make the move. Beginning in 1817, the college petitioned the legislature to remove the stipulation of a site relocation. After capturing the governorship in 1818, DeWitt Clinton (Columbia, 1786) supported the college in this request and persuaded the legislature to pass a bill the following year removing the site stipulation and granting the college $10,000 in cash. The cash grant was in lieu of the revenue the legislature had thought the garden would generate.

Thus Hosack's dream of a publicly supported garden had been lost in the New York assembly, and the garden became a political consolation prize passed to institutions that showed little interest in its care. Although Columbia thought the garden a burdensome expense, its property-minded trustees held onto it. One day the "country" land might become valuable. Eventually this did happen, and by 1857 the college was realizing a substantial revenue of $80,000 from the land. By 1900 the property was to have a value between six and eight million dollars; later in the twentieth century it became the site for Rockefeller Center. The state grant of 1814 was to become the principal endowment of Columbia University.

Financial support was not the only issue that concerned Columbia and the assembly before 1820. The contract between Columbia and Trinity Church, which required the president to be an Episcopalian, had never brought public

18. For a full description of the history of the Botanical Garden, see Addison Brown, *The Elgin Botanical Garden* (Lancaster, Pa., 1908).

favor to the college.[19] To establish a broader base of support for Columbia in the state, friends of the college, including Governor Daniel Tompkins (Columbia, 1795), tried to effect a plan in 1817 whereby the college could sever its Episcopal connection. Tompkins suggested that the trustees of Columbia ask Trinity Church to take back one-fourth of the land it had given the college, endow a theological seminary, and remove the stipulation that the president be an Episcopalian. After doing this Columbia should consolidate both its resources and trustees with those of newly chartered Washington College and move to Staten Island. The Tompkins plan included the intimation, but not the promise, that the legislature would look favorably on such a consolidated and nonsectarian college in the southern district.[20]

Columbia was no more disposed to merge with a new college than it had been to be amalgamated into the state university. The trustees responded that a move to Staten Island would violate Columbia's duty as a college for the city of New York. Moreover, the trustees were irritated that Columbia was always being accused of sectarianism and responded to the legislature:

> It may be proper for your Committee to further observe that Persons of all sects both in Politics and Religion have been uniformly educated in Columbia without any invidious distinctions or any illiberal attempts to induce a change of either their political or religious principles.[21]

Whether the trustees were genuinely distrustful of the state or merely annoyed at the affront to institutional integrity in-

19. The acts of 1784 and 1787 did not allow an Episcopalian to be president by charter right, which had been true in the 1754 document. However, since the contract between Trinity Church and Columbia required that the college return the land grant of 1754 if the president was not an Episcopalian, the assembly did not make the college renounce the gift. It simply refused to write this relationship into the charter. This really meant that the state conferred no privileges on Trinity Church, otherwise the college could do as it pleased.

20. This plan is recorded in CCT Minutes, Mar. 3, 1817.

21. CCT Minutes, Mar. 27, 1817.

herent in the suggested merger, they concluded their refusal
with the words:

> Your committee are indeed sensible that the legis-
> lature from their respect and esteem for the proposer of
> the plan may be led to exercise more liberality in their
> grants to the college at Staten Island, than to any other
> in the Southern district. But still considering the diffi-
> culties of the situation of the legislature, the pressing
> calls for the public money, the enormous expense that
> must attend the favorite plan of a great canal, the natural
> jealousy of other parts of the state as to any large appro-
> priations for the immediate benefit of the Southern dis-
> trict and the opposition to those appropriations which
> such jealousy must engender, there is too much reason
> to apprehend that any great expectations from legis-
> lative bounty ought not be indulged and would prob-
> ably end in disappointment.[22]

Once again Columbia had refused to be part of an educational system it did not completely dominate even if the favor
of the state might come from this.

There was something both noble and tragic in Columbia's
negotiations with New York from the Revolution to 1820.
The fierce stand of institutional integrity in defiance of what
may well have been the indifference of the state to higher
education may be viewed as a noble stand for learning in a
country only half convinced of the need for well-educated
citizens. On the other hand, this institutional integrity kept
Columbia tied to the Episcopal Church, which was beginning to lose interest in the college, and led her trustees to
reject all compromises of educational control which might
have won greater public favor.

Columbia's "tragedy" went even deeper. While a refusal
to curry public favor might be viewed as noble if other values
were maintained, this was not really the case at Columbia.

22. Ibid.

Professor Dwight C. Miner has suggested that after 1790 Columbia began to lose its "sense of identity." This loss was related both to the college's role in New York City and that city's place in the affairs of both the state and the nation.[23]

When Columbia asserted its quasi independence from the state university in 1787, New York City was the capital both of the state of New York and of the United States. With its classical curriculum, which emphasized oratory, Columbia could entice as students young men interested in politics, who could listen to the debates of state and nation by taking only a short walk from the college's Park Place campus. Also, the political fame of such prominent Columbia graduates as John Jay and Alexander Hamilton was an added attraction of the college. It was probably for these reasons that young DeWitt Clinton, who had stopped briefly in the city on his way to Princeton, decided to enroll at Columbia in 1784.

But in 1790 the national capital moved to Philadelphia, and six years later Albany became the state capital. Not only did New York City lose the physical presence of these capitals, but gradually it even lost influence in the political affairs of the state and nation, although it gained in commercial importance. As New York declined as a center of governmental activity, Columbia, whose students were almost exclusively New Yorkers, lost its identity as a seminary for future politicians; it consequently was unable to secure the interest of state politicians in its welfare. Miner has noted that the only Columbia graduate after 1800 to achieve national or state prominence in politics was Hamilton Fish (1827). Even DeWitt Clinton (1787) found that his attention shifted to upstate projects such as the Erie Canal after his election as governor. That he could obtain a grant of only $10,000 for Columbia in 1819 was indicative of the loss of influence of New York City in the state legislature.

Of course, politics was not the only face Columbia could present to the world; the college also attracted students inter-

23. This "loss of identity" theory was suggested in a conversation between J. S. W. and Dwight C. Miner, Mar. 17, 1971.

ested in law, medicine, and the clergy, and possibly a few "professional gentlemen" who wanted to pursue a life of scholarship or acquire social polish. Unfortunately, Columbia lost influence in both medicine and theology before 1820. In 1813, only six years after the regents had chartered the College of Physicians and Surgeons in New York City, Columbia discontinued its own medical department.

Although the college refused to alter its relation with Trinity Church in 1817, in the same year the General Convention of the Episcopal Church established the General Theological Seminary in New York City to train its clergy; the church had decided that Columbia was no longer a "safe" place for its future ministers. The college's former alliance with the Episcopalians was further shaken in 1820 when the convention moved the seminary to New Haven to be near Yale! Two years later the institution returned to New York and received a corporate charter after hearing that Jacob Sherred, a former vestryman of Trinity Church, had bequeathed $60,000 for its support. So even Columbia's ancient benefactor, Trinity Church, had forsaken her.

With its links to politics, medicine, and the clergy dissolved, Columbia appeared to founder for a purpose. Its enrollment remained at a low level for the entire antebellum period, and its trustees' principal activity seemed to be property management. In later chapters, this "loss of identity" and the subsequent search for a new purpose will recur as a constant theme in the history of Columbia throughout the nineteenth century.

Like Columbia, Dartmouth became involved in the statehouse negotiations over higher education in the Revolutionary years. But in 1777 Dartmouth found itself in a unique situation: it was not sure with which state to negotiate—the mother state of New Hampshire or the newly proposed state of Vermont.[24]

24. I will call Vermont a state though it was not connected with the other thirteen until 1791. Various parcels of the land known as Vermont were

When Eleazar Wheelock heard that the 1777 constitution of Vermont specified that "one University in this State ought to be established," he became fearful that a rival institution might arise in the new state just across the Connecticut River from Dartmouth. Wheelock hastened to Vermont to suggest that the legislature might save money by patronizing Dartmouth and dropping any plans for a new university.

By June, 1778, it looked as if more than just Dartmouth College would be under the care of Vermont. The sixteen western New Hampshire towns along the Connecticut River had always felt a greater kinship to the river towns on the Vermont or New York side than to the more populous seaboard region of their own state; this affinity had increased in the last few years. In 1775 the New Hampshire constitutional convention, dominated by eastern merchants, had called for a system of government with an assembly apportioned on the basis of population. Since the western men viewed New Hampshire as a confederation of towns and desired an assembly with one vote for each town, they feared they would be subjected to eastern rule by the 1775 plan. So in March, 1778, the river towns asked the Vermont assembly to admit them to the new state. The legislature approved this request in June of that year; thus Dartmouth became a Vermont institution.

Wheelock was elated. Now Dartmouth College would be the favored college of Vermont. The assembly voted to take Dartmouth under its care and gave Wheelock civil jurisdiction over the college district by making him a justice of the peace, a favor which New Hampshire had refused to extend him.

---

claimed by New Hampshire, New York, and Massachusetts during the colonial period. In January, 1777, a group of men led by Ira Allen declared Vermont a free and independent republic; in July, 1777, they adopted a constitution. Vermont failed to gain admission to the Confederation and existed as an independent republic for fourteen years. In 1790 New York relinquished its claims for $30,000 and conceded the independence of Vermont. In 1791 the state was admitted to the Union.

The Connecticut River union did not last. New Hampshire was so angered at this move that Vermont backed down and voted the towns out in 1779. Some men proposed that both the New Hampshire and Vermont river towns bolt and form another state, to be called New Connecticut. This plan never materialized, and in 1781 Vermont voted the towns back in. John Wheelock, who had assumed the leadership of the western New Hampshire cause when his father Eleazar died in 1779, was influential in the second admission.

The drama was not over. The dominant party in Vermont, the Bennington party led by Ethan Allen, heard that the Continental Congress would not admit Vermont with the New Hampshire towns included. As part of an attempt to gain the support of New York and New Hampshire, the Bennington faction tried to oust the river towns once more. The college party retaliated by accusing the Allen men of a conspiracy to unite with Canada, and Dartmouth even sent one of its professors to the Continental Congress to petition for the admission of Vermont. The college party received the same reply as the Bennington party: no admission would be granted with the New Hampshire towns. In 1782 matters reached a head. Unless the river towns went back to New Hampshire, the Continental Congress would divide Vermont between New Hampshire and New York. With its very survival at stake, the Vermont assembly dissolved the connection with the river towns and Dartmouth was back home in New Hampshire.[25]

One might think that the vacillation of Dartmouth between two states would have generated animosity and put an end to any future college-state alliances. The opposite was the case. John Wheelock immediately jumped back into statehouse politics in both New Hampshire and Vermont. Fearful that Vermont might charter a college now that Dartmouth

---

25. A full account of the Vermont-New Hampshire merger can be found in John L. Rice, "Dartmouth and the State of New Connecticut, 1776–1782" (pamphlet, DCA).

was out of the state, Wheelock returned to the Vermont assembly in 1785. He first sought a financial grant for the college and persuaded the legislators to give Dartmouth 23,000 acres of land, which would yield the college a good revenue in rents. Next he turned his attention to the men drafting a new Vermont constitution to see if he could help the college there. Ultimately, he wished to make Dartmouth the favored college of Vermont, but at least he wanted to prohibit any constitutional mention of a state duty to erect another institution. In the revised constitution of 1786 Wheelock proposed a clause that would prohibit the use of state resources for colleges other than Dartmouth. Though he failed in this move, Wheelock did succeed in preventing the inclusion of a clause that would require the state to establish a university. In hindsight, one of the most intriguing parts of Wheelock's endeavors was his belief that constitutional mention of higher education would lead to state support.[26]

With Vermont neutralized for the moment, Wheelock and his trustees directed their attention to the mother state, New Hampshire. The college had not realized the benefits it had hoped from Wentworth's 1769 gift of the township Landraff. Many people claimed possession of the land, and the college found it impossible to rent land to which it had no clear title. The trustees petitioned the legislature in September, 1788 either to intercede for Dartmouth in defending its claim to the Landraff grant or to give the college a new township. While the legislators were thinking, the college sought to curry the favor of the governor by reminding him of his ex officio position on the board of trustees and soliciting his interest in the college. The trustees' minutes noted, "Resolved as the opinion of this board that the President of this state, for the time being, [is] in virtue of the Charter, of right a trustee of this College and it is the desire of this board that

26. An account of Wheelock's dealings with the Vermont legislature appears in Julian Lindsay, *Tradition Looks Forward: The University of Vermont* (Burlington, 1954), pp. 6–11.

he attend our meetings as such so far as his situation will from time to time admit." [27]

New Hampshire responded to Dartmouth with a land grant of 42,000 acres in 1789. The trustees grew bolder and awarded honorary degrees both to the president of New Hampshire and to the governor of Vermont. Feeling confident that regular state support was coming, they renounced the Landraff township in 1791.

Further aid was slow in materializing. For a decade the only favor shown the college was a $15,000 lottery in 1796, which Dartmouth failed to organize successfully. The college pushed harder in 1803 and appointed agents to lobby in the General Court for a grant of land and/or money. Some success was realized in 1804 when the state awarded the college $900. By 1806 Dartmouth was ready to make concessions to the state in return for aid. In their September meeting the trustees formed a committee:

> to take into consideration the expediency of apply[ing] to the General Court of New Hampshire for an enlargement of this board by authorising the President of the Senate, the Speaker of the House of Representatives and the Chief Justice of the Superior Court, for the time being, or any other officers of the State Government to act in this board.[28]

Of their own volition, the trustees of Dartmouth had proposed an alteration of the college charter. Indeed, they had anticipated a charter change ten years before the legislature of New Hampshire tried such a move. In 1816 the legislature would not be an innovator. That body merely enacted a previous suggestion of the college trustees.

But in 1806 the college did not have to amend the charter. It received a grant of land in 1807 but was able to compromise on a charter revision. Rather than becoming a per-

27. DCT Minutes, December, 1789.
28. DCT Minutes, September, 1806.

manent addition to the board of trustees, the state officers would sit and vote with the trustees only on matters directly concerning revenues from state land grants.

The land grant of 1807 was the last negotiation between Dartmouth College and New Hampshire until the beginning of the famous Dartmouth College case in 1815, which will be discussed in the next chapter. As a prelude to that event one should remember that for forty years before 1815, both the trustees and the presidents of Dartmouth had conducted continual negotiations with state governments. They had even suggested charter changes to facilitate college-state relations. Dartmouth College was hardly a neutral little institution of learning unaccustomed to the machinations of politics and legislative maneuvering.

While the American Revolution brought the concerns of constitutions and new universities to college men and politicians in New York, Massachusetts, and New Hampshire; Connecticut and Yale were not as directly affected by the cataclysm of independence. As Connecticut had not been a royal colony, there was no royal governor or government to replace. The people of the state claimed their royal charter of 1662 required no replacement. Since Yale's charter had been granted by the General Assembly, the separation from monarchy brought no uncertainty as to Yale's standing. With no new state constitution to be written, no question of constitutional mention or protection for the college arose.

Even if the Revolution itself did not cause new negotiations between college and state, there were a number of issues in Yale's colonial past that were carried over into the first years of independence. Animosity between Yale and Connecticut had reached a high point during the reign of Yale president Thomas Clap (1740–66). Clap had viewed Yale not as a college for the teaching of the liberal arts to men headed for a variety of professions and callings, but as a religious society for the training of ministers of a definite sectarian stripe.[29] Among other illiberal moves, Clap had introduced in 1754 a provision that all officers (professors) and members of the corporation must subscribe to the Westminster Confession of Faith. Richard Hofstadter has described Clap's regime as "an attempt . . . to reduce one of the major colonial colleges to the status of a severely sectarian agency." [30]

Beginning in 1758, the Connecticut legislature had attempted to assert visitorial power over the college. Clap successfully resisted this move, claiming that the state had not founded the college and held no visitorial rights by the granting of a charter. He also asserted that the college had been founded by the ten ministers who had given their books at Branford. He was able to keep the state out of Yale, but finally unable to keep himself in. Tensions mounted and a group of students stormed the president's house in the fall of 1765. The following year Clap resigned. Animosity was so high that the corporation dared not name a new president. Instead, Napthali Daggett presided over the college as president pro tempore for the next eleven years.

By 1777 it had become evident that Yale must make some attempt at a reconciliation with the state. The opposition to Yale on religious grounds was combining with an opposition on geographic grounds which sought to charter a second college in the Hartford area. Fearful of the threat of competition, the Yale trustees looked for a president who could conciliate the assembly as well as run the college. Ezra Stiles (Yale, 1746) was the man.

Stiles was well aware of his role in placating the state. He noted in his diary, "the fellows elected me to prevent the Assembly's building another college." [31] Even before assum-

---

29. For Clap's views see Thomas Clap, "The Religious Constitution of Colleges" (1754), in Richard Hofstadter and Wilson Smith, *American Higher Education: A Documentary History*, 2 vols. (Chicago, 1961), 1: 111–17.

30. Richard Hofstadter and Walter Metzger, *The Development of Academic Freedom in the United States* (New York, 1955), p. 163.

31. Franklin B. Dexter, ed., *The Literary Diary of Ezra Stiles*, 3 vols. (New Haven, 1901), 2:209 (Sept. 19, 1777).

ing the presidency in July, 1778, he drafted a plan that would
turn Yale from the narrow sectarian mold Clap advocated
into a broadly useful institution. In Stiles's words, Yale would
ripen from a college into a university "When in addition to
the languages and liberal arts provision is made for studium
generale and it exhibits instruction in the highest literature,
especially in the learned professions of Divinity, Law, and
Physic." [32] This "Plan of a University" proposed professorships in divinity, law, physic, Hebrew and Oriental languages, mathematics and natural philosophy, civil history,
and oratory. The future president wanted to secure the favor
of the state toward the college but made it clear that the state
was merely to be one of a number of partners in the support
of the college/university. "It is rather to be desired," he explained, "in order to cement a Seat of Learning with the
public that some of the principal Foundations should be
instituted by the State, tho not to the exclusion of personal
Foundations."

The professorships of law and of physic were those suggested for endowment by the state. Pointing out the "utility"
of these professorships, Stiles noted that the physic professorship would directly train doctors, a strictly professional task.
The professional training of barristers or lawyers was not so
much the purpose of the law professor as the education of
wise civilians. According to Stiles's plan:

> Fewer than half of the young Gentlemen educated at
> College enter into either of the learned professions of
> Divinity, Law or Physic. By far the greater part of them
> after finishing their academic course, return home, mix
> in with the body of the public, and enter upon com-
> merce or the cultivation of their estates. And yet per-
> haps the most of them in the course of their lives are
> called forth by their country into some one or other of

32. Ezra Stiles, "Plan of a University" (1777), in Beinecke Library, Yale
University.

the various branches of civil improvement in the public offices of the state.

The professorship of law that would try to guarantee a succession of wise men in the councils of state committed Stiles's university to nothing less than the welfare of the political life of the state. The president readily accepted this duty, saying, "How happy a community abounding with men well instructed in the knowledge of their rights and liberties."

In his university proposal Stiles made no mention of a change in college government. He did not want to commit himself to one plan, as there were many being discussed at the time. At a meeting early in 1777 between the assembly and the corporation, it was suggested that the state should merely have a voice in appointing the professorships it might endow. Later in 1777 Stiles was led to believe by Governor Trumbull that assembly radicals would be assuaged only by filling the next four vacancies on the ten-man corporation. This proposal frightened Stiles, as he feared the four state men would gradually remove all Congregational ministers from the board as vacancies arose. But in 1778 an assembly-corporation committee thought there would be no need to alter the corporation if an adjunct state board was appointed to oversee funds given to Yale.

Negotiations on the best form of college government continued for more than a decade. While a group known as the Nocturnal Stellegeri wanted to purge the ministers and appoint the corporation as they would judges of the superior court, others were not interested enough in Yale to want to purge it. Some wanted the assembly to forget Yale and build a college in Hartford. In 1782 Stiles mused on all of this, "Thus differently men talk upon the matter." [33]

Meanwhile Stiles managed the college well. He wanted to keep Yale an ecclesiastical institution but assumed that some laymen, probably state officials, would be added eventually

33. Dexter, ed., *Diary of Ezra Stiles,* 3:9.

to the corporation. Knowing that one day he might have to accept the dictates of the legislature on a charter change if Yale became dependent on state funds or if students deserted the college, Stiles strengthened the college's financial position and kept the student body large during the decade of the 1780s. The president also prepared the college itself for the arrival of laymen by having the seniors debate, first in 1786 and then in subsequent years, "Whether Civilians ought to be joined with Ecclesiastics in the Corporation of Yale College." [34]

Events outside of the president's control finally led the state and Yale toward compromise in the 1790s. First, the religious solidarity of Connecticut was weakening. In 1782 Stiles had noted, "There are not 10 out of the 180 or 200 ministers in this State who are for a change in the Constitution of Yale College and putting it into the hands of Civilians." [35] In 1792 he was advised that the "College [is] obnoxious to above half the ministers because Corporation don't choose New Divinity men." [36]

While clerical division lessened opposition to a state merger, the assembly was becoming mellow in its demands upon Yale. Connecticut's neighbor states, New York and Massachusetts, had formed some sort of college-state alliance or made provision for the support of higher education. Connecticut legislators did not want to appear less enlightened than their neighbors. So in 1791 the assembly appointed a visitorial committee to look into the affairs of Yale College. Finding a prosperous college with a large student body and a treasury yielding £1,200 annually, the committee suggested that the assembly give financial support to the college whose reputation was known throughout the country.

In May, 1792, the state offered Yale a financial grant of over $30,000, representing part of a federal refund for the

34. Ibid., p. 231.
35. Ibid., p. 73.
36. Ibid., p. 451.

state's expenses in the Revolution; technically, the state allowed Yale to collect a tax authorized by the federal government. In exchange for this money, the state asked for eight ex officio seats on the corporation; the governor, lieutenant governor, and six senior assistants would be the civilian members.[37] This would enlarge the board to nineteen members (president, ten clerics, eight civilians). Though such an addition constituted more than the one-third civilian representation Stiles desired, at least it did not constitute a civilian majority. The corporation decided that this measure was a palatable compromise and accepted it. They knew that a rejection of the money offered by the assembly would probably result in the chartering of a competing college, thus causing injury to Yale.

A rejection might have had religious repercussions as well. Connecticut was in the throes of a fight for religious toleration and Congregational disestablishment in the 1790s. Dissenters attacked the granting of state aid to the college of the Congregational church. But a rejection of this aid by Yale would have been interpreted as an insult to the state. It would have conjured up images of Clap's sectarian rejection of the visitorial committee of the 1760s. This might have generated more enemies for the college than already existed.

Stiles believed the compromise an advantageous move for the college, but he was not necessarily overjoyed with the change. "I anticipate that this will bring forward Professors obnoxious to me and who will at length enterprise Mischief to me personally," sighed Yale's diplomat.[38] Still, he realized that the very existence of Yale or any other college depended on public confidence and goodwill. In 1792 the way by which a college could be linked with the world outside its institutional walls or beyond the confines of a band of clerics was

37. In 1792 the General Assembly of Connecticut was composed of a governor, lieutenant governor, twelve assistants, and a house of deputies. In 1818 the twelve assistants became the senate.

38. Dexter, ed., p. 456.

through legislative visitation or representation. The idea of a confederation of alumni as the extrainstitutional balance-wheel had yet to be conceived.

From 1792 to 1818 Yale's relationship with the state was closely tied with the movement toward religious freedom. Although dissenting groups, principally Episcopalians, Methodists, and Baptists, were irate at the 1792 grant of money to Yale, the Congregational-controlled assembly aided Yale again in 1796 by turning over the remaining proceeds of the Revolutionary refund partially granted Yale four years earlier. This appropriation particularly upset the dissenters, as they had won a victory over the use of funds from the sale of Western Reserve lands a year earlier. While the "Standing Order," as the Federalist-Congregational establishment of Connecticut was called, had wanted to turn the western funds over to ecclesiastical districts and Yale in 1791, the dissenters had objected and had successfully diverted the money to local school districts in 1795. The Western Reserve funds became the endowment of the Connecticut Common School Fund. The forces of both "democratic education" and disestablishment had thwarted Yale.[39]

Not only were the dissenters irritated by state grants to Yale, they were also uneasy about sending their sons to the Congregational institution. The election of the Reverend Timothy Dwight, the principal spokesman of the "Standing Order," to the presidency in 1795 only heightened their concern. The president was such a powerful figure that he was known in the state as "Pope Dwight." And when Yale declared in 1810 that it would appoint a local guardian for all students whose homes were outside New Haven, the chance for the son of a dissenter to receive an untainted education appeared grim indeed.[40]

As the Episcopalians were more concerned with college

39. An account of the dispute over the Western Reserve lands appears in Maria Louise Green, *The Development of Religious Toleration in Connecticut* (Boston, 1905), pp. 368–92.
40. YC Minutes, September, 1810.

education than the Methodists or Baptists, they began to push for a chartered institution of their own. In 1795 they started an academy but did not ask for a charter, as they thought this would rouse strong opposition from the Yale interests: a chartered academy was always a potential base for launching a rival college. For a while it even appeared as though a Yale-Episcopal compromise might work, when the Congregational college agreed to award advanced standing to Episcopal Academy graduates. But the dissenters wanted a place of their own, not advanced placement at Yale. Spurred on by their success in securing an academy charter in 1801, they petitioned the assembly for a college charter in 1804. They were denied the grant in that year, and again in 1810 and 1811. Undaunted by these initial defeats, the Episcopalians sought to link their collegiate goals with economic interests.[41]

In 1814 a group of Episcopal laymen in Hartford organized the Phoenix Bank and offered the state a bonus of $50,000 for a charter of incorporation. The group suggested the bonus be used for the Medical Department of Yale College, the Bishop's Fund (Episcopal), and "any purpose whatever which to your Honour's may seem best." The Episcopalians meant a college. The assembly voted $20,000 to Yale but turned down any appropriations to the Episcopalians. No worse action could have been taken. The assembly had publicly rejected the Episcopalians, consequently infuriating all dissenters. As for Yale, the college was again in politics as a stronghold of the "Standing Order" — a position from which it never sought to hold itself aloof.

The 1814 insult caused the Episcopalians to bolt from the Federalist party and fuse with the Republicans to form the Tolerationist party. In 1816 the Tolerationist candidate for governor was Oliver Wolcott, a 1778 graduate of Yale who had been an arch-Federalist until 1814, when he split

41. For a full account of the efforts of the Episcopalians to start a college in Connecticut, see Glenn Weaver, *History of Trinity College* (Hartford, 1967), pp. 5–12.

with the party because of his defense of the War of 1812. Though Wolcott was not elected in 1816, the Tolerationists made substantial gains in the assembly.

The Federalists were frightened at these victories and sought to pacify the dissenting groups with financial support. Using a $14,500 refund from the federal government for the state's expenses in the War of 1812, the assembly voted "An Act for the Support of Literature and Religion," apportioning the money as follows:

1/3	Congregational societies
1/7	Bishop's Fund
1/8	Baptists
1/12	Methodists
1/6	Yale
1/6	To remain in the state treasury.

Again the Federalists had blundered. In 1816 the dissenters were opposed as much to state support for any church as for just a favored one. As a historian of Connecticut has noted:

> The passage of the Act for the Support of Literature and Religion, raised, as the Congregationalists ought to have known, a violent protest from every dissenter and every political come-outer. Some of the towns in town meeting opposed the bill as unnecessary for the support of schools and clergy; as wasteful when it would be wiser to create a state fund; and unduly favorable to Yale where the policy was to create an intellectual class and not to advance learning and literature among the commonalty.[42]

In 1817 the Congregationalists lost their majority in the assembly, and Wolcott was elected governor. In 1818 Connecticut at last found herself with a state constitution, and one that disestablished the Congregational church. Fortunately, Yale was not injured by this change in state government. The 1745 charter with all of its privileges was con-

42. Green, p. 468.

firmed by the 1818 constitution. This was not really surprising. After all, Wolcott was a Yale graduate, and, somewhat symbolically, "Pope Dwight" had died along with his party in 1817. Though Yale did not renounce the Westminster oath until 1823, its new president, Jeremiah Day (1817–46), formerly professor of mathematics and natural philosophy, had not been a minister until he accepted ordination to become president. To some extent, Yale itself had been disestablished.

Strangely enough, the Episcopalians did not rush to a favorable assembly for a college charter. A few years later, however, they did bring an end to Yale's monopoly position in higher education by receiving a charter for Washington College (later Trinity) in 1823.[43]

It should be remembered that in the struggle for religious toleration, Yale never attempted to be neutral. With its faculty oath, its clerical trustees, and "Pope Dwight," Yale never disassociated itself from the interests of the Congregational order. From the "Compromise of 1792" to the Constitution of 1818, Yale was a participant in the political maneuvers of the "Standing Order" versus Dissenters. The college was no innocent outpost of learning that unavoidably became a political football in the hands of partisan politicians. Yale was partisan itself. And, like Harvard, Yale profited from this position. The state grants from 1792 to 1816 totaled about $70,000. If the grants were erratic rather than annual, this was partially caused by the fact that the assembly found it difficult to tax the people. Most grants to education at any level were made when the state found itself with funds to appropriate that required no taxation—federal refunds, land sales and bank bonuses. With the exception of the sale of Western Reserve lands, Yale fared well with the legislature.

So from 1776 to 1820 the alliances between college and state continued to vary from college to college and to change

43. See chapter 3 for the story of the chartering of Trinity College.

within each college, as they had in the colonial period. In regard to control, Harvard and Yale were more closely allied to their respective states in 1820 than they had been in 1776. And though Columbia had drawn closer to New York only to separate from the state university, it still considered itself entitled to state support.

Throughout this period a definite feeling existed on the part of both college and state officials that some alliance between the two was necessary, regardless of the changes the alliance might undergo. Thus it was not unnatural for John Wheelock to attempt to draft a constitution for Vermont or for Ezra Stiles to be in continual negotiation with committees of the General Assembly of Connecticut. It was also natural for graduates of the colleges to form interest groups in the state assemblies. Harvard men and Columbia men viewed their colleges as interests to be protected and supported by the state. They were not just well-educated men who had a general interest in education but men educated in particular colleges supporting the interests of particular institutions. In New York this could be seen in the movement for, and later against, a state university. Whereas Ezra L'Hommedieu, a Yale man in New York, had a general interest in higher education for the state and wanted the state to appoint the trustees of particular colleges, Alexander Hamilton, a King's College man in New York, was clearly representing the institution in blocking this move.

The contrast between Hamilton and L'Hommedieu might lead one to believe that the mixed public-private nature of our four colleges was a reactionary result caused by the resistance of older institutions in the state. Nothing similar to a modern state-controlled, state-financed institution developed in any of our states before 1820, with the possible exception of the three-year experiment in New York.[44] Would state universities have developed had there been no opposition from existing institutions?

44. The abortive attempt to create a state university in New Hampshire in 1816 will be discussed in chapter 2.

Only a guess could answer the question in New York. There is evidence, however, that the mixed character of higher education was the rule also in those states which lacked an institution of higher education at the outset of the Revolution. The kind of alliance that existed at our four colleges was not unique to the Northeast.

Eight so-called state universities were established between 1785 and 1820. Five of these were founded in states that had no other college or university. In matters of finance and control the majority of these universities resembled the colleges we have examined.[45]

The first state university, University of Georgia, had been founded in 1785 by a state endowment of 40,000 acres of land. This had not been the spontaneous action of the legislature, but the result of a petition by some recently arrived Yale graduates led by Abraham Baldwin (Yale, 1772). "The plan of a college or university for the state," explains historian E. M. Coulter, "was none of Georgia's making; it was imported." [46] The corporation chartered to receive this land was a self-perpetuating board of trustees supervised by a state appointed board of visitors. Together the two boards were called the Senatus Academicus; this dual form of government was similar to that at Harvard.

The land grant from the state in no way signified a commitment to continuing support. In fact, the original grant was not really an indication of support or enthusiasm for higher education at all. As Coulter has noted, "The legislature was willing to do this small favor for those who wanted a college, for what was 40,000 acres of land when compared with the vast areas extending to the Mississippi; and after all what was the price of land in Georgia — any head of a

45. Georgia (1785), North Carolina (1789), Vermont (1791), South Carolina (1801), Ohio (1804), Miami (1809), Maryland (1812), and Virginia (1819). Competing colleges existed at the time of founding in Virginia, South Carolina, and Maryland.

46. E. Merton Coulter, *College Life in the Old South,* 2d ed. (Athens, 1951), p. 2.

family who cared to settle in these same counties could have
a thousand acres free." [47] Perhaps it was not surprising, then,
that from the founding date to 1820 the state assumed no
financial responsibility for the university. The college had
been launched; now it must float on its own. On occasion the
state did consent to loan the college money at interest!

The southern pattern was repeated in the North. After
Vermont freed herself of Dartmouth and sent Wheelock back
to New Hampshire in 1785, men in the state pushed for a
university of their own. The University of Vermont, chart-
tered in 1791, received state lands set aside for education in
1787, but the institution received more support from the
£4,000 grant of a private citizen, Ira Allen, and other subscriptions from various towns.

The people of Burlington, who wanted the "state" university in their town, fully realized that the legislature would
not support the institution. In their argument to locate the
institution in Burlington, they openly explained:

> It is also evident that a University cannot be established
> in any place, unless the people shall so far agree in it
> as to be willing to bear ye expense for it. The govern-
> ment of ye State has no monies to advance for this pur-
> pose. Nor would the people consent to have a Tax raised
> upon them for this purpose. Such a Tax would operate
> very unequally. It would be of great advantage to that
> part of the people who lived near the college; it would
> be of little advantage to those who were in the remote
> parts of the state; and none at all to those near other
> seminaries. It cannot be expected that ye Government
> of ye State should raise the monies necessary for this
> purpose.[48]

In Vermont the functions of the legislature were to charter
the institution, select the site, and appoint a board of trustees
who would then become self-perpetuating.

47. Ibid., p. 4.
48. Lindsay, *University of Vermont,* p. 24.

In Ohio higher education was promoted with land grants from the federal government. By the terms of a contract signed July 23, 1787, between the Continental Congress and the Ohio Company of Associates, two townships were allotted "to be given perpetually for the purpose of an University . . . to be applied to the intended object by the legislature." [49] When Ohio became a state in 1803, the legislature took possession of these two townships, plus a third which had been granted John Cleves Symmes for the promotion of higher education.

Ohio established two universities with these grants — Ohio University at Athens (1804) and Miami University at Oxford (1809) — and viewed both as "state" institutions even though the governing boards differed in composition. Ohio University was managed by a state-appointed board of trustees, while Miami's guardians were self-perpetuating and remained so until 1842. Regardless of the form of control, neither university received financial support from the legislature, except for the proceeds from the land grant sales. In Ohio, as it was also to be in the other states carved from the Northwest Territory, the role of the state was that of receiving agent and protector of federal lands rather than direct supporter of higher education.[50]

Besides making provision for future "state universities" in the Northwest Territory, the Continental Congress also considered creating a national university. Such an institution, according to Benjamin Rush's proposal of 1787, would undertake both scientific research and the education of civil servants. Rush even went so far as to propose that a degree from

49. The Northwest Ordinance of 1787 included the passage "Religion, morality, and knowledge being necessary to good government and the happiness of mankind, schools and the means of education shall forever be encouraged in not less than three nor more than five states to be founded in the Territory," but made no specific provision for support. It was in the contract to the Ohio Company, and upon the specific insistence of the company's leader, Manasseh Cutler (Yale, 1765), that the townships were given.

50. A discussion of state universities founded after 1820 in the Northwest appears in chapter 3.

the university be required for entry into the federal service.

Though the Congress had no clear plan as to how the university would be financed, one prominent sponsor of the proposal, George Washington, envisioned funds coming from public appropriations, private endowments, and student fees; he even bequeathed some of his own property to the Congress for the use of the institution. Like Stiles's university in New Haven, the national university would be endowed by individuals and by "public communities."

Because of opposition from existing colleges on the grounds that a national university would be "godless" and a possible competitor, the 1787 plan was not enacted. A similar plan proposed by Joel Barlow and Thomas Jefferson in 1806 met a similar fate.[51]

So in its proposals for national and state universities, the Congress suggested alliances between college and state that were not significantly different from the patterns emerging at our older colleges at the same time.

In the minds of many men, the connotation "state university" did not really signify that a state government had undertaken responsibility for higher education. Under those terms only South Carolina and Virginia could qualify in the period before 1820.[52] Generally speaking, state universities were founded by a group of men who wanted the initial support or land grant and protection of the state in organizing a quasi-autonomous institution. The founding group could be called state men only in that they represented the interests of higher education for a particular state rather than a par-

51. A full account of the national university can be found in Edgar Bruce Wesley, *Proposed: The University of the United States* (Minneapolis, 1936) and David Madsen, *The National University* (Detroit, 1966).

52. Virginia and South Carolina are discussed in chapter 3. Their omission from chapter 1 may appear to be a move to withhold evidence that might disprove my theory of state universities. My purpose in chapter 1 is to show that the term *state university* did not necessarily require state control or state support. In chapter 3, I will try to show that Virginia and South Carolina were exceptional, even as state universities.

ticular religious sect. "Non-denominational" or "civil" might have been as apt descriptions as "state."

This state interest was as evident in Connecticut as in Georgia. In the older state the interest challenged the clerical monopoly of higher education at Yale. In both states the institutions that emerged were similar in their mixed character of government and support. One might even say that Yale, with its single governing board of civil and clerical members, was more closely connected to the state government than Georgia with its dual boards.

In understanding the various alliances between college and state, whether at our colleges or at the new state universities, it must be remembered that rarely, if ever, did anyone doubt the legitimacy of state support or the right of the state to supervise an institution it had chartered. While a group of ministers might privately conclude, as they did at Yale, that they were the best body to administer a college, they recognized a necessary bond with the state. No college wished to exist without the state-granted charter that allowed it to induce students to enroll with the offer of a degree. And since the colleges viewed the education of civil leaders as one of their principal functions, they wanted to secure the interest of the state in this activity.

The states naturally took an interest in the affairs and government of a college that might produce future legislators. They did not want the colleges to advocate values inimical to republican government. Thus, to some extent the college was trying to protect the state by providing well-educated leaders and the state was trying to protect itself from the kind of leaders the college might produce — and no one doubted that the colleges were teaching values. In our states, the truly "private" institutions, or those in which the legislature showed virtually no interest, were the academies and proprietary schools that taught accounting and modern foreign languages. These were skills for the use of men going into commerce or business rather than subjects that might have an implication for government.

College leaders realized that the alternative to a recognition of public interest would be a schoolhouse presided over by a cleric with a small group of students. This was hardly an institution that would have an effect on the society of the time. Our colleges viewed themselves as institutions with a societal purpose as well as a desire to impart wisdom to individuals. Though Ezra Stiles might look askance at the inclusion of state senators on the Yale Corporation, he had no intention of affirming Thomas Clap's idea that Yale was a school solely for the training ministers.

The most well known and best-documented event in college-state relations in the 1776–1820 period was the Dartmouth College case. The case is generally thought of as the defense of a private college against the invasion of a state that wanted to transform or change the institution. When viewed in the light of the constant negotiations between colleges and states after the Revolution, the case takes on new dimensions. It will be my contention that the defense given by Daniel Webster was an innovation, that the case broke rather than defended the tradition of higher education at Dartmouth — and for that matter at most other institutions in the United States. In examining what Webster had to disprove about college-state relations, one may more clearly see the nature of the alliance.

2 Dartmouth: A Small College

It is . . . a small college. And yet, there are those who love it.

Daniel Webster, 1818

Brilliant and useful as its career has been, illustrious as its alumni are, and ample as its endowments have become, it has suffered for the greater part of the nineteenth century from the needless and hurtful estrangement of the mass of the people.

F. B. Sanborn, 1908

In a collective view, they appear . . . to be . . . tending to one end; to complete the destruction of the original principles of the college and school and to establish a new modified system to strengthen the interests of a party or sect, which by extending its influence, under the fairest professions, will eventually effect the political independence of the people and move the springs of their government.[1]

This was a plea for the defense of Dartmouth College made not by Daniel Webster to the United States Supreme Court but by John Wheelock, president of the college, to the legislature of New Hampshire in 1815. The first interaction between college and state, which would eventually result in John Marshall's famous Supreme Court decision of 1819, began not because the state acted on its own accord to change a "private college" into a "state university," but because the college president asked the legislature to investigate the abuses done to the institution by its trustees. And it should be noted that in May, 1815, Wheelock's plea was that of a Federalist president against a Federalist board of trustees brought before a Federalist legislature and a Federalist governor.

1. *Documents Relative to Dartmouth College, Published by the Legislature* (1816), DCA.

What sent Wheelock to the legislature? Although there may have been religious differences between the president and the board, the problem revolved around a question of power — would Wheelock or the trustees control Dartmouth College? The question was not what should be taught but who would make the appointments to teach. Both sides readily admitted that this was the issue. Wheelock simply claimed that the trustees had no right to assert authority over him.

The president's problems had been over two decades in the making. As members of the pliant board of trustees his father had appointed before the Revolution began to die, new men joined the board who sought to challenge the authority of the Wheelock dynasty. The transformation began in 1793 with the appointment of Nathaniel Niles (Princeton, 1776). New trustees were named in 1802, 1804, and 1806. Finally, the arrival of Charles Marsh (Dartmouth, 1786) on the board in 1809 gave control to the anti-Wheelock group. As a group, the trustees were absolutely convinced of their right to govern Dartmouth. One chronicler has noted, "Nothing short of divine power could control such men." [2]

It was almost inevitable that a man as headstrong as Wheelock would come into conflict with such a board. Shortly after the trustees had elected Roswell Shurtleff (Dartmouth, 1799) to the professorship of divinity, Wheelock tried to curtail his importance by refusing to let him preach in the church at Hanover as the professor before Shurtleff had done. But the professor went on preaching with the support of the trustees, who continued to pay him from the Phillips Fund. Enraged at this affront to his authority, Wheelock charged the trustees with a misappropriation of funds to sponsor a church for a particular sect.

The breaking point between the president and the trustees finally came in 1814 when the board relieved Wheelock from the instruction of the senior class. This was too much for him. Convinced that the trustees were trying to get rid of

2. John M. Shirley, *The Dartmouth College Causes* (St. Louis, 1879), p. 84.

him and were violating the charter to do it, the president published in May, 1815, his "Sketches of the History of Dartmouth College and Moor's Charity School," in which he gave his account of the decade-old struggles.

Throughout the years of this struggle for home rule, the trustees had never pretended that they liked Wheelock. Pressed to state their objections in 1815, they claimed he was typical of a certain breed of men: "Such men are always the heroes of their own story. Every measure which places them in the foreground of the picture, promotes their views, honor or interest is right in itself. Every measure which in any degree thwarts their view or lessens their importance is precisely so far wrong." [3] The board added that Wheelock was so intent upon controlling Dartmouth that "he will be willing to make the college his heir; but upon the condition that the institution, its authorities and funds should pass, like a West India plantation with the slaves and cattle upon it, to his actual heirs and descendants according to his own destination." [4]

It was precisely this sense of proprietary right which the trustees were avowedly trying to dispel. They claimed that Wheelock had no charter right to instruct the senior class and that he had decided the Phillips Fund had been misappropriated only after he realized the trustees were against him.

By 1815 Wheelock feared, with some justification, that he was about to lose his power. A few months before he published his "Sketches," a friend had advised him that once they were published, "you must go forward, then you must kill or *be killed*." [5] Wheelock did not wait for the trustees to answer his charges. He proceeded to the legislature in June with his grievances and asked Governor John T. Gilman (Dartmouth, 1794 M.A.), a Federalist and a trustee of Dart-

---

3. *A Vindication of the Official Conduct of the Trustees of Dartmouth College* (1815), p. 16, DCA

4. Ibid., p. 33.

5. Elijah Parish to J. Wheelock, Mar. 7, 1815, DCA.

mouth,[6] to appoint a committee to investigate his charges and make changes in the college if necessary.

Why had he gone to the legislature? Why had he not made a legal case against the trustees and brought them to court for violation of the charter? The trustees claimed that this would have been the proper course and explained why Wheelock chose the assembly:

> The President well knows that there is no foundation for the complaints set up in the Sketches; but has nourished the vain hope that by exaggeration, colouring and misrepresentation, he can prejudice and hurry the Legislature into some hasty and violent measures which will favor his views and again place the whole Institution with its government and its funds and resources at his disposal.[7]

Some of Wheelock's friends thought otherwise. To them the legislature, not the courts, was the proper body to approach for aid. Colonel Josiah Dunham, secretary of state of Vermont, announced, "What then remained for President Wheelock to do? He had but one alternative — either to be contemptuously trodden in the dust — or to appeal to the sovereign of the state — to the legislature of New Hampshire." [8]

After all, why should Wheelock not have gone to the legislature? He had been going to the assemblies of Vermont and New Hampshire all his life to advance his own and the college's interests, which were often indistinguishable from each other. The legislature was a natural arena for college concerns. Even the trustees did not deny Wheelock's right to go to that body or the right of the legislature to investigate them.

6. Gilman had been a trustee of Dartmouth ex officio from 1794 to 1805. In 1807 he was elected to the board. Thus when he returned to the governorship in 1813 he did not become a "double trustee"—there were only eleven members, and votes, rather than twelve.

7. *A Vindication*, p. 78.

8. Josiah Dunham, *An Answer to the Vindication of the Official Conduct of the Trustees of Dartmouth College in Confirmation of the Sketches* (1815), p. 80, DCA.

They simply thought they would fare better in a court — which they eventually did.[9] Governor Gilman accepted Wheelock's memorial and appointed a committee to look into his charges — a committee dominated by Federalists.

The summer of 1815 saw both sides — trustees and Wheelock — preparing for a showdown. The trustees issued a pamphlet defending their actions, and Colonel Dunham produced a tract vindicating the president. Advised to secure a lawyer, Wheelock sent a twenty-dollar check to Daniel Webster. Though Webster accepted the check, he failed to come to Wheelock's aid when he realized that most of his political allies were among the trustees.

With both parties ready for battle, a few men tried to act as peacemakers. Fearing that the trustees might try to fire Wheelock at their August meeting, Jeremiah Mason (Yale, 1788) wrote to his cousin Charles Marsh, a Dartmouth trustee, and advised him against any action of this kind. Mason, who was later to defend the college against the state in the New Hampshire Superior Court, thought the legislative committee would find Wheelock's charges baseless, thus vindicating the trustees. And in 1815 Mason looked favorably on the legislature, holding few reservations about its power: "The legislature, I think, for certain purposes have a right to inquire into an alleged mismanagement of such an institution, a visitorial power rests in the State, and I do not deem it important for my present view to determine in what department or how to be exercised. The legislature may, on proper occasion, call it into operation." [10] A year later he reversed this opinion.

While Mason tried to dissuade the trustees from any rash action, Josiah Dunham wrote Webster imploring him to ex-

---

9. In fact, Webster argued that the problem was that the legislature of New Hampshire had no right to interfere with Dartmouth because it was necessary that the Vermont legislature join in the action. Baxter P. Smith notes, in his *History of Dartmouth* (Boston, 1878), that Wheelock really just chose the wrong legislature. Smith says Wheelock should have gone to the U.S. Congress (p. 116).

10. Jeremiah Mason to C. Marsh, Aug. 15, 1815, DCA.

tricate himself entirely from the affair if he was not going
to defend Wheelock. Dunham's plea was motivated by the
split that had occurred in the New Hampshire Federalist
party. The Dartmouth trustees belonged to the faction that
wished to support their own Timothy Farrar (Harvard, 1767)
for governor and to remove Gilman, who was friendly toward
Wheelock. Dunham warned, "The trustees and their friends
[are] trying to give this college business a political turn in
order to draw *all Federalists* to help them pull down the
President. The Democrats will try to make use of it to help
their party I well know." [11] He thought the trustees would
lose, thus injuring Webster's reputation in the state. Webster
replied on August 25 that Dunham was overexcited.[12]

Neither Mason's nor Dunham's advice was heeded. At their
August meeting the trustees appointed a committee to investigate the authorship of the "Sketches." The committee reported on August 25 that President Wheelock was the "principal, if not sole, author of the pamphlet entitled 'Sketches
of the History of Dartmouth College and Moor's Charity
School.' " [13]

Wheelock was furious at this investigation. At a meeting
of the trustees on August 26 he accused the board of creating
a political issue. He noted that the legislature was currently
investigating the college and suggested that the trustees ask
that body or "any proper council or tribunal" to look into
the accusations against him. Standing on what he felt were
his rights of office, Wheelock exclaimed, "I hereby protest
against the proceedings of your board and utterly deny your
right of jurisdiction in this case." [14]

The board quickly took a vote and decided 10–0 that they
did have a jurisdiction. Announcing that Wheelock had committed "gross and unprovoked libel on the institution," the
board dismissed him as president, trustee, and professor of

---

11. J. Dunham to D. Webster, Aug. 16, 1815, DCA.
12. D. Webster to J. Dunham, Aug. 25, 1815, DCA.
13. Dartmouth College Trustees Minutes, Aug. 25, 1815.
14. Ibid., Aug. 26, 1815.

history. The vote was 8–2, with Governor Gilman and Stephen Jacob (Yale, 1778), a Vermont judge, dissenting.

The trustees wasted no time in finding a successor. On August 28 they elected the Reverend Francis Brown to the president's post and inaugurated him September 27, 1815.

The dismissal of Wheelock thrust Dartmouth College into the political arena. The upcoming elections revolved, among other things, around the question of religious liberty. The Congregational church was tax-supported in 1815 and the "Standing Order" in religion was equated with the Federalist party. The Democrats or Republicans who supported William Plumer for governor ran on a promise of disestablishment, which they eventually fulfilled with the Act of Toleration in 1819. Like their counterparts in Connecticut, the New Hampshire Federalists had entwined the affairs of the college with those of party politics.

Whether the trustees really had a religious difference with the president, as he had claimed in his memorial to the legislature, was not important. His dismissal convinced the public that the charge was true. Immediately after the trustees made their move, Jason Dana wrote to his friend Tristram Gilman:

> a deep impression is made on the minds of the citizens through the state that all of the trustees who have acted against the President are rigid Calvinists or Hopkinsians and are endeavoring to establish those doctrines as the *Law Religion* of the State. This has roused sectarian feelings to the highest pitch and keenly animated political zeal.[15]

The Democrats openly espoused sympathy for Wheelock and won the elections in March, 1816 for both the governorship and the legislature. Many Federalists who were friends of Wheelock voted for the Democrats. Again there were similarities between New Hampshire and Connecticut. In both states the downfall of Federalism was caused by a split in

15. J. Dana to Tristram Gilman, Sept. 2, 1815, DCA.

the party resulting from an incident involving a college that was interpreted as an act against religious liberty.

In April, 1816, the Federalists were in their last month of power. The Dartmouth investigating committee presented its report to Governor Gilman. Just as Mason had predicted, they found no reason for the legislature to take any action against the trustees or to modify the governing structure of the college. But the matter did not rest with Gilman; he was not to be the man to present the report to the legislature. When the assembly convened in June, William Plumer would be governor.

There was much discussion in the air as to what would happen. Some thought the affair would all be over. T. Farrar wrote Francis Brown:

> The difficulties at the college have almost ceased to excite conversation or attention here and I do not know but it is the same at Hanover. I have always supposed that the Democrats cared nothing about them and wished to make no other use of them than to make Dr. Wheelock and his friends help them into power. This has been effected and the Dr. has rendered them all his assistance he is capable of rendering. . . . I expect their interest in the business will end.[16]

The legislature might have followed this course, but the new governor was a different matter. William Plumer had been a staunch member of the Federalist party and a United States senator from 1802 to 1807. During Jefferson's second administration he became disenchanted with his party, bolted, and supported Madison in 1808. Elected governor of New Hampshire in 1812, he lost the annual election to Gilman for the next three years, and finally returned to office in 1816. Having switched from Calvinism to the Baptist persuasion at age twenty, he had long been an advocate of religious freedom. And though he was not a well-educated man,

16. T. Farrar to Francis Brown, Apr. 8, 1816, DCA.

he believed in the value of colleges. Dartmouth historian Leon Burr Richardson has noted:

> One man alone seems to have been interested . . . from the point of view of a proper fundamental basis for a college, and that man was Governor Plumer, who, if we may judge from his correspondence, appears to have been honestly concerned with that part of the situation.[17]

Plumer shared the ideas of Thomas Jefferson; Plumer thought institutions should be flexible and governed by a representative body rather than by a group of men of like political and religious views. Had the Wheelock incident occurred a decade later with a Jacksonian governor, the state might have shown no more interest in Dartmouth College. But a Jeffersonian could not let the matter rest.

In his June 6, 1816 message to the legislature, Plumer advocated that the state patronize the college but criticized the charter:

> As it emanated from royalty, it contained, as was natural it should, principles congenial to monarchy among others, it established trustees, made seven a quorum, and authorized a majority of those present to remove any of its members which they might consider unfit or uncapable and the survivors to perpetuate the board by themselves electing others to supply vacancies. This last principle is hostile to the spirit and genius of free government.[18]

Plumer thought the number of trustees should be expanded to "increase the security of the college" and as a "means of interesting more men in its prosperity." He advised the legislature that it had authority to act upon the trustees, noting, "In this country a number of states have passed laws that made material changes in the charters of their colleges." [19]

17. Leon Burr Richardson, *History of Dartmouth College*, 2 vols. (Hanover, 1932), 1: 319.
18. Shirley, *Dartmouth College Causes*, p. 105.
19. Ibid., p. 106.

He was right. Yale, Harvard, and Columbia could have been cited as examples. A copy of the speech was sent to Thomas Jefferson, who applauded it and wrote to his friend Plumer, "It is replete with sound principles and truly republican." [20]

Webster and some of the trustees had foreseen Plumer's actions and tried to divert the attention of the assembly away from Dartmouth. To do this they suggested that the legislature found a new college, the University of New Hampshire, with a board of trustees chosen by the state and a board of overseers composed of state officials. As John Shirley, the leading chronicler of the Dartmouth College case, has commented, "Mr. Webster seems to have thought that a board of overseers numbering nineteen, and religious toleration, were adapted to every institution but Dartmouth College." [21]

The legislature was not interested in a new college. The governor had asked them to amend the charter of Dartmouth, and that they intended to do. The assembly proposed a bill, "An Act to Amend the Charter and Enlarge the Corporation of Dartmouth College," which would change the name of the corporation to the Trustees of Dartmouth University, increase the trustees from twelve to twenty-one, create a board of overseers, and require the trustees and officers of the college to swear allegiance to the constitutions of the United States and of New Hampshire. The governor would appoint men to the nine vacancies on the board of trustees. The board of overseers would have as ex officio members the president of the senate and speaker of the assembly from New Hampshire and the governor and lieutenant governor from Vermont. The New Hampshire governor would appoint the other members.

Oddly enough, once the governor appointed the men to fill the board of trustees and the overseers, both bodies would become self-perpetuating. As historian John K. Lord has pointed out:

20. Ibid., p. 107.
21. Ibid., p. 104.

It will be noticed that this Act preserved the "monarchical" features which the governor thought so dangerous in the old charter. The board of trustees was still a close corporation, after the first injection of new blood in nine new members, though there could of course be no guarantee that the process of legislative interference might not be repeated as often as party whims might dictate.[22]

The trustees made another attempt to propose an alternative bill in the legislature that would create a board of overseers for Dartmouth but leave the trustees unimpaired. The college board even announced that it had no "objection to the passage of a law connecting the government of the state with that of the College and creating every salutary check and restraint upon the official conduct of the trustees and their successors that can be reasonably required."[23]

Unfortunately, Dartmouth had no Ezra Stiles to mediate the situation. The legislature passed the original bill, and the governor signed it into law on June 27, 1816.

It was the passage of this bill which most historians call the attempt of the Republicans to transform a "private college" into a "state university" and return John Wheelock to power with a sympathetic board of trustees.[24] Yet none of

22. John K. Lord, *A History of Dartmouth College* (Concord, N.H., 1913), pp. 90–91.

23. "Trustees of Dartmouth College to the Legislature," 1816, DCA.

24. Among historians taking this view see the following:

Donald Tewksbury, *The Founding of American Colleges before the Civil War* (New York, 1932), p. 149: "The Act of 1816 transformed the college into a state university, under the name of the Dartmouth University, with a dual system of control dominated by the state."

Freeman Butts and Lawrence Cremin, *A History of Education in American Culture* (New York, 1953), p. 265: "the Republican state legislature passed legislation in 1816 making Dartmouth a state university, enlarging the board of trustees by eleven members, and appointing Wheelock as president of the new Dartmouth University."

Claude Fuess, *Daniel Webster* (New York, 1930), p. 219: "Thus for all practical purposes, the college was placed under the thumb of the legislature and the Board of Trustees was to be packed by Wheelock's friends."

the old trustees nor President Brown was dismissed by the act. The old trustees would still have been a majority on the new board. Even if one considers that Plumer, as governor, would not be acceptable to the old trustees, the ten plus President Brown would still have formed a majority. Dartmouth had no more been transformed into a state university than Yale had been in 1792.[25]

Transformed or not, the new Dartmouth University did not appeal to the old trustees. On August 25, 1816, the board — minus Stephen Jacob, John Gilman, and Governor Plumer[26] — voted not to accept the Act of 1816. Like the Harvard Corporation in 1812, they were distressed that their assent to the act had not been necessary to implement the bill. Still another quandary plagued the board. Plumer had appointed William H. Woodward, secretary-treasurer of Dartmouth College, as a trustee of the university. Woodward had accepted and delivered the seal and charter of the college to the enlarged or improved board of trustees.

The governor was also in a predicament. When he convened the trustees of Dartmouth University on August 26, a quorum of eleven failed to appear. Plumer then wrote Brown on August 27, asking why he and the old trustees would not meet with the board. On the same day the old board claimed again, as it had two days before:

> We cannot see the expediency of accepting the provisions of the said act, considering the circumstances under which it passed and considering the unwieldy number of overseers and trustees it proposes and the great increase of expense it will necessarily occasion.[27]

What was the governor to do? Could he dismiss the old trustees and appoint successors? He asked the New Hamp-

25. The Yale Corporation had been expanded from eleven to nineteen, or 73% (8/11); Dartmouth from twelve to twenty-one, or 75% (9/12).

26. Jacob decided to join the university board; Gilman declined to participate with either board during the controversy but remained a trustee of the college until April, 1819. Plumer obviously met with the university board.

27. DCT Minutes, Aug. 27, 1816.

shire Superior Court if the June act gave him such power. The court thought not and suggested that the governor needed additional legislation. So in November and December of 1816 Plumer addressed the legislature and persuaded them to pass bills that would lower the number of trustees necessary for quorum to nine, allow the governor to fill the vacancies created by the absence of the college trustees, and fine the old trustees $500 each if they continued to exercise the privileges (e.g. degree-granting and property-holding) of the original charter.[28]

Facing a fine of $500, the trustees were forced to act. In many ways they were in the position of their Harvard friends in 1812. They claimed the new law had no effect on them, but what should they do? Acquiesce and hope that a new legislature might right the situation? In January, 1817, they were no more ready or eager for a court case than the Harvard Corporation had been in 1812. Although the trustees were prominent men who claimed their "private" rights had been violated, they were not ready to contribute their personal funds to a legal defense. Fortunately for them, John B. Wheeler, a country merchant and farmer who had never attended a college, had offered them $1,000 back in September to test their rights. Wheeler said he made the gift "not as the effect of personal friendship but as resulting from a conviction that all mankind are morally bound to use their endeavour to support the cause of science and virtue." [29] With the prospect of being taken to court themselves under the governor's penalty legislation, the trustees decided to use Wheeler's money and take their case to a New Hampshire tribunal.

On February 8, 1817, the board brought its case before

---

28. The two additional acts were "An act in addition to and in amendment of an act entitled An Act to Amend the Charter and Enlarge the Corporation of Dartmouth College," Dec. 18, 1816; and "An act in addition to an act entitled An act in addition to and in amendment of an act entitled An Act to Amend the Charter and Enlarge the Corporation of Dartmouth College," Dec. 26, 1816.

29. J. B. Wheeler to the Trustees of Dartmouth College, DCA.

the court of common pleas in Grafton County whence it was transferred to the May term of superior court, the highest court in New Hampshire. Of course, the case was against the act of the New Hampshire legislature, but it is interesting to note the technicalities of *Trustees* v. *Woodward* — the old board sued their own secretary, William H. Woodward, who had defected to the university, for the return of the seal and charter. Such an action is known as trover.

While the college trustees were bringing suit against Woodward, the university trustees finally held their first legal meeting under the new quorum requirements on February 4, 1817. On February 14 the board brought charges against President Brown and the old board for their failure to attend the university board. On February 22, they discharged Brown as president of the university and elected Wheelock to this position. The trustees and professors who had refused to join the university were also discharged.[30]

Eight months had elapsed between the passage of "An Act to Amend the Charter and Enlarge the Corporation of Dartmouth College" and the election of Wheelock. Nothing in the original act dictated this development. Francis Brown was president of the university until he was dismissed in February. It is true that the bill had been passed the preceding June by a Democratic house, voting along party lines, but the bill did not oust the Federalists from the new university. The Federalists ousted themselves by refusing to assent to a new organization in which they could have been the dominant element.[31] Like the trustees of Columbia in 1787, they no doubt felt that if they did not have a monopoly of the board they might eventually be replaced — probably in the same manner that they had revolutionized the old board

30. Of the eight recalcitrant trustees, three were removed on Feb. 22, 1817; four on Aug. 26, 1817; and one on Aug. 25, 1818.

31. It should be understood that, although the full twelve members of the old corporation would form a majority on the new board, the number who objected (eight plus the president) would be a minority.

from a group acquiescent to the Wheelock dynasty to a group that ended it.

Now the fortunes of the college moved to the courts, first to the New Hampshire Superior Court and later to the United States Supreme Court. The trustees had carried their dispute with Wheelock to the arena in which they felt most comfortable — the court. The Federalists had lost their college, along with their political power, in the legislature; they intended to regain at least the college in the courts.

The case in New Hampshire was elaborate. Not only did counsel for the college argue that the Act of 1816 impaired the obligation of contracts which the federal constitution protected; they claimed that the act violated the New Hampshire constitution by depriving citizens of their property rights without trial, and that it was outside the proper and legitimate scope of legislative action. In New Hampshire the Federalists were trying to pare down the authority of the legislature. Their real achievement here and later in Washington was to de-emphasize, not the importance of the legislature but of Dartmouth, by insisting that it was a college rather than a university. The "smallness" of Dartmouth was created in the courtroom.

The college was represented by a galaxy of legal talent: Jeremiah Mason, Jeremiah Smith, and later Daniel Webster. Mason opened the argument, declaring, "The question is whether the acts are obligatory and binding on the plaintiffs; they never having accepted or assented to them." [32] He next claimed that the Act of 1816 had abolished the old corporation because "It was neither expected, nor desired that the old trustees should unite with the new ones. The intention doubtless was, in this indirect way, to abolish the old corporation and get rid of the trustees." [33] Hence the private

32. Timothy Farrar, *Report of the Case of the Trustees of Dartmouth College against William H. Woodward* (Portsmouth, N.H., 1819), p. 29.
33. Ibid., p. 31.

rights of the trustees had been violated by the legislature. Mason had begun his defense by reading the minds of the legislators.

Although he had thought only a year before that the legislature held certain rights over the college, he now attacked the encroaching, usurping authority of state legislatures. Quoting Hamilton, Mason announced, "We have seen, that the tendency of republican governments is to an aggrandizement of the legislative, at the expense of other departments." [34] Sounding the alarm bell he added, "Permit the legislature, in this instance, to abolish a charter of corporate privileges and there will be no ground left on which they can be restrained from abolishing patents of land. The great principle of security for private property will be destroyed." [35] His companion Smith was even more concerned about the danger of legislative authority and announced:

> For myself, I do not wish to see the time when the government of this or any other literary institution . . . shall be closely connected with the government of the state. Changes in the latter, if not desireable, are always to be expected; permanence in the former is every way important. There is besides something in political men, generally speaking, which unfits them for the management of an academical institution, or to be useful fellow-workers with instructors of youth.[36]

One wonders if Smith and Mason thought all legislatures unfit, or merely Democratic or Republican legislatures.

The court had not convened to decide whether political men were evil or benign; to nullify the Act of 1816 the plaintiff had to prove that the college was a "private" corporation or that the trustees had "private" rights. It was acknowledged that legislatures, regardless of the character of their members, could alter the charters of municipal cor-

34. Ibid., p. 34.
35. Ibid., p. 52.
36. Ibid., p. 155.

porations. Dartmouth needed to show that a college was different from a municipality, and also different from a "university." It was acknowledged in English law that Parliament could legislate for Oxford and Cambridge without their consent.

The college lawyers tried to prove that Dartmouth was an eleemosynary institution, or a charity whose principle of organization was the distribution of bounty or funds given by a private donor. A college, according to their argument, was merely the perpetual corporate form of a wealthy individual or group of individuals. The trustees were usually the principal donors or the representatives of the donors. Thus the private rights of the trustees were the same as the private right of an individual to distribute his money as he pleased. Neither Smith nor Mason dwelt on the fact that whatever bounty Dartmouth possessed had not been the gift of the present trustees or any of their predecessors.

By this argument the privileges of the charter did not really empower the trustees to educate but merely to distribute funds so that students could be educated — but where? In England the colleges were originally charitable organizations that supported and housed poor students at Oxford and Cambridge. Later the colleges took over the teaching function and prepared their scholars for the university examinations and degrees. Mason and Smith tried to place Dartmouth College in the category of an English college and then to cite the precedent in English law which protected those colleges.

But in New Hampshire where was the university of which the college was a part? College and university were the same. Indeed, the charter allowed the trustees to hold gifts and distribute charity, but it also granted them the right to confer "any such degree or degrees to any of the students of the said college, or any others by them thought worthy thereof, as are usually granted in either of the Universities or any other college in our realm of Great Britain." State counsel Ichabod Bartlett noted that the trustees of Dartmouth College "have not only exercised the powers of a university but have used and even preferred that name as the most appropriate until, by some coincidence, it became the legitimate title by the act of the legislature." [37] He was right. In their minutes the trustees had referred to themselves as early as 1782 as the Trustees of Dartmouth University. And from 1801 to 1814 the catalogue had called the college Dartmouth University.

The state argued that Dartmouth was a public corporation like a municipality. State attorney George Sullivan went on to assert that even if it were a private corporation like a banking or turnpike company, the state held the right to legislate and alter the charter when the public good was in question. Citing an 1807 case in which the legislature had forbidden a bank to issue bills not payable on demand, Sullivan stated, "the legislature of the states, perhaps of all of them, have taken from private corporations some of their rights and privileges when the welfare of the community has required it." [38] The state claimed that the trustees had no rights as individuals: "When a man gives property for a particular object he intends that it shall be applied to that object but it is a matter of no importance to him whether the application be made by twelve trustees or twenty." [39] Hence the rights of the trustees and the object of the charity had not been affected by enlarging the board. The New Hampshire Constitution had not been violated.

Strangely enough, the college argued that banks and turnpike companies were less "private" than Dartmouth. The former were private civil corporations while the college was a private charity. The college continually claimed that its only function was to distribute alms for a charitable purpose such as healing the sick or educating the ignorant rather than actually healing or educating, which might be an area of public concern.

37. Ibid., p. 183.
38. Ibid., p. 77.
39. Ibid., p. 95.

Sullivan and Bartlett responded to the Federalist attack on the fitness and ability of legislatures. According to them, the legislature could not possibly injure Dartmouth because it would be against its own interest to do so: that is to say, the government and the trustees would have no separate, no distinct interests to guard — their interests were precisely the same:

> when the interests of legislators are united with those of the objects of their laws; when bad laws will produce as much injury to those who make them as to those on whom they are intended to operate, there is the most perfect security that such laws never will be made.[40]

The value of Dartmouth to the people of New Hampshire was so great that they would remove from power any legislature which tried to harm it. The virtue of the people, not a royal charter, was the best protector of the college.

Rebutting the college's case that political men were somehow evil, Bartlett wondered why it should be taken for granted that the trustees were men whom "No passions can ever move — no intrigue ever influence." To him the trustees were the potential enemies of both college and state. "The triumph of liberty and justice and equal rights," he announced, "proclaim the publick care and patronage of education. . . . There is no alternative, the government must controul these institutions, or they shall controul the government." [41]

So in New Hampshire much more had been argued than the case of a college. Two theories of government, Federalist and Republican, had been on trial. In regard to higher education the Republicans had held to that necessary connection between college and state which had characterized the development at least of our four colleges. Two decades before, the Federalists might have argued the same case. They might not have proclaimed the virtues of legislatures, but certainly

40. Ibid., p. 87.
41. Ibid., p. 186.

they would not have tried to argue the college completely away from the state into the hands of private donors. The Federalists had reversed themselves in 1816. While Federalist supporters at Yale, Harvard, and Columbia — and Dartmouth before 1815 — had all been involved in the movement to raise the American college to university status, the Dartmouth Federalists now tried to pull the emerging university back to the level of a college which probably would have met the approval of Thomas Clap.

The two sides completed their arguments in November, 1817, and in the same month Chief Justice William M. Richardson (Harvard, 1797) handed down a unanimous opinion in favor of the university. "The decision of the cause," explained Richardson, "must depend upon whether the legislature had a constitutional right to authorize the appointment of new trustees without the consent of the corporation." [42] The judge concluded that it had that right, as Dartmouth was a public corporation because of its public purpose. A private corporation would be one created solely for the interest of the corporators. The right of the legislature was then self-evident because, "All publick interests are proper objects of legislation and it is peculiarly the province of the legislature to determine by what laws those interests shall be regulated." [43]

Richardson then addressed himself to other questions raised by the case. He claimed the only private right the trustees could possess was the right to be members of the expanded board. They could no more stipulate the number of trustees than a citizen could the number of people living in a municipality. As the act did not remove them, their rights had not been violated. The judge also decided that the charter was not a contract as defined in the United States Constitution.

The chief justice tried to convince the Federalists that, like it or not, they should learn to live with legislatures: "If these acts be injurious to the public interests, the remedy

42. Ibid., p. 208.
43. Ibid., p. 216.

is to be sought in their repeal, not in the courts of law." [44]
He pointed out that public goodwill was necessary for the
health of a college. Although the plaintiffs were free to appeal
the case, he warned, "It would avail these institutions nothing
that the publick will was wrong, and that their right could
be maintained in opposition to it, in a court of law." [45]

Possibly the college Federalists felt they had permanently
lost the public goodwill and the ability to repeal the act in
the New Hampshire legislature. Whatever their reasons, they
appealed the case on writ of error to the United States Supreme Court on the ground that the New Hampshire court
was not qualified to render an opinion on the definition of
a contract in the United States Constitution. The appeal was
granted and Webster carried the case to Washington in
1818.

Mason and Smith did not accompany Webster. Joseph
Hopkinson, a congressman from Pennsylvania, aided him
in the college cause. The university made a tragic mistake
in its selection of counsel. Thinking there was really no new
case to be presented, they failed to send Sullivan and Bartlett, who were well-informed on the history of both Dartmouth and educational legislation. They asked William Wirt,
attorney-general of the United States, and John Holmes, a
Brown graduate and a congressman from Maine, to represent the university. Both men admitted that they knew little
of the case before entering court.

Webster waxed eloquent in Washington and presented essentially the same argument that had been made in New
Hampshire. He emphasized the private nature of the college
on the ground that it was equivalent to an English college.
The visitors or trustees were the representatives of the donor,
not merely public-minded men. Quoting English law, Webster declared:

44. Ibid., p. 217.
45. Ibid., p. 233.

The case before the court is clearly that of an eleemosynary corporation. It is in the strictest legal sense a
private charity. In *King v. St. Catherine's Hall,* that college is called a private, eleemosynary, lay corporation.
It was endowed by a private founder and incorporated
by letters patent. And in the same manner was Dartmouth College founded and incorporated.[46]

After establishing that the trustees had "private" rights
which were violated by the state, he argued that the charter
was a contract. "There are in this case," Webster contended,
"all the essential parts of a contract. There is something to be
contracted about; there are parties, and there are plain terms
in which the agreement of the parties, on the subject of the
contract, is expressed." [47] A necessary condition to a contract
is some mutual consideration, usually a tangible consideration (i.e. money or property). Webster knew this and carried
his contract definition to a point that marked a true Federalist innovation in the interpretation of property. Webster
claimed that the founder, for his part, "agreed to establish
his seminary in New Hampshire, and to enlarge it, beyond
its original design, among other things for the benefit of that
province." Contracting for this gain, the governor (Wentworth) had given the founder a charter. Had the governor
given lands for this purpose rather than a charter, he, and
later the state legislature, could not revoke them. Similarly,
Webster reasoned, "And is there any difference, in legal con-
templation, between a grant of corporate franchise and a
grant of tangible property?" [48] Webster had expanded the
concept of property to include the granting of privileges.

The case presented by Wirt and Holmes had little merit.
The university trustees were so distressed at the performance
of the two that they employed William Pinckney, one of the
leading lawyers in the United States, to reargue the case when

46. Ibid., p. 255.
47. Ibid., p. 279.
48. Ibid.

the court returned in 1819 from its recess. The court had decided in 1818 that they could not reach a decision at the end of Webster's argument.

Some authors have claimed that the case was decided not in the chambers of the justices but in drawing-room intrigues during the 1818–19 recess. College officials met with Chancellor Kent in Albany to enlist his aid in convincing Justices Livingston and Johnson of the college cause. They had to convince the chancellor himself, as he had already gone on record in support of Chief Justice Richardson's New Hampshire decision.[49]

Whatever the intrigues of the recess, the court reconvened on February 2, 1819. Before William Pinckney could ask for a reargument, Chief Justice Marshall announced that the court had arrived at a decision: 5-1 in favor of the college. Marshall claimed that Dartmouth was a private corporation and that the charter was a contract under the terms of the constitution. The Act of 1816 had impaired that contract because "the will of the state is substituted for the will of the donor." [50]

Marshall admitted that such a charter-contract was not exactly what the framers of the constitution had had in mind but concluded:

> Although a particular and a rare case may not, in itself, be of sufficient magnitude to induce a rule, yet it must be governed by the rule, when established, unless some plain and strong reason for excluding it can be given. It is not enough to say that this particular case was not in the mind of the convention when the article was framed, nor of the American people when it was adopted. It is necessary to go farther and to say that had this particular case been suggested, the language would have been so varied as to exclude it, or it would have been a special exception.[51]

49. See Shirley, *Dartmouth College Causes,* p. 250.
50. Farrar, *Case against William H. Woodward,* p. 329.
51. Ibid., p. 322.

Marshall had turned the justices into mind readers of the past.[52]

In Hanover the trustees of the college were ecstatic. The students, most of whom had remained loyal to the college, fired a cannon in jubilation. Judge Woodward returned the seal of the college, and the buildings the university had held throughout the case were also put back into college hands. Unfortunately the case took its toll in human life. John Wheelock had died in April, 1817, and Francis Brown followed him in 1820.

So, Dartmouth had been returned to its "private" trustees and the state had been routed — or had it? Strangely enough, the first recorded act of the restored trustees was to appoint a committee to petition the legislature "for indemnity or further aid on account of losses and injuries they have sustained in consequence of late legislative acts." [53] Why were the trustees so ready to return to that assembly which Mason and Smith had argued was so evil? Were the victorious trustees trying to exact retribution from the now vanquished oppressor? Or were they just negotiating with the legislature as they had always done? In the 1780s the trustees had asked the assembly to indemnify them for the expenses incurred in defending the title to the state-granted Landraff township. Had the Supreme Court really effected a separation of college and state or merely defended the rights of the trustees and returned college-state relations to a status quo ante-1816?

Almost every historian of American education has accepted the former interpretation. The Dartmouth College case, ac-

---

52. The justices were indeed guessing. None of them had been delegates to the Constitutional Convention of 1787. None of the records of the convention or the papers of James Madison had been published. Years later when the records were published, critics of Marshall's decision claimed that, if Nathan Dane, the author of the contract clause, had thought it might be interpreted as Marshall did, he would never have proposed it and certainly the convention would never have approved it.

53. DCT Minutes, April, 1819.

cording to these scholars, sanctioned the spread of small private colleges and quashed state attempts to reshape existing colleges. "The Dartmouth College decision," states Frederick Rudolph, "by encouraging college-founding and by discouraging public support for higher education, probably helped to check the development of state universities for half a century."[54] The facts, particularly at Dartmouth, do not entirely support this interpretation.

If the Dartmouth College decision deterred the state from seeking an alliance with the college, it did not deter the college from seeking an alliance with the state. Mills Olcott, treasurer of Dartmouth, wrote Daniel Webster in June, 1821:

> Some of the friends of old Dartmouth College who are here have thought that her real interest might be subscribed by some legislative arrangement whereby not only state patronage but state funds should be obtained. They have thought of a Board of Overseers of 20 to include the President of the Senate, the Speaker of the House, the others to be appointed by the governor and council — to have a veto upon the appointment of the trustees and afterwards fill up the vacancies themselves and to be somewhat on the footing of Cambridge — a tax is expected to be raised for the state Treasury this session from Banks and from this fund have say $5,000 annually for ten years appropriated for Dartmouth College.[55]

54. Frederick Rudolph, *The American College and University* (New York, 1962), p. 211. Also see:

Tewksbury, *Founding of American Colleges before the Civil War*, p. 151: "The decision implying, as it did, a victory for the religious interests in the country at large, gave these interests an unprecedented degree of freedom to develop educational institutions without fear, in general, of molestation on the part of the state."

Butts and Cremin, *History of Education in American Culture*, p. 265: "In the first place, it guaranteed the philanthropic endowment of private colleges from the encroachment by the states, thereby encouraging private donors to contribute freely to the causes they supported."

55. Mills Olcott to Daniel Webster, June 13, 1821, DCA.

Webster advised against the move. "All would be political," he replied, "nothing literary. My impression is that if the college must die, it is better it should die a natural death." [56] He thought the state would readily appoint the overseers and then give no money to the college.

But Dartmouth needed money and was willing to make concessions to obtain it. Since Webster and his friends did not rush forward with endowments, the college turned to the most lucrative source, the state. The New Hampshire Literary Fund of 1821 (the bank tax in Olcott's letter which had been voted for the support of higher education) was only one source of public funds that might be tapped; there was also a movement among the original eastern states (i.e. those which had never been a federal territory) to induce Congress to grant them western lands for the endowment of a university in each state. The states, including New Hampshire, argued that the university land grants in the Northwest Territory had shown federal preference for a particular section. New Hampshire supported this land grant move for the eastern states.

The possibility of a federal grant also raised the specter of a second college to compete with Dartmouth. There was bitterness among many in the state toward the Dartmouth College decision, and at least one faction in the legislature wanted to set up a rival college under state control. Richard Bartlett wrote Jared Sparks, "Such an appropriation would soon lead to the establishment of an University in this town [Concord] under the auspices and control of the legislature and in opposition to that fountain of Calvinism, Dartmouth." [57] If there was one thing a college feared more than state interference, it was competition. There were not enough students in New Hampshire to share.

The Supreme Court decision may have protected Dartmouth's charter, but outside the courtroom the interests of

56. Webster to Olcott, June 17, 1821, DCA.
57. Richard Bartlett to Jared Sparks, Nov. 23, 1821, DCA.

college and state were as entwined as ever. Webster was now safely in Massachusetts, but Dartmouth had to exist in New Hampshire. The trustees really could not let the college die a natural death as her defender suggested. But what should they do? Dartmouth was in much the same position as Yale had been at the inauguration of Stiles. Could her new president, Bennett Tyler, negotiate with the legislature as well as Stiles had done?

Fortunately, Dartmouth had friends in the state government. Governor Samuel Bell (Dartmouth, 1793) thought that two colleges would not be in the state's best interest. In 1822 John Church advised Olcott of the governor's persuasion and also noted, "I have no inclination to put the college under the control of the legislature. . . . But if we can consistently do anything to conciliate the Government and secure the patronage of the State I view it important that it should be done." [58]

Some pressure was removed from the college-state negotiations in 1823 when the federal land grant bill was defeated in Congress because western congressmen feared absentee ownership of land. But by 1825 Dartmouth was involved again in legislative maneuverings, when a bill was presented in the New Hampshire senate to establish a rival, New Hampshire University. In the same year another bill appeared entitled, "An Act to amend the charter of Dartmouth College and to make an appropriation for the encouragement of that institution." Had the legislature not heard of the Dartmouth College decision?

The latter bill acknowledged the duty of the legislature to "cherish the interests of literature" and noted the existence of the Literary Fund. Concluding that a second college "would rather tend to check than to promote these great interests," the bill proposed a plan whereby Dartmouth College would receive one-half of the fund if a board of overseers was appointed. The provisions of the bill were similar to

58. John M. Church to Mills Olcott, Mar. 12, 1822, DCA.

the Act of 1816 except that the board of trustees was unaffected. The bill failed to come to a vote in 1825, the reasons for which are not entirely clear. Bennett Tyler, president of the college, wrote trustee Charles Marsh, "I found it impossible to obtain a grant to the college on any terms which the trustees would be likely to accept." He also reported that many Republicans felt a second college would be a bad idea, "But many have not forgotten the old controversy and they are unwilling to do anything for the college without a surrender of the charter or something equivalent." [59]

The Dartmouth-New Hampshire cause, round two, continued to occupy the attention of the legislature for the next three years. In 1826 Governor David Morril supported Dartmouth and implored the legislature to rescue the college in the eyes of the people. "The relation and intercourse between that [Dartmouth] and the legislature ought to be such, as to command the entire confidence of the people in that institution." [60] The assembly was split over its goals for higher education; the house presented the bill to amend the charter while the senate resolved to create a new institution that would be united with Dartmouth, a precursor of the union of Dartmouth and the New Hampshire Agricultural School after the passage of the Morrill Act in 1862.

In 1827 the senate passed a bill to establish the New Hampsire University, but it failed in the house. A year later the legislators must have been getting tired of this controversy. Governor John Bell addressed the body and announced that the college could get along on its own funds; New Hampshire did not need to aid Dartmouth or any new college. In December, 1828 the legislature changed the design of the Literary Fund and diverted its resources from higher education to the common schools. As had happened in New York in 1805, "democratic education" won the attention of the assembly — and permanently. Dartmouth would not receive

59. Bennett Tyler to Charles Marsh, June 20, 1825, DCA.
60. *Journal of the House of Representatives of the State of New Hampshire* (Concord, 1826), p. 22.

state aid, with the exception of the Morrill grant, until the 1890s. But if there was now no new money for Dartmouth, there were also no funds for a rival university. The legislature allowed Dartmouth to retain its monopoly on higher education in New Hampshire — which was no inconsiderable privilege.

Dartmouth's trustees must have seen the end coming. In January and August, 1828, they had organized committees to petition the legislature for aid from the Literary Fund. In October they resolved:

> that Rev. Wheeler, a member of this Board and now gone to Europe for his health, be hereby requested and authorized to apply for benefactions in aid of the college funds in England and elsewhere in his discretion.[61]

Dartmouth was returning to the pre-Revolutionary fund-raising methods of Eleazar Wheelock.

Bennett Tyler had not been as successful as Ezra Stiles; he had been unable to effect a compromise of control for financial support. But he had been more successful than his contemporary at Yale, Jeremiah Day, president from 1817 to 1846. He had at least prevented a rival institution from appearing in New Hampshire. In 1828 Yale was in competition with Washington College at Hartford. Three years later it would have another competitor in Wesleyan College at Middletown.

For a full decade after Marshall's decision, both Dartmouth and the state had initiated action to reshape the college. Reflecting on this in 1932, Dartmouth historian Leon Richardson tried to explain these events by saying, "The trustees were slow in recognizing the full implications of the decision in the Dartmouth College case, namely that an institution not under state control should not look to the state for support." [62] But does it really seem likely that the trustees

61. DCT Minutes, October, 1828.
62. Richardson, *History of Dartmouth College*, 1: 374.

did not understand the implications of the decision? Or does the problem lie with the modern historians' understanding of the early nineteenth century?

From the vantage point of the twentieth century, historians seem obsessed with the idea that nineteenth-century state governments wanted to control higher education. But what did the states want to control — the curriculum, the life of the students, the expenditure of funds? There is little evidence that the states had any interest in control. What they were interested in was making the governing boards of the colleges representative of the state at large. Antagonism to sectarian colleges had been an issue since the 1750s. The broad representative structure written into the charter of King's College in 1754 had been an attempt to stave off sectarianism through charter stipulations. Yet in the period from 1776 to 1820, when religious liberty had become an important political issue, our four colleges became identified in the popular mind with particular denominations — Yale and Dartmouth with the established Congregationalists, Harvard with the dissenting Unitarians, and Columbia with the disestablished Episcopalians.

The state was trying to regulate the colleges to make them representative of a new balance in society. The legislation was a corrective measure to create a balance which the charter alone could not maintain. No state wanted to take over a college and run it without a charter as a branch of government. The governor of New Hampshire had explained the state's role well in 1826 when he announced that the state should secure the confidence of the people to the college and make whatever structural amendments were necessary to effect such an end.

The state would have little to gain by controlling a college. There were few, if any, jobs to be distributed as patronage. And if there were jobs, the state might have to pay the salaries. To paraphrase Richardson, one could say the states were coming to realize that if they controlled a college, they might have to support it. The state supported and controlled

university we know today was not an idea in the minds of
legislators before or after the Dartmouth College decision.
It did not appear until after the Civil War.[63] Dartmouth and
New Hampshire were no more separated after the Supreme
Court decision than they had been after the unsuccessful
secession attempt to Vermont in 1782. People were irritated
at the college on both occasions. Whence comes the fame of
the 1819 event?

The decision received little widespread attention in the
reportings of the day. An article by Warren Dutton in the
North American Review, however, did praise the decision
and the college trustees for protecting their rights: "They
have encountered the difficulties and expenses of a protracted
law suit, in maintaining their chartered rights; they have
their reward in the approbation of wise and good men." [64]
But this praise did not mean that the *Review* had taken a
stand against public support or had heralded the separation
of college and state. Appearing in the same January 1820
issue, an article by the *Review*'s editor, Edward Everett,
praised state patronage for the University of Virginia, which
had not yet opened, and advocated that other states and the
federal government support colleges. According to the *Review*
it was the duty of the state, not of private individuals, to
finance higher education. In fact, the *Review* took a stand
against private gifts:

> But does it become a mighty nation rising fast into an
> importance, destined to throw a shade over the decay-
> ing greatness of Europe, does it become us to depend
> on charity for the education of our sons, and the uphold-
> ing of our national character? . . . This dependence on
> single and private bequests of rich individuals is a relic
> of a state of society, which never existed among us, and
> to which we have nothing else corresponding.[65]

63. Again the exceptions would be Virginia and South Carolina, which
are discussed in chapter 3.
64. *North American Review,* no. 26 (January, 1820), p. 83.
65. Ibid., p. 135.

Was Everett unaware of the implications of the Dartmouth College case? If it is remembered that the Supreme Court decision only forbade states from implementing a piece of legislation without the college's consent, it should not be difficult to realize that this provision in no way ended that sense of necessary connection between college and state which had existed for decades. There was nothing inconsistent in the thinking of the Dartmouth trustees when they asked the state for an indemnity, or in the juxtaposition of articles praising the decision on the one hand and advocating state support on the other.

This reasoning will help us to understand the implications of Chancellor Kent in his 1826 *Commentaries on American Law*. Only seven years after the decision Kent wrote:

> The decision in that case did more than any other single act, proceeding from the authority of the United States, to throw an impregnable barrier around all rights and franchises derived from the grant of government; and to give solidity, and inviolability to literary, charitable, religious and commercial institutions of our country.[66]

Did he mean by this that the decision had effected a separation of college and state? If so, he should have explained the negotiation and potential new alliances between New Hampshire and Dartmouth at the time of his writing. He did not mention the affairs in New Hampshire, and he did not have to. As with the *North American Review*, to praise the inviolability of literary institutions did not mean that their historic alliance with the state had to be dissolved. At least it did not mean this before the 1870s.

It was after 1870 that the case drew extensive legal attention because it was used as the precedent forbidding state regulation of railroad freight rates — the Granger cases. Articles concerning the decision and its relation to business

66. James Kent, *Commentaries on American Law*, 4 vols. (New York, 1826), 1: 392.

corporations could be lumped into two groups between 1874 and 1917. Those coming before 1900 tended to deplore the case, claiming that the decision was incorrect and that the United States Constitution did not intend for legislatures to be so restricted. After 1900 the arguments ameliorated, the tenor being that the case was not really very important because the Supreme Court essentially overruled it in the 1875–1900 period by allowing legislatures a regulating function over business corporations that affected the public interest.[67] The post-1900 authors expounded a thesis that the true "genius" of American government was its ability to change its laws as times changed. Hence no Supreme Court decision was really binding or should be considered an overstep of judicial authority. Strangely enough this idea that the court would overrule its outdated decisions was nearly the same argument given by New Hampshire in 1816 to establish the virtue of legislatures — that a legislature will automatically repeal a law which conflicts with the public interest.

Still, these articles in legal journals paid little attention to the effects of the case on education or on the separation of college and state. The first mention of the case, as far as I can find, appears to have been in a 1903 University of California monograph by Elmer E. Brown entitled *The Origin of American State Universities*. According to Brown, "The decision in the Dartmouth College Case put an end to efforts directed toward governmental regulation of educational close-corporations; but in so doing it turned the

---

67. A sample of the articles includes: "The Dartmouth College Case," *American Law Review* 8 (1874); Aldace Walker, *A Legal Mummy or the Present Status of the Dartmouth College Case* (1886); Seymour Thompson, "Abuses of Corporate Privileges," *American Law Review* 26 (1892); Alfred Russell, "Effect of the Dartmouth College Case as Precedent," *Dartmouth Magazine*, 1910; John K. Lord, "Dartmouth College Case," *Dartmouth Magazine*, 1901; William Trickett, "The Dartmouth College Paralogism," *American Law Review* 40 (1906); Jesse F. Orton, "Confusion of Property with Privilege: Dartmouth College Case," *Independent*, 1909; Charles Warren, "An Historical Note of the Dartmouth College Case," *American Law Review* 46 (1912); J. C. Jenkins, "Should the Dartmouth College Case be Recalled," *American Law Review* 51 (1919).

full force of this movement into that other possible course
of governmental agency, namely the establishment and maintenance of colleges and universities under full state control." [68]

More than eighty years had elapsed before this dual theory
of the withdrawal of state interest in the older colleges and
the blossoming of that interest in other states for universities
gained currency. Later we will see that such a theory could
only have developed after the 1870s. For almost fifty years
after the Dartmouth College decision our states, in varying
degrees, continued to be interested in and even attempted
to remake the old colleges — and the new states in the Midwest showed little if no interest in establishing state universities.

After the appearance of Brown's monograph, which, inci-
dentally, praised the state university and asserted that the
private college was "a public institution in the highest sense
when its members give themselves continuously, as a matter
of principle to the whole people," little was written on the
educational effects of the case. Charles Thwing made no mention of the "private-public" issue in his *History of Higher
Education* (1906). Charles Warren mentioned no such effect
in his *History of the Supreme Court* (1922), nor did Albert
J. Beveridge in his *Life of John Marshall* (1916–19). However, both men cited the effects of the decision on business
corporations. Franklin Benjamin Sanborn, a New Hampshire
historian, cited the case in his 1908 address, "Dartmouth
College: Its Founders and Hinderers." Calling Webster the
principal hinderer of the college, Sanborn saw the decision
as retarding the development of Dartmouth into a state university of the late nineteenth-century variety. This happened
because the case alienated the "people" of the state from
the college, not because of any legal impediments it created.
It was not until 1930 and after that historians began to write
about the "private" significance of the case. Differing from

68. Elmer E. Brown, *The Origin of American State Universities* (Berkeley,
Calif., 1903), p. 34.

both the legal critics and Brown, they were the first to think the case had a beneficial effect; that the protection of the college from the state helped the institution to prosper and to advance the cause of learning. Freeman Butts and Lawrence Cremin noted in their 1953 *History of Education in American Culture:*

> In the first place, it guaranteed the philanthropic endowment of private colleges from the encroachment by the states, thereby encouraging private donors to contribute freely to the causes they supported.[69]

This was quite a different view of the case than that which the *North American Review* had espoused in the 1820s. The reason is not hard to find. It was Americans in the 1930s and 1950s, not in the 1820s, who valued the "private" college.

If my view of the Dartmouth College decision's impact is correct, should the case then be dismissed as a factor in the story of the separation of college and state in the nineteenth century? Not at all. The case was important, but its importance lay not in its legal implications but in the line of argument the college trustees were willing to espouse. In order to remain the sole guardians of Dartmouth, they were willing to renounce the university movement generated by the Revolution and even to cast aspersions on the virtue of civil government. One might interpret the actions of the Dartmouth trustees as a desperate attempt of the Federalists to retain power in some segment of American society. As defenders of an established church, they were losing ground. As a political party that could succeed in state elections, their days were numbered. One of their last areas of influence was higher education. One could well argue that the Federalists simply did not want the Republicans to beat them in this arena. They argued Dartmouth away from a state they could no longer control. To do this they were willing to break an alliance they had once sought with enthusiasm.

69. Butts and Cremin, *History of Education in American Culture*, p. 265.

Dartmouth did not have to link its fate to the reasoning of Webster and the dying Federalists. But until the 1850s that college and our other three seemed determined to perpetuate the type of thinking used in Dartmouth's defense, by standing on a narrow base of support both in regard to religion and to curriculum. Some of the colleges continued to appeal for state support, but they did not seem to understand that legislators found it difficult to support institutions that frankly admitted, and were frequently somewhat proud of, their narrowness of purpose. Even supporters of higher education found that a college which rebelled against being called a university was a difficult product to market in statehouse chambers. From 1820 to 1850 it was the state that was separating itself from the college. In many cases the colleges wanted to maintain the alliances. The 1819 decision eventually freed not Dartmouth from the state but the state from a small college.

3 The Estrangement of College and State 1820–1850

Our academies and colleges add superficial instruction in the dead languages, without the philosophy of our own; scientific facts, without their causes; definitions, without practical application; the rules of rhetoric, without its spirit; and history, divested of its moral instructions.

William H. Seward,
governor of New York, 1839

But the cry everywhere is, "Numbers, numbers." "These," everyone exclaims, "are the evidence and element of success." All this is very natural in a republic. Under such a form of government, power and superiority are reckoned by the head. No account is taken of the nature of those heads, or of their material.

Josiah Quincy,
president of Harvard, 1845

For more than forty years after the American Revolution our colleges and states had maintained that alliance forged earlier in the colonial era. In fact, all four of our couples had become more intimate at one time or another after the Revolution: New York and Columbia had drawn closer together in the 1780s, Yale and Connecticut in 1792, Harvard and Massachusetts at varying times between 1780 and 1814, and finally Dartmouth and New Hampshire after 1815.

Though too much intimacy generally seemed unacceptable to the couples, the need for some kind of alliance remained. New York did not forsake Columbia after the state university was pared down in 1787. And after the Supreme Court decision, New Hampshire and Dartmouth appeared to be heading for an alliance almost as intimate as the one Marshall had broken up.

The competing claims of Federalists and Republicans had tugged at and strained the alliance, but they had not destroyed it. Harvard had received its largest state donation, the $100,000 bank tax of 1814, as a sort of reparation for serving as a combat zone for the two parties. Yale had more or less been the paid retainer of the "Standing Order" in the struggle for toleration in Connecticut. Dartmouth's trustees seemed to have thrown the college into politics as if by plan and purpose. Despite the seeming strength of the alliance up to 1820, the connection began to wane, not to break but to wither away, in the thirty years after that date. Our couples gradually, often imperceptibly, were becoming estranged from one another.

Of course, it is always difficult to describe the precise nature of any estrangement. With our colleges and states, one thing was clear: legislatures were no longer willing to make financial grants — a grant of $7,000 to Yale in 1831 was the last grant made to any of our colleges until 1850. But what did this inaction mean — hostility, apathy, or insolvency? The colleges said the states "should" continue to aid them. Most of the legislatures expressed pride in the colleges but concluded that financial grants would be "inexpedient at the present time." Strangely enough, although financial support ceased, there was no corresponding change in the state connections with college government. The Massachusetts senate still sat with the Harvard Board of Overseers; the Connecticut senators remained on the Yale Corporation; the governor of New Hampshire was an ex officio member of the Dartmouth trustees; and Columbia was as "supervised" by the New York Regents between 1820 and 1850 as it had been in 1787. Since financial support and state representation had increased jointly in the earlier years, why did these two components of state influence not wane together?

What caused this somewhat disjointed estrangement, and what did it mean? Did the states lose interest in the colleges and in the men who studied there? Or were the states overwhelmed by other concerns that claimed priority over the colleges? And what kind of new priority was necessary to weaken that alliance which had once been considered essential to a healthy government? We might also ask if the estrangement was mutual. Did the colleges lose interest in the the states? Were the colleges now trying to gain independence from the disorder of the political imbroglios to which they had been willing accomplices?

The answers to these questions are not entirely clear. Contemporary observers, though they perceived the estrangement, were not able to give explanations that satisfied either themselves or the historian who reads their accounts today. Still, there are a number of clues we can pursue. Even before 1820 we saw competitors vying with the colleges for the favor of the legislatures. Common schools had successfully challenged the colleges' hold on the state treasury in Connecticut in 1795, and in New York in 1795 and again in 1805. Competing colleges had appeared in New York and Massachusetts. Still, before 1820 the common schools had not completely won the state treasury, nor had competing colleges diverted the attention of the legislators from the older institutions. Harvard, not Williams or Bowdoin, received the largest share of the 1814 bank tax. But after 1820, and particularly in the 1830s and 1840s, common schools and social welfare activities such as insane asylums and institutes for the deaf and dumb began to monopolize the assemblies when the time came for the state to distribute its bounty.

If the colleges faced new and more vigorous competitors they also encountered a barrage of criticisms which asserted that the higher institutions were unworthy of support — regardless of the needs of the competitors. The critics, who were more often college graduates than those illusive "common men" of whose "rise" at that time many historians remind us, claimed that the colleges were anachronistic — small, aristocratic, and sectarian in a country that was growing large, democratic, and supposedly tolerant. Unfortunately, the response to this criticism by spokesmen for the colleges sounded so reactionary to the popular mind that many people thought the colleges really confirmed the charges of their critics.

In addition to the pressure exerted by critics and competitors, the old ties between college and state may have been strained by more general forces and trends in American society. Some historians have pointed out that the "private" business corporation emerged in the period between 1820 and 1850. Does it not sound logical that the private college was just a reflection of this trend appearing in the business world? Yes, it sounds logical; but did it happen that way? And what about the extension of the suffrage? Was it not the common man who wanted the common school? That too sounds plausible; but can the assertion be supported? Was it the common man who lobbied in the legislature? Finally, we cannot dismiss the Dartmouth College decision. Was it Marshall's ruling which caused the states to abandon interest in the colleges? In chapter 2 an attempt was made to discredit this thesis. We should see if activities in our states and in the West after 1820 affect the argument.

It should be clear by now that the causes of the estrangement of college and state will be somewhat hard to grasp. Competitors, critics, private business corporations, and the common man all exerted some influence. But if some of these elements wielded influence before 1820, what combination caused the change in state support and interest after 1820? Later these various elements will be weighed and assigned priorities. But before embarking on this exercise, let us first examine the facts which do exist about our colleges and states in the years between 1820 and 1850. It is possible to tell when the states ceased to aid the colleges, what the critics said, and how the colleges responded.

Harvard received its last financial grant from Massachusetts in 1823, when the bank tax of 1814 expired. The Federalists, who had granted that tax and were friends of Harvard, lost the election that year. Undaunted by the change in party, the Harvard Corporation petitioned the new Republican legislature in 1824 for a renewal of the grant at the reduced rate of $6,000 annually for the next five years. The funds were to go for scholarships and an observatory. Though the senate committee appointed to consider the petition responded favorably to the request and also recommended that Williams receive support of $2,000 per year for the same period, the legislature failed to heed the committee's advice.

In 1825 the Republicans took a step which, at first glance, might have been interpreted as an action against Harvard and Williams; it chartered a new college in Massachusetts — Amherst. The chartering of Amherst did pose a threat to Williams. In fact the president of the older college had left Williamstown in 1821 with fifteen students (one-fifth of the college) for the express purpose of transforming the Amherst academy into a college. But Harvard was little affected by this new competitor. Modeled along Congregational lines, Amherst did not compete with the Unitarian institution for students on denominational grounds. As Harvard had not depended on a flow of students from central Massachusetts for some time, the new college was not a competitor for geographic reasons. And in terms of state support, the legislature had in no way created a new rival. Also, the Republicans stipulated in the act of incorporation "that the granting of this charter shall never be considered as any pledge on the part of the Government that pecuniary aid shall hereafter be granted to the college." This was a strange gesture toward a college whose advocates, according to Samuel Eliot Morison, had led a campaign to win central Massachusetts for the Republicans.[1]

Even though the chartering of Amherst did not directly injure Harvard, the loss of state funds caused a financial panic at the college. Harvard's budget, mostly composed of salaries and building maintenance, was largely fixed. Without state aid the college quickly ran into debt, as it was difficult to lower expenses, even though undergraduate enrollment decreased from 267 in 1824 to 199 in 1826. In 1825 the college's loss amounted to $4,000. The situation improved

1. Morison, *Three Centuries of Harvard*, pp. 218–19.

slightly in 1827, but the $3,265 deficit of that year was still too large a debt to service out of a $34,564 budget.

The trustees did not want to embark on a permanent policy of deficit finance. At first they thought they would gamble and lower the tuition fee from $55 to $30 with the hope of attracting more students. Possibly they realized that their market was limited. In any case, they maintained the $55 tuition fee and economized by reducing the president's salary from $2,550 to $2,250. The professors' salaries were lowered from $1,700 to $1,500.[2]

Harvard's problems in the 1820s were not induced by the state alone. Just as the college was hit from without by loss of state support, it was threatened from within by its own faculty. In the years 1824 and 1825 the resident instructors tried to gain control of the Harvard Corporation by claiming that a nonresident board of fellows was illegal. The faculty asserted that the "fellows" mentioned in the charter of 1650 were meant to be the same as the fellows of English colleges, that is, residents who received an income from the funds of the corporation.

The corporation refuted the charge by using much the same argument as the state of New Hampshire had employed in the Dartmouth College case. Rejecting the English definition of *fellow,* the trustees asserted, "The laws of Massachusetts abound in names of officers borrowed from those of England, while at the same time only a general resemblance and sometimes a very remote one is found in their qualification and duties."[3] They then announced that the fellows at Harvard derived their authority not, as in England, from the bounty of the founder but from the legislature. The corporation finished its reply to the faculty with a reference to the virtue of the legislature. The representatives of the people certainly would not have made grants of money to an illegal body that had violated a publicly granted charter.

2. HC Minutes, Aug. 19 and Sept. 28, 1827.
3. HC Minutes, Jan. 11, 1825.

Unlike John Wheelock, the resident instructors at Harvard did not resort to a legislature or to a court to press charges against the alleged violations of the charter by the corporation. This was fortunate for the college, as it prevented even the possibility of a Republican legislature adjudicating a difference between two Federalist tribes, the faculty and the Harvard Corporation. In the light of the Dartmouth College case, it is interesting to wonder if the Federalist trustees realized that in noting the power of the legislature they had espoused a Republican argument to save themselves?

While neither the faculty nor the corporation had asked the legislature to intervene in the attempted "Revolution of 1825" and while the failure of the assembly to renew the bank tax had been most dismaying, the college did not lose interest in seeking the aid of the public body. It still viewed the assembly as a protector and a potential source of financial support. In 1832 the corporation petitioned for funds to build a fireproof building to house several valuable collections in the college library. Extolling the utility of these holdings, the trustees pointed out, "In the recent controversy between the United States and Great Britain, relative to the boundaries of the State of Maine, charts and works were found in it which could not be obtained elsewhere in Europe or America, and which being deemed in some respects conclusive in favor of the right of the United States by its counsel." [4] As in 1824, a senate committee commended the project and the legislature failed to appropriate the money. Fortunately, the trustees were able to build the library with the $100,000 bequest of former Massachusetts governor and corporation fellow Christopher Gore, who had died in 1827.

Despite this refusal, Harvard still believed that the legislature's lack of interest was only temporary. In 1840 it tried to revive enthusiasm for the observatory, which the assembly had rejected in 1824 and again in 1837 in spite of the backing of Governor Edward Everett. While the college had

---

4. *Report of the Committee on the Petition of the President and Fellows of Harvard College* (1832), HUA.

raised money for a building through private subscriptions, it thought the legislature might want to aid in staffing the facility. It might be easier to obtain money for jobs than for bricks. Such was not the case. The assembly rejected the "lighthouse in the skies" a third time.

Meanwhile, Harvard's fellow colleges were also asking the legislature for support. Williams appealed unsuccessfully in 1837, 1839, and 1842. Amherst advocates evidently believed that the Republicans did not intend to adhere to the "no aid" clause in the college charter. The college petitioned, with no success, annually from 1827 to 1832 and again in 1837 and 1838. Finally, the legislators loosened their purse-strings in 1847 and granted $5,000 a year for five years to Amherst. The college was not selfish with its good fortune and agreed to make a joint appeal with Harvard and Williams in 1848.

The trio composed a grand and painless plan for state support — the decades-old dream of a perpetual fund that would impose no taxation on the people and require no annual approval on the part of the legislature. Rather than create a separate fund for higher education, the colleges thought it best to build on the base of the Massachusetts common school fund, which had been established in 1834 with the proceeds from the sale of state-held lands in Maine. By statute the fund was limited to a capital of $1 million. In 1848 the fund had reached $850,000, and it appeared as if the land revenue would soon bring the fund to its statutory limit. The colleges proposed that the state raise the limit to $1,500,000 and distribute the interest on the additional $500,000 ($30,000 per annum) to higher education. The funds would be used to subsidize, but not to abolish, tuition. Harvard's fee ($75) would be lowered so that "young men of moderate circumstances" could go to college without undue financial sacrifice.[5] The colleges would gain permanent support and virtuous young men would be spurred to higher achievements.

5. For the full details of the plan, see *Report of State Aid to Colleges 1848* (Massachusetts House Document no. 112, HUA).

No money would be taken from the common schools, and no new taxes would be levied. Could the legislature refuse such a perfect offer?

The assembly could and did refuse the proposal. College officials concluded that the rejection could not have been caused by any fault in the plan. Clearly, the people of Massachusetts did not understand the value of higher education. If the memorial was to be presented again in 1849, someone must inform the public of their need for colleges. Samuel Eliot, treasurer of Harvard, accepted the assignment and addressed the people of Boston through six articles in the *Boston Advertiser*. Like Edward Everett in the *North American Review* of 1820, Eliot asserted that public support for colleges was much more desirable than reliance on private philanthropy. The state should never allow the rich to undertake what should be a public responsibility, or force the poor to accept private charity. If this happened, the treasurer warned:

> There would be no gratitude to her for that which was accomplished without her aid; and she would be justly regarded as a parent who instead of providing as she was well able to do for all her children, placed the least fortunate in a state of dependence upon the others, and thus fomented, as far as she could, mutual jealousy, instead of mutual respect.[6]

Eliot felt it necessary to reply to a number of the current arguments against public support. He explained that colleges were not competing with common schools but were complimentary to them, as the higher institutions supplied teachers for the lower ranks. Acknowledging the fact that some men of true genius (e.g. Benjamin Franklin) had never gone to college, Eliot countered, "Was there ever one of these self-made men, as they are called, who did not lament over his want of means of early education?"[7]

6. Samuel A. Eliot, "Our Schools and Colleges," *Boston Daily Advertiser,* 1848 (clippings in HUA).
7. Ibid.

After speaking in terms of abstract values, the treasurer thought it might be wise to offer a concrete example of the benefits of public support. He could have pointed to Harvard at the time of the American Revolution; instead, he chose West Point as his illustration. The victories of trained officers in the Mexican War proved the value of highly educated men in a democratic society: "Unfailing victory over long-practised soldiers, in every conflict and the capture of every position, however ably fortified, were not the consequences of uninstructed valor. They were the result of educated bravery, of scientific courage. And why should not similar effects be seen in the more peaceful arts of production?" [8]

Despite the sound reasoning in the above arguments, Eliot made other assertions in his articles which may have done more harm than good. In addressing the working man, the treasurer in no way portrayed Harvard as an institution with expanding courses of study for everyone. According to him, it was Harvard's mission to offer education to only a limited number of students. "It results from the unavoidable constitution of human society," reasoned Eliot, "that a portion only of its members require the more extended education which is given in colleges." Harvard College was not for all men, only for those going into the professions. To Eliot, public support for these occupations was as wise a policy in 1848 as it had been to Ezra Stiles in 1777. It constituted a part of the common good: "It is for the interest of *all* then that *some* should be carefully and thoroughly prepared for the pursuits referred to, by the best education that can be given them." [9]

To secure a public grant, Harvard needed to influence groups other than just the general public. After all, it was not the people but their representatives who would grant the needed funds. An advocate of greater fame than Eliot undertook the statehouse assignment. When the colleges repeated their petition in 1849, Edward Everett summoned his su-

8. Ibid.
9. Ibid.

preme oratorical ability on their behalf. He had resigned as president of Harvard (1846–49) and announced to the assembly that he was speaking merely as a citizen interested in the Commonwealth of Massachusetts, which he had served as governor (1836–39).

Everett explained that support for higher education did not mean that the funds would be taken from the common schools, as a minority report from a senate committee had asserted. Everett pointed out that he had helped create the Massachusetts Board of Education in 1837 and had never dreamed that the common schools should replace the colleges as the sole recipients of state aid. All levels of education should be supported. The ex-governor then reminded the legislators that their failure to support the college constituted a rejection of both their public duty and their Massachusetts heritage. In response to the current popular theory that college men should pay for their own education, Everett exhorted:

> This, Sir, is not Massachusetts doctrine. It is not the doctrine of the Pilgrims. This Commonwealth was founded by college-bred men; and before their feet had well laid hold of the pathless wilderness, they took order for founding an institution like those in which they had themselves been trained, the Universities of Cambridge and Oxford. . . . It is not the doctrine of the stern Puritan fathers, who, for a hundred and fifty years, and through the darkest periods of our colonial and provincial history, withheld not a frugal bounty from the cherished Seminary. It is not the doctrine of the Revolutionary worthies. Amidst all the popular susceptibilities of the day, it never entered into their imaginations, that Academic education less than School education was the interest of the entire people.[10]

10. Edward Everett, *Speech in Support of the Memorial of Harvard, Williams, and Amherst Colleges Delivered before the Joint Committee of Education, February 7, 1849* (HUA), p. 25.

Regrettably, neither Pilgrims nor "Revolutionary wor-thies" formed the majority in the legislature of 1849. Even though a joint committee presented a bill that approved the memorial and tried to make it more politically attractive by augmenting the common school fund by an additional $250,000 for the support of normal schools, the legislature rejected the proposal.

But though Harvard and the other colleges in Massachu-setts were defeated in the assembly, the world of learning, by a strange twist of fate, may have gained. The bill of 1849 was presented in the assembly by John Lothrop Motley, an 1831 Harvard graduate serving his one and only term as a state representative. Motley was distressed at the failure of the bill and even more by the fact that George S. Boutwell, a man with only a common school education, had displayed greater oratorical ability in opposing the bill than he him-self had in sponsoring it. As a result he left Massachusetts politics and in 1851 departed for Europe, where he wrote his *Rise of the Dutch Republic.* In exile Motley probably ac-complished more within the world of scholarship to bring fame to his college than he could have done in Massachusetts politics.

Like Motley, Harvard grew disenchanted with the legisla-ture after 1849 and ceased to appeal for support. Possibly the college had foreseen this end in 1824. Yet for twenty-five years the college had viewed itself as a natural object of patronage by the state. The state had separated from the col-lege in the area of finance. There had never been the first suggestion at Harvard that the college would benefit by being wholly independent.

Columbia's experience with public disinterest and the dry-ing up of state support was similar to, but more severe than, that of Harvard. The $10,000 grant made by New York to Columbia in 1819 proved to be the last instance of state aid for that college. Like Harvard, Columbia had no way of knowing that this was the last grant and continued to appeal to the legislature. The trustees petitioned annually from 1820 to 1827. In 1823 it looked as if aid might materialize, but the assembly wanted to tie the grant to a professorship appointed by the regents. The trustees refused the offer, not on any grounds of academic freedom or state interference, but for the reason that they had intended to cancel the college debt with the funds.[11]

Although all of our colleges incurred financial losses at one time or another, the college debt played a particularly significant role in the affairs of Columbia. Unlike Bostonians, New Yorkers were not accustomed to making donations to their college; Columbia received only one personal donation before 1850 — a gift of $20,000 in 1843 to endow the Gebhard Professorship of German. The college thus realized its income almost entirely from tuition and from land rents dating to the colonial period; the former source provided about two-thirds of the budget. Since enrollment fluctuated as much as 20 percent from year to year, budget deficits frequently occurred. Even in years of relatively high enrollment (110–30 students), tuition revenue was not sufficient to erase the losses of the leaner years. In order to cover these deficits and to acquire capital for construction and maintenance costs, the trustees borrowed the needed funds. As early as 1824 the debt stood at $15,000.

Without state support, the debt, and the interest required to service it, became such a burden that the trustees decided to improve the financial situation by raising income and lowering expenses. After increasing tuition from $50 to $100 in 1824, they economized by cutting the salaries of the college officers. The president, who had enjoyed a salary of $3,500, was given $2,600;[12] the professors' income decreased from $2,500 to $2,200.

11. CCT Minutes, Feb. 17, 1823.
12. It is interesting to note that the $3,500 salary paid the president of Columbia was the second-highest sum paid to any civil official in New York. Only the governor received a higher salary, $4,000. The chief justice was paid only $2,000.

Columbia's financial difficulties were serious enough while it was the only college in New York City. Its problems increased after 1831 when Columbia found itself in competition with a second college, the University of the City of New York (later New York University). The chartering of this competitor was an act of the state and reflected a change in the state's educational policy during the last decade.

Although the regents possessed no funds they could grant to Columbia, they had long recognized a responsibility to protect the city college and other colleges in the state by withholding charters from potential competitors. The regents had reported in 1811 "that colleges are to be cautiously erected and only when called for by strong expediency." At the same time the board had established the principles that no charter would be granted to a sectarian institution and that any group desiring a college charter must have raised a capital endowment of $50,000.

In 1822 the regents were beset by petitions for college charters from a number of denominational groups. Despite their reasoning in 1811, after considerable debate they decided that competition, even denominational competition, might be good for higher education. They recognized the fact that many people still thought education could best be promoted by a concentration of funds, libraries, and professors in a few institutions, but asserted, "in this country such establishments are neither applicable to the state of society, congenial to the manners and character of the people or consistent with the form or principles of the government." A diffusion of knowledge was the desirable goal even if it did not produce "perfect and accomplished scholars." [13]

Acting under the principles of this new egalitarian philosophy, the regents reversed their previous policy and agreed to charter more than one college in any given geographic area. Future college organizers would not be required to show an increasing demand for higher education on the part of

13. Hough, *Historical and Statistical Record of the University of the State of New York*, p. 94.

prospective students; only the $50,000 capital requirement would remain in force. Geneva College (later Hobart) was the first institution to be chartered under this policy. Sponsored by Episcopalians, it was incorporated by the regents in 1825.

But the regents had gone too far in their egalitarianism; in the process they had unknowingly stripped themselves of their power. Since the state university had, in essence, renounced its desire to control the chartering of colleges, many men in the legislature thought there was no longer a reason to delegate this power to the university. So the legislature reasserted its coequal authority to grant charters and exercised this prerogative for the first time in 1831 by incorporating the University of the City of New York.[14] The regents were unable to reassert themselves until 1851.

So New York was again to have a university. This 1831 project was not organized by denominational or even popular interests. Instead, it had been planned by some of the leading men in New York City who were distressed at the lack of adequate professional and technical education in the metropolis.

The opening of the technically oriented University of London in 1828 had caused many New Yorkers to realize that their city was behind in its provision of educational facilities. In December, 1829, a group of nine men, including two Columbia trustees, met and decided to found a university on the London model.[15] The funds for the institution were to

14. The legislature had never completely delegated its power to the regents. After the reorganization of the state university in 1787, both the legislature and the university had the power to charter colleges. The legislature deferred to the university until 1831. After that date no college was chartered by the regents until 1851. College organizers sought a legislative charter because it did not contain the $50,000 capital stipulation.

15. The two Columbia trustees were The Right Reverend Jonathan Wainwright (Harvard, 1812) and The Reverend James Mathews (Union, 1803; and Yale, DD, 1823), who became chancellor of the new university. Both men resigned from the Columbia board in 1830. Wainwright returned in 1853 after becoming Episcopal bishop of New York. In addition to these two trustees, there were two Columbia graduates among the founders of the university, John Delafield (1802) and Hugh Maxwell (1808).

be obtained by selling shares of stock in the new corporation. No dividends would be declared but subscribers could endow and name the recipient of a scholarship for $1,500; a similar arrangement for a professorship could be obtained for $10,000.

Knowing well the need to generate enthusiasm for the new institution, the founders decided to organize a convocation of the leading minds in America to discuss the problems of education. The meeting opened on October 20, 1830, in the council chambers of the City of New York. Indeed, most of the leading minds in America were there. Albert Gallatin, Francis Lieber, Thomas Gallaudet, Edward Livingston, Benjamin Silliman, Theodore Dwight Woolsey, and Jared Sparks headed the galaxy of intellects.[16]

After surveying the state of American education, a number of men, including Gallatin, Lieber, and Gallaudet, concluded that the level of learning in America was not high enough. In order to stimulate intellect, large numbers of students must be attracted to institutions of higher education. The way to achieve this, they thought, was not to make tuition free but to abolish Greek and Latin as mandatory requirements; the old classical curriculum was the principal stumbling block to the diffusion of knowledge. Some men declared that 800 to 1,000 students would flock to a New York institution that offered a course of study excluding the classics.[17]

The Literary Convention of 1830 clearly gave the founders of the university a mandate to proceed with their plan. The new institution would offer instruction without the ancient language requirements and would provide a place where

16. The assorted speeches delivered at this meeting, compiled as *Journal of the Proceedings of a Convention of Literary and Scientific Gentlemen, Held in the Common Council of the City of New York, October, 1830* (New York, 1831), form what may be the most important educational document of the antebellum period. The educational philosophy in the *Journal* offers a striking alternative to the Yale Report of 1828.

17. Theodore F. Jones, ed., *New York University 1832–1932* (New York, 1933), pp. 12–13.

all men of literary and scientific interests could give public lectures on a wide variety of topics.

The founders claimed they were not building a competitor for Columbia College but creating an institution that would supply the needs the older college failed to fill. Columbia's guardians felt otherwise. Despite the "university" plans, the "college" trustees feared that the new institution would soon offer the same classical education as Columbia. After all, when the college had been a part of the state university, the regents had developed similar dreams for an institution with many professors offering instruction in every branch of knowledge. The trustees reasoned that New York City was no better prepared to support such a grand scheme in 1830 than it had been forty-five years earlier. They were doubtful about the supposed thousand young men who would flock to the university. The trustees believed they had already tapped New York's supply of men interested in higher education; a new university would simply divide the attention and patronage of a limited clientele between the two institutions.

Even before the Literary Convention convened, Columbia had taken a number of steps to forestall the founding of a second institution. To dispel the idea that the college was wedded to a classical curriculum or that it was uninterested in attracting a diversified clientele, Columbia had established in January, 1830, a literary-scientific course and had proposed lectureships in more than fifteen subjects ranging from Greek to mineralogy. At the same time the college had created a number of free scholarships to be awarded to students from the different educational societies in the city — two apiece to the Corporation of the City of New York, the High School of New York, the New York Public School Society, the Clinton Hall Association, the Mercantile Library Association, the Mechanic and Scientific Institute, and the General Society of Mechanics and Tradesmen. Also one free scholarship was offered to every religious denomination.

After authorizing these "household" improvements, the trustees appointed different committees in February, 1830, to meet with the outside world. One delegation tried to convince the founders of the university to merge their interests with Columbia's. Others sought to strengthen Columbia's position with potential benefactors of both institutions.

The trustees approached the City of New York and agreed to accept public officials on Columbia's board in exchange for financial support. If the city would patronize Columbia as the "city college," the mayor and recorder would become ex officio board members, and "for every $20,000 in money or in real estate granted or conveyed to the trustees . . . the said city shall have the right to appoint one trustee." [18] Under this arrangement the trustees were willing to admit twenty-two new members in addition to the mayor and recorder. They suggested that the city could immediately appoint ten trustees by donating the almshouse, valued at $200,000.[19] In a burst of democratic rhetoric the board concluded its proposal to the city:

> The advantages of the above proposal in respect to the city are, that *all* the citizens, merchants, mechanics, working men, as well as professional men, all who are entitled to vote at the city and county elections will have a real and substantial voice in the concerns of the college through their representatives in the Common Council of the City.[20]

An advantage to Columbia would be that the gift of the almshouse would spoil the plans of the university men, who also wanted this city facility.

The city was not the only public body the trustees approached in February, 1830. To secure students for the literary-scientific course, the board offered a plan to the

18. CCT Minutes, Feb. 3, 1830. The concept of selling trusteeships was not new. When the state university was first organized in 1784, a position known as Founders Regent was available to anyone who made a financial contribution equivalent to 1,000 bushels of wheat.

19. CCT Minutes, Feb. 3, 1830.

20. Ibid.

United States Navy whereby up to forty-five midshipmen at the New York naval yard could receive a scientific education for a group tuition fee of $3,500 per year. The trustees did not want to neglect any opportunity for additional support and added, "Should it enter into the views of the government to provide instruction for its young officers in literature or modern languages, Columbia College stands prepared to furnish these also on equally moderate terms or the classes are open to them individually on the payment of a moderate fee." [21]

In many ways the trustees had proposed a revolution. The college was ready to become a combination of modern-day City College, Annapolis, and Columbia. Literally, Columbia College was for sale; almost any reasonable offer would have been accepted.

Unfortunately, all of these efforts failed; there were no buyers for any of Columbia's offers. Commodore Chauncey of the naval yard liked the proposal but could not secure the assent of the Department of the Navy. The city was uninterested in being the patron of scholarship, and the organizers of the University of the City of New York went forward with their plans to erect a second institution of higher education. Columbia did succeed, however, in persuading the city not to give support to the university. If the two were to compete, at least it would be an even match.

All of Columbia's fears about a rival materialized, at least in the first years of competition. In November, 1830, 133 students, of whom 119 paid tuition, had matriculated in the college.[22] When the university opened in the fall of 1832, 127 students appeared at Columbia, but by January, 1833, only 112 remained. The trustees were particularly depressed because, "Several of our former students, indeed, applied for their dismissals for the avowed purpose of entering the Uni-

21. Ibid.
22. As a result of the full scholarships authorized in 1830, the number of paying students was always lower than the total number who matriculated each fall.

versity of the City of New York." [23] The drop in enrollment precipitated even greater financial distress than the college had previously encountered; the college debt reached $31,650 in 1833. An appeal to Columbia's friends and alumni in 1835 for $50,000 went unanswered. The following year the debt rose to $48,300. To whom could the college turn?

The president and trustees were prepared to espouse progress or reaction. In January, 1837, President William Duer suggested that the college strive for university status and appoint faculties of law, medicine, and divinity. Yet knowing that part of Columbia's problems stemmed from its reputation as an Episcopalian college, Duer looked away from the university path and wondered if it might not be best for Columbia to declare itself a sectarian college. "It may be worthy of consideration," he proposed, "whether some measure cannot be derived for obtaining such support from Episcopalians as may at least counterbalance the disadvantages under which the college at present labours from the sectarian character unjustly imputed to it." [24]

Specifically, Duer envisioned some type of union between Columbia and the General Theological Seminary. Like the city and the navy, the church did not choose to accept responsibility for the college. After this defeat, the trustees decided to approach the state again. An appeal to the legislature in 1842 also failed to bring support. This rejection was particularly insulting because the assembly had been distributing cash grants from Andrew Jackson's 1837 treasury surplus to Hamilton, Geneva, and even the University of the City of New York since 1838. Though it is difficult to understand why one New York City institution was aided but not the other, the chancellor of the University of the City of New York claimed he had persuaded the legislature that the university was more than a mere college.

In 1850 Columbia's future appeared bleak. Enrollment

23. CCT Minutes, Jan. 7, 1833.
24. CCT Minutes, Jan. 4, 1837.

was low; the number of paying students had rarely exceeded a hundred for the past thirty years, and the University of the City of New York had usually surpassed Columbia in its ability to attract students.[25] The trustees anticipated a deficit of $5,200 that year, which would raise the total debt to $68,000, a level they thought would seriously impair the efficiency of the college. Columbia had been rejected by its alumni, the church, the city, the state, and the United States Navy. Would anyone come to its aid?

The college was to be rescued, but not as it had hoped and not by any one person. Within the next decade the growth and expansion of New York City and the consequent rise of land values soon made the Botanical Garden a better endowment than the gift of any merchant prince, community, or government.

Though Columbia stagnated in the second quarter of the nineteenth century, this was not without effect on the trustees. By 1850 the governing board fully realized that the institution would never prosper as a small college — in terms

25. Comparative Undergraduate Enrollment between Columbia and the University of the City of New York.

	Col	UCNY		Col	UCNY
1825–26	134		1838–39	149	56
1826–27	128		1839–40	131	81
1827–28	103		1840–41	121	122
1828–29	88		1841–42	104	135
1829–30	101		1842–43	95	151
1830–31	133		1843–44	104	143
1831–32	127	42	1844–45	114	131
1832–33	100	a	1845–46	124	135
1833–34	99	a	1846–47	125	146
1834–35	97	a	1847–48	124	151
1835–36	99	a	1848–49	136	135
1836–37	107	153	1849–50	113	115
1837–38	114	122			

a Figures not available

Note: Only between 1833 and 1837 did the presence of the university cause a marked dip in Columbia's enrollment.

Source: *Annual Report of the University of the State of New York* (Albany, (1828–50).

either of enrollment or curriculum. So when the Botanical Garden rents began to fill the Columbia treasury in the late 1880s, the funds were not spent to recruit students from distant states in order to expand the size of the college, but to transform a small college into a university with professional and graduate facilities. This university expansion was not hampered by undergraduate advocates as at Yale and Dartmouth. Unlike Harvard where the university movement succeeded because of Charles Eliot's ability to overcome the conservative college forces, Columbia's later expansion resulted from a positive response by trustees and presidents to the failure of the institution as a classical college.

While Columbia declined after 1820, both Yale and Dartmouth attracted large numbers of students. Despite this quantitative success, the two Congregational colleges were unable to engage the support of the state.

Yale's enrollment in 1820 stood at 319. In the late 1830s it rose to more than 430 and still hovered around 400 in 1850 — the number of students from Connecticut reached a high point of 194 in 1836. With a student body of this size, the Connecticut institution was the largest college in the United States throughout this thirty-year period. In the 1790s the aspect of a large, flourishing academic center had attracted the attention and support of the state. But in the decade following 1820, no money flowed from the state coffers to Yale.

At the beginning of the decade Yale seemed unconcerned that its Federalist party had lost control of the state and continued to petition the legislature for support. In 1822 President Jeremiah Day (1817–46) asked for aid and emphasized that Yale could secure Connecticut's reputation and prestige in an expanding nation. "While she can never be distinguished for extent of territory, commerce, wealth or magnificent cities," explained the president, "her college, her asylum, her academies and her schools, if wisely managed, and liberally supported, may command respect and admiration abroad." [26] This plea did not even arouse the enthusiasm of an assembly committee, much less the entire legislature. The committee found Yale "the pride of our state" but was "of the opinion, that at present it would be inexpedient to make the grant." [27]

It may have been "inexpedient" for a number of reasons. The Episcopalians were still planning a college of their own and the legislators may well have thought it wise to wait until that group made a firm decision. A grant to Yale could have been interpreted as an act against the Episcopalians. Also, the legislators may have hoped that they could induce Yale to loosen its orthodoxy by withholding support. If this was their intention, they succeeded. In 1823 Yale feared the assembly would charter a second college and consequently decided to abolish the rule that all instructors subscribe to the Westminster Confession of Faith — a move that was also necessary to receive a $5,000 benefaction from Sheldon Clark. Unfortunately, the Congregationalists had waited until it was too late. They made their decision the day before the assembly was to vote on a charter for Washington College (Trinity). The legislature was unmoved by Yale's "midnight" gesture, and chartered Connecticut's second college on May 23.

Although Yale's 122-year-old monopoly of higher education was broken, the presence of a competitor yielded an unexpected profit. Supporters of the Episcopal college maneuvered an educational bank bonus through the assembly in 1831 which netted Yale $7,000. This bank bonus, the gift of a Republican assembly, was the last Connecticut grant to Yale — and the last grant to any of our colleges until the proceeds of the Morrill Act were distributed after the Civil War.

26. Jeremiah Day, *The Memorial and Statement of the President and Fellows of Yale College* (1822), Beinecke Library, Yale University.

27. *Report of the Committee to whom was referred the memorial and statement of the President and Fellows of Yale College* (1822), Beinecke Library, Yale University.

The Democrats captured the assembly in 1833. Yale had no way of predicting the action of the new party, but probably assumed that, at worst, the Democrats would be indifferent to higher education. Possibly the college thought its fortunes would rise in 1834 when the Whigs dominated the legislature. But much to Yale's surprise, the assembly removed the tax-exempt privileges on property held by Yale instructors. Since the officers had to pay a new tax, the state had, in effect, lowered salaries — a negative appropriation. The exact impact of this penalty became evident in 1837 when the corporation resolved "that the Professors of the Academical Department in this College be each annually allowed forty dollars in consideration of their liability to the payment of taxes." [28]

Despite this negative action of the legislature, Yale, like Harvard, continued to view the state as a potential source of aid for more than a decade. [29] This was particularly interesting because Yale found in the 1830s that it could depend on its alumni for financial support; they had raised $100,000 between 1831 and 1836. [30] Still, in 1838 Ebenezer Baldwin announced in his *Annals of Yale College,* "This institution ever has been and we confidently hope ever will be, the pride of our State, whose legislatures have from time to time extended a fostering hand." But he was appalled that "Its natural guardians, the legislators of the state . . . look on with

28. YC Minutes, August, 1837.

29. In contrast to my theory of a negative state action, Brooks M. Kelley has suggested, in his forthcoming *Yale: A History,* that Yale may actually have sought the Act of 1834. Not all exemptions granted by the 1754 charter were removed. Nonrevenue-producing property (i.e. college buildings), and even revenue-producing property yielding up to $6,000 a year, remained exempt. And a new exemption not mentioned in the charter was added in 1834; all funds of the college, which were rising in the 1830s, were also to be exempt. Thus Kelley thinks the corporation may have traded professorial exemption for the exemption on funds. However, I know of no state or municipal tax on funds, as opposed to real estate, in the 1830s. Also, there is no mention in the corporation minutes of Yale seeking this act, though all other advances to the legislature in this period are noted.

30. See chapter 5 for more on the Centum Milia Fund and the activities of Yale alumni in fund-raising.

strange apathy and extend no cheering hand for its relief." [31] And in 1846 when a donor offered a gift of $5,000 to the corporation for a professorship of agricultural chemistry with the stipulation that $20,000 be raised elsewhere, it was to the Connecticut legislature that the trustees turned. Possibly they thought an appeal for such a practical project would arouse state enthusiasm. They miscalculated; the assembly was uninterested.

This state refusal to support agricultural education marked a watershed in the history of higher education. When Ezra Stiles had contemplated the addition of professional instruction in law and medicine in 1777, he had intended that the state should pay for this appendage. The grant of 1792 endowing a professorship of law had partially fulfilled this intent. In the 1840s many people in Connecticut were calling for instruction in the mechanical arts and agriculture, as well as legal and medical training. Since neither the state nor the college wished to assume financial responsibility for this instruction, an impasse developed. In the 1840s and 1850s Yale broke this deadlock by instituting the fee system to maintain and expand its offerings in the professions and science. Thus the trustees were able to create a Department of Philosophy and Arts — later Sheffield Scientific School — and to appoint a professor of practical chemistry and a professor of agricultural chemistry, with the stipulation that their only salary would come from fees paid directly by the students. The college also appointed a number of law instructors under the same fee stipulations. Support for professional and scientific training had shifted from the state to the individual. The college would now be an agent for individuals rather than for the state. Later, the funds for this education would be endowed by professional associations, wealthy industrialists, and the federal government.[32]

While this expansion of nonclassical education, even by

---

31. Ebenezer Baldwin, *Annals of Yale College,* 2d ed. (New Haven, 1838), p. 211.

32. For more on scientific education and methods of finance, see chapter 4.

fee, might have appeared to be a liberal change at orthodox Yale, the clerics still exerted a strong influence on the character of the college. It had been necessary to ordain Jeremiah Day in 1817, and in 1846 the trustees were still unwilling to relinquish this requirement when their choice for president was again a layman — Theodore Dwight Woolsey, professor of Greek language and literature. Woolsey had actually studied theology and was licensed to preach, but he had never been ordained. One Yale historian has suggested that "humility as to his fitness for the work of the ministry had kept him from accepting ordination." [33] However, Woolsey had once written his father, "One thing, however, remains in my mind unchanged and that is an utter repugnance and a fixed decision not to engage in the work of the ministry." [34] The corporation was not so much concerned with his humility or repugnance as with his lay status. Despite this reservation, they elected him president but resolved "that Professor Woolsey be requested, in case of his acceptance of the office of President of this College to unite with the Prudential Committee in making the necessary arrangements for his ordination and installation." [35] Woolsey concluded, no doubt in the manner of Henry IV of France, that Yale was worth a clerical collar, and acquiesced to the corporation's stipulation. Even if Yale could no longer lean on its "natural guardian," the state of Connecticut, it could at least feel it had kept God on its side.

By 1850 Dartmouth, like its sister colleges, found no fountain of support in the state legislature. Yet, while the other three had continually petitioned for aid, Dartmouth had turned its back on the state. Neither John Marshall's decision nor the ensuing negotiations with the state legislature had

33. Ralph Gabriel, *Religion and Learning at Yale* (New Haven, 1958), p. 117.

34. Theodore Salisbury Woolsey, "Theodore Dwight Woolsey," *Yale Review* 2 (1912): 636.

35. YC Minutes, August, 1846.

brought about the rift. Rather, a resurgence of religious orthodoxy in the person of Nathan Lord had severed the college-state relationship that had survived two Wheelocks and
Daniel Webster.

Lord, a graduate of Bowdoin and a Congregational minister in Amherst, Massachusetts, had been a Dartmouth
trustee since 1821. In 1828 he was elected president of the
college. His inaugural address of that year clearly set forth
his educational goals: Dartmouth would remain a small college. The new president was distrustful of the "inventions of
this restless age." Even though he admitted that some of the
educational experiments which "the wise have devised or the
popular voice demanded" might have value, Dartmouth was
not the place for change. He wanted the college to forsake
any university ideas and to maintain a course of study "merely
introductory to professional education." His college would
expand neither upward to offer professional studies nor out-
ward to prepare students for mechanical and agricultural
occupations. The president's address was a little strange in
light of the fact that ninety students were currently enrolled
in the college's medical department.[36]

Despite the presence of this department, which clearly gave
Dartmouth some claim to university status, Lord went on
in his inaugural address to point out the dangers of universities. When defined as a union of college and professional
studies, such institutions should be viewed with caution:

> The examples of other times, when the learning of uni-
> versities all had respect to the future political and ec-
> clesiastical relations of the student, and these institutions
> became little better than panders to allied despotism
> and superstition, may teach us to cultivate our youth
> in the elements of general knowledge, and impart vigor

36. The medical department existed at Dartmouth College throughout
Lord's administration. Enrollment remained at a level around 90–100 until
the late 1840s, when it dropped to the level of 50 where it remained until
Lord left in 1863.

and force and freeness to their minds in the course of sound fundamental study, before they are permitted to engage in any merely professional acquisitions.[37]

As one might imagine, that "fundamental study" was a classical education.

Lord's theories of education were tied to a certain obsession with evil. In his mind, even a classical education was potentially dangerous. "The very cultivation of the mind," he warned, "has frequently a tendency to impair the moral sensibilities." To ward off this danger, piety had to be the order of the day at Dartmouth. "The relations which every individual student sustains to God and to eternity," announced the president, "call imperiously and aloud, that the great principles of moral obligation, the everlasting distinctions between right and wrong, the methods of Divine administration, should be kept before him, in all their significancy, and enforced by the constraining motives of the gospel of Jesus Christ, without which all secondary authority and influence will be comparatively vain." [38]

When Ezra Stiles had proposed to raise Yale from a college to a university in 1777, he had thought that a "happy community" resulted when men were well-instructed in their "rights and liberties." Fifty years later, Lord returned to the thought of Stiles's predecessor, Thomas Clap. Though he abjured sectarian motives, he advocated a college, rather than a university, so that "the destined alliance between religion and learning shall be perfected, and their united influence shall be employed and shall prevail to raise a world from ignorance and sin and wretchedness to the dignity of sons of God." [39] Belief in God, not the laws and mind of man, was his prescription for American higher education.

Since the state of New Hampshire had never created religion and no longer even supported it, Lord saw no need

37. Baxter P. Smith, *History of Dartmouth College* (Boston, 1878), p. 148.
38. Ibid., p. 155.
39. Ibid., p. 156.

for a connection between college and state. Leon Burr Richardson has noted, "Good feeling and sympathy activated by the clergy, leading to private financial support, rather than appropriation of public money was the goal at which he aimed." [40] Under the influence of Lord, the trustees made no appeal for funds to the New Hampshire legislature until after they had expelled the president in 1863. [41]

In turning his back on the state and opening his arms to the faithful, Lord did the college no harm in regard to student enrollment. During his administration (1828–63) Dartmouth more than doubled in size from 125 in 1828 to a peak of 340 in 1840. Enrollment dipped to 179 in 1845 but rose steadily thereafter to a level of 275 in 1860. By the yardstick of numbers, Dartmouth was one of the "largest" colleges in the United States. About 60 percent of the students were from New Hampshire; the remainder came from neighboring states. [42]

So Lord had replaced the alliance between liberty and learning, which had once drawn college and state together, with an alliance between learning and religion. On the surface it appeared as if Dartmouth had profited from the change. But little more than a decade after 1850 Lord's special orthodoxy, which sanctioned slavery, was to bring the unlikely response of a union of trustees and churches against Lord and in support of the federal government.

We have now seen the "fever charts" of the estrangement. At three of the four colleges the waning of interest appeared

40. Richardson, *History of Dartmouth College,* 2 vols. (Hanover, 1932), 1:392.

41. The story of Lord's expulsion appears in chapter 4.

42. The percentage of students from New Hampshire remained fairly constant throughout Dartmouth College's rise and fall in enrollment. Although the rate fluctuated as much as 5% a year, when enrollment began to rise in about 1833, the percentage was sixty and remained there until enrollment decreased ten years later. In the 1850s the percentage was nearer to fifty.

to be that of the state for the college. But what caused the illness? Our colleges had not grown to a size that required greater state support than had been given in the past. Columbia was no larger in 1850 than it had been in 1820. When the three colleges of Massachusetts appealed for aid in 1848–49, they were speaking for only 350 state students, of which about 200 were at Harvard. The student bodies at Yale and Dartmouth had grown, but the number of state students whom the legislature would have aided remained small, again less than 200 at each college.

The size of the appropriations or endowments the colleges requested had not risen. The $20,000 Yale requested for an agricultural chair in 1846 was no more than the bank bonus the state had given in 1814. Although the $30,000-a-year revenue which an expanded school fund would have produced for Massachusetts's three colleges in 1848 was larger than the $16,000 a year provided by the bank tax of 1814, the colleges would certainly have settled for the lower sum if it had been offered.

Were the states without money to give? It is true that legislative journals and gubernatorial messages in the years between 1820 and 1850 were filled with pledges to lower state expenditures and to avoid any form of taxation. New York levied no taxes from 1825 to 1835 and paid the expenses of government from a general fund supported by the revenue from land sales. In the 1840s governors John Davis and Marcus Morton of Massachusetts expressed alarm at increasing expenses — pay for the militia, grants to charitable organizations, and the support of paupers. Retrenchment was the keynote of every address to the legislature. "The people expect it and demand it. The times favor it, and the depression of prices and the stagnation of business justify it," were Morton's words in 1843.[43] Even Edward Everett had advised in 1839, "too much watchfulness cannot be exercised in pre-

43. *Address of His Excellency Marcus Morton to the Two Branches of the Legisature* (Boston, 1843).

venting new calls on the treasury for other purposes and beyond the present available resources of the state." [44]

But the states had not supported the colleges with direct taxes before 1820. If they had continued to grant aid from windfalls of bounty, the colleges would have flourished. The largest refund or bounty ever given by the federal government came in 1837 when Andrew Jackson announced a $37,468,859 surplus in the treasury and ultimately distributed $28,101,644 to the states. New York received $4,014,520; Massachusetts, $1,338,173; Connecticut, $764,670; and New Hampshire, $669,086. Only New York made appropriations from this treasury surplus to any of its colleges — and only $100,000 or about 2½ percent. Despite the protests of Edward Everett, who wanted to distribute $250,000 directly to the colleges and another $200,000 for an observatory, the Massachusetts assembly allotted the money to the towns on a per capita basis to be used as they saw fit. In Connecticut the towns also received the surplus, but they were required to apply one-half to common schools (the Town Deposit Fund). New Hampshire devoted the surplus to "general purposes of government." Clearly, the failure of the states to support colleges from Andrew Jackson's bounty indicated a lack of interest rather than a disability.

The presence of competing interests, particularly the common schools, provides one of the most persuasive explanations for the estrangement of college and state. Revenues raised from state land sales after 1820, again a source that required no taxation, were usually applied to the common schools. In fact, George S. Boutwell stated emphatically in the 1870s that Motley's 1849 bill had failed because of the competition of common schools. In a letter to Motley's biographer, Oliver Wendell Holmes, Boutwell explained:

> In truth he [Motley] espoused the weak side of the
> question and the unpopular one also. His proposition

44. *Address of the Honorable Edward Everett to the Two Branches of the Legislature* (Boston, 1839).

was to endow the colleges at the expense of the fund for the support of the common schools. Failure was inevitable. Neither Webster nor Choate could have carried the bill.[45]

Still, was it just the *presence* of the common schools which increasingly attracted the total attention of the state after 1820? The schools had been *present* before that time. In the 1840s there were vastly more students in the common schools than in the colleges — hundreds of thousands more — but the number of students in common schools had always been greater. When the states had given equal support to colleges and common schools before 1800, it had not been because the same number of students were in each. And before 1820, particularly before 1800, the common schools had been considered the responsibility of local authorities; colleges were the wards of the state. What changed after 1820 to alter this relationship? It was not the mere presence of the schools.

One of the most important changes after 1820 was the organization and systematization of the common schools. With these systems the schools gained administrators (state superintendents of schools or secretaries of boards of education) who could be advocates and who could protect and expand the school funds that legislatures had provided.

In most of our states a common school fund had been created before a state board of education; some states had done this before 1820. Connecticut had authorized such a fund from the sale of Western Reserve lands in 1795 and had made the first appropriation from it in 1799. New York had established its common school fund — as distinguished from the five-year grant of 1795 — through a series of legislation passed between 1805 and 1812.

New Hampshire's Literary Fund of 1821, discussed in chapter 2, was originally earmarked for higher education but was diverted to the common schools in 1828. Massachusetts was the last of our states to start a fund. In 1834, ten

45. Oliver Wendell Holmes, *John Lothrop Motley* (Boston, 1878), p. 56.

years after the last grant to Harvard, the General Court authorized support for the common schools with revenue derived from the sale of Maine lands.

Although Massachusetts was the last state to establish a fund for common schools, it was the first to organize a state board of education. The board began its operations in 1837, with Horace Mann as its first secretary. Two years later Connecticut created a board of commissioners for common schools with Henry Barnard as secretary, but ended this organization in 1842. In 1845 the state authorized the commissioner of the common school fund to be ex officio superintendent of schools, and in 1849 the principal of the state normal school replaced the commissioner as ex officio superintendent. Interestingly enough, Barnard was the normal school principal.

The state boards were later in coming to New Hampshire and New York. The former state appointed a state school commissioner in 1846, but abolished the post in 1850 and authorized the county school commissioners to act jointly as an ex officio state board of education. And though New York had named a superintendent of schools as early as 1812 only to discontinue the position in 1821, the state did not permanently organize a state department of instruction and appoint a superintendent of schools until 1854. Possibly this late organization of the department of instruction partially explains why New York was the one state of our four that continued to grant money to colleges in the 1830s and 1840s.

The alliances between the states and their boards of education, and particularly the permanence of those alliances, differed from state to state. Similarly, the influence and power of the boards and their secretaries varied. In Massachusetts, where the board was strong, it is easy to see how the organized competition of the common schools diverted state funds from the colleges.

While the colleges in Massachusetts always argued that higher education and common schools should not be thought of as competitors for state funds but as complementary parts of a system of education, college-educated advocates of the

common schools claimed that the state need not aid the
colleges if it supported the lower schools. Horace Mann
(Brown, 1819) took this position during his tenure as secretary of the board of education (1837–48). In his first annual
report (1837), Mann argued for aid to the common schools
and then stated, "seminaries for higher learning, academies,
and universities should stand ready to receive, at private
cost, all whose path to any destination may lie through their
halls." [46]

This statement might indicate that Mann had come under
the influence of a laissez-faire doctrine of education. But if
that was the case, why did he advocate state support for
common schools? Many people, including the "common
man" as well as the wealthiest taxpayers, objected to such
support because it taxed the property of one man to support
the children of another. A true advocate of laissez-faire would
not have espoused support for either level of education.
Mann did not disavow the state's responsibility for education.

But why should the state have to choose? The only plausible reason would have been a scarcity of funds. Mann must
have thought that the state could not finance a complete
system of education. To obtain aid for common schools, he
argued that the state need support only a part of the educational system. [47]

Of course, this was the argument Edward Everett tried so
valiantly to refute in his 1849 appeal to the General Court.
There was enough money for all, he thought. But whom were
the legislators to believe — Everett or Mann? Both men were
college graduates, both advocated support for common
schools, and both knew the available sources of state funds.
One, however, said support should stop at the lower level,

46. "First Report" (1837), in Lawrence A. Cremin, ed., *The Republic and
the School* (New York, 1957), p. 33.

47. It should be noted that the states were in no way assuming the total
cost of the schools. The school funds provided less than 10% of the budget,
the rest coming from local taxation.

while the other wanted all levels supported. The legislators could believe Mann, refuse aid to the colleges, and still feel they had shown an understanding and appreciation for all levels of education — while saving money. Mann's way was the least expensive and probably the most attractive; it was the path the assembly chose.

So, in the years between 1820 and 1850 the colleges faced not merely the competition of common schools, which had appeared as early as the 1790s, but also an organized and systematized competition. Legislators were not influenced just by a vague or abstract feeling for "democratic education," though such a feeling no doubt existed, but by common-school advocates who were appointed by the state. Only New York appointed men to speak for the colleges.

Despite this state-sanctioned competition, it still appears that the states could have supported the colleges if they had wanted to. Despite Mann's assertion that funds should not be given to the colleges, there was ample bounty from the 1837 treasury surplus. And the logic behind the 1849 college bill in Massachusetts was sound. The General Court could have expanded the fund to $1,500,000; the lower schools would not have been injured. There was more to the estrangement than just competition or organized competition. For some reason the "people" and their representatives did not *like* the colleges. And again, the "people" who expressed their dislike most vocally were frequently college graduates.

The doubts of the people rested on three major contentions — that the colleges were aristocratic, that they were sectarian, and that they were only for the "professional classes." All of these objections were alike in that they explained why the colleges were small; they were for the "few." The colleges continued to claim that they restricted no one on the basis of social and economic class or religious belief. This response only enhanced the doubts of the people. If the colleges were not actively restricting entry and students still failed to appear, then there must be something basically wrong with the institutions. And statistics showed that after 1840 the college enrollments were not keeping pace with the growth of the population.[48] Was there any validity to these claims? Did the populace have good reason to believe that a narrow perspective on the colleges' part had caused the low increase in enrollment?

Sectarianism would have explained low enrollment if all colleges had been under the influence of one church. This, however, was not the case. The multiplication of denominational colleges, ably documented in Donald Tewksbury's *The Founding of American Colleges Before the Civil War* (1932), established colleges for many religious persuasions. Unfortunately, this growth in collegiate units did not induce a proportionally larger number of American youths to strive for higher education. In Connecticut, for example, the ratio of college students to the total population fell after 1838 despite the existence of Congregational, Episcopal, and Methodist colleges. F. A. P. Barnard noted in his 1870 report that in 1838 the proportion was 1:1,101; in 1855, 1:1,860. Also, our colleges were really less sectarian than in the days when

48. In the 1840s such men as George Bancroft claimed that college growth had not kept pace with population growth. In the 1860s and 1870s educators published tables confirming this claim. F. A. P. Barnard, president of Columbia, noted in his 1866 presidential report that, on a national scale, the proportion of males 16–20 years of age in college had changed from 1:64 in 1840 to 1:83 in 1860. He published even more statistics in his 1870 report, reprinted as *Analysis of Some Statistics of Collegiate Education* (New York, 1870). In 1877 Amherst professor Edward Hitchcock published a pamphlet entitled "On the Decrease of the Relative Number of College Educated Men in Massachusetts during the Present Century," which gave the following statistics for the number of college students per 100,000 population:

1800–04	86	1855–59	61
1805–14	90	1860–64	56
1815–24	82	1865–69	51
1825–34	85	1870–74	53
1835–44	76	1875–76	55
1845–54	56		

Hitchcock concluded that the average increase in population for each period had been 15%, while the increase in students had been only 8%.

they received aid; Yale had dropped the Westminster oath in 1823.

The aristocratic argument was also weak. True, the wealthy boys, and those who emulated wealth, were the most visible. They were the ones who spent money lavishly at taverns and accumulated large bills with local merchants. But an ample number of "young men of moderate circumstances," and even poor students, attended all of our colleges. Tuition or cost alone was not the deterrent to numbers. In fact, Josiah Quincy pointed out that the expenses of a Harvard education were no greater in the 1840s than they had been in 1813–14.[49] Of course, cost may have kept some from going to college if they could see little advantage, present or future, in spending four years with the classics.

The criticism that the colleges catered only to the "professional" classes was the most convincing. According to this attack, the classical curriculum was suited only for those students who wished to enter the professions of law, medicine, divinity, and teaching; it was virtually useless for young men seeking other occupations, particularly those involved with manufacturing, farming, and commerce.[50] The "professional" critics, such as Yale trustee Noyes Darling, who asked the college to discontinue its Latin and Greek requirements in 1827, wanted the colleges to offer a more flexible and broader curriculum, usually including the modern languages and scientific and industrial training, to attract students with nonprofessional career plans.

The colleges responded to this criticism in a number of ways. Harvard and Dartmouth frankly admitted that the classical curriculum was intended for the professional classes and

49. Quincy provided extensive tables to support this claim in *Speech of Josiah Quincy President of Harvard University Before the Board of Overseers of that Institution* (Boston, 1845), pp. 53–58.

50. For example, at Yale the proportion of graduates entering the "professions" (law, medicine, clergy, education) was almost the same for classes graduating 1834–49 (76%) as for the classes of 1797–1833 (77%). The percentage in trade or manufacturing rose only from 7% for the 1797–1833 classes to 10% for the 1834–49 group. Farming was a constant 5% in both groups.

saw the education of that group as their only duty.[51] On the other hand, the Yale faculty claimed, in the famed Yale Report of 1828, that a college education was preparatory to any future life, be it the professions, "or the operations which are peculiar to the higher mercantile, manufacturing or agricultural establishments." Emphasizing the need for all men to attend college, the report explained, "Merchants, manufacturers and farmers as well as professional gentlemen take their places in our public councils. A thorough education ought therefore to be extended to all these classes." [52]

But what kind of education was suitable for every class? Was only one curriculum acceptable? Yale announced that the education must be "thorough" and "excellent." No one argued with that; no one had asked Yale to offer an inferior education. What they had requested was the elimination of the classics in exchange for modern languages. Could this not also have been an excellent education?

Yale concluded that only one curriculum, the classical curriculum, could be excellent. Ancient literature not only formed the best preparation for professional study but was also superior to the modern languages "both as respects the general estimation in which it is held in the literary world and its intrinsic merits." The faculty foresaw the gravest consequences from any change:

> If it should pursue a course very different from that which the present state of literature demands; if it should confer its honors according to a rule which is not sanctioned by literary men, the faculty see nothing to expect for favoring such innovations, but that they will be considered visionaries in education, ignorant of its true design and objects and unfit for their places. The ultimate

51. Samuel Eliot had emphasized Harvard's duty to the professional classes in his articles in the *Boston Advertiser* in 1848. Lord had emphasized Dartmouth's role as a college for those bound for the professions in his 1828 inaugural address.

52. "The Yale Report of 1828," in Richard Hofstadter and Wilson Smith, eds., *American Higher Education: A Documentary History*, 1:287.

consequence, it is not difficult to predict. The college would be distrusted by the public, and its reputation would be irrevocably lost.[53]

This statement led some people to wonder if Yale was sincere in its desire to educate the many. By affirming the classics on the ground of the faculty's reputation in the "literary world," the report of 1828 almost refuted its case for the general value of the liberal arts. While announcing that it actively sought students from all present and future walks of life, the Yale faculty affirmed the fact that its curriculum was peculiarly suited for the professions and rejected as "visionary" a curriculum based on modern languages, which it acknowledged as desired by a larger number of students. Is it difficult to understand that many people, including many well-educated people, found such a position narrow-minded, if not contradictory?[54]

Not all colleges were as inflexible as Yale. As early as 1830 Columbia instituted a literary-scientific course to satisfy students who wanted an alternative to the classics. So few students enrolled that the course was discontinued within a few years. Similar results occurred at other colleges that offered a nonclassical course.[55]

Whatever the merits of the sectarian, aristocratic, and professional criticism directed at higher education, the overriding objection was the failure of the colleges to grow. George Bancroft (Harvard, 1817), a leading critic of his college, made it perfectly clear in an 1845 minority report of

53. Ibid., p. 291.

54. In fairness, it should be mentioned that historian Richard J. Storr has noted in *The Beginnings of Graduate Education in America* (Chicago, 1953), pp. 29–33, that the Yale Report was not so much opposed to an expansion of the curriculum in principle as it was to the expense that would be necessary to offer alternate and advanced programs.

55. The nonclassical or literary-scientific plan proved unsuccessful at those colleges which offered no degree for the course and frankly announced that it was "second-class" education. A few colleges, such as Union, offered a degree for the scientific or classical course. At Union, students in the scientific course comprised 25% of total enrollment at some times.

the board of overseers that low enrollment was his major complaint. Though Bancroft railed about the Unitarians and the high cost of an education at Harvard, he explained:

> The undersigned, acting as one of your Committee, has been more deeply impressed than ever with disproportion between the magnificent endowments and the comparatively small number who derive a benefit from them. The increase of students has not kept pace with the population of the Commonwealth.[56]

Bancroft went on to add, in the same paragraph, that of 184 Massachusetts residents at Harvard, 104 were from Boston and its suburbs; eight Massachusetts counties supplied the college with no students at all. "This desertion of the College, by half of the Commonwealth," Bancroft asserted, "is most deeply to be regretted." He believed, somewhat naïvely, that if only Harvard would reduce the cost of tuition and renounce its Unitarian connections, "universal confidence" would return to the college.

Harvard's president, Josiah Quincy, well understood the problem of numbers. But in defending Harvard from Bancroft's attacks he espoused a rhetoric that smacked of the aristocratic pretensions which irritated so many people. According to the president:

> Numbers bring not merely honors, reputation and equivalent income to a literary institution, but something else. They bring increased care, anxiety, labor in instruction, and supervision, greater danger of noisy assemblages, more materials for the engendering of idle, dissipated, rude, and ill-regulated habits and manners. Numbers bring also increased expenses, require necessarily more instructors, cause more difficulty in arranging hours for study, more minute division of the labors of

---

56. *Speech of Josiah Quincy President of Harvard University Before the Board of Overseers of that Institution* (Boston, 1845), p. 61.

instruction, and a less proportion of direct instruction to each individual.[57]

So in 1845, at a time when most of the country was obsessed with growth in all areas of national life and with the somewhat vague concept of a "general diffusion of knowledge" in the realm of education, Harvard announced that growth was not to be desired because it might lead to "ill-regulated manners" and "difficulty in arranging hours of study." Though one should not completely belittle Quincy's fear of a "crisis in manners," this 1845 response was hardly one to gain the confidence and goodwill of a representative assembly. To proclaim smallness a virtue was really more than the popular temper could bear.

The "spirit of the age" emphasized expansion and diversity. Jeremiah Day's Yale Report of 1828 and Josiah Quincy's 1845 reply to Bancroft were both attempts to belittle this "spirit." These men were annoyed at the criticism directed at their institutions by this muse and reacted by labeling it superficial, transitory, or mediocre. They resented being told that they must keep pace with the times.

Of course, they may have had a case. It may well have been true that before 1850 the American youth who did not want a classical education saw no need for higher education of any kind — modern or classical. After all, there was no occupation of any kind, professional or otherwise, that required a college degree, or even a particular course of study. Even the Federalists of the 1790s had rejected Benjamin Rush's proposal that a degree from a national university be a prerequisite for government service. And Herman Melville's Ishmael spoke for many young men who congratulated themselves on being "self-made" when he asserted, "a whaleship was my Yale College and my Harvard." [58]

57. Ibid., p. 19.
58. For a discussion of the aversion to higher education among "self-made" men, see Irvin G. Wyllie, *The Self-Made Man in America* (New Brunswick, N.J., 1954), pp. 101–15.

Possibly Yale was correct in stating, "We are not sure that the demand for thorough education is, at present, sufficient to fill all the colleges in the United States with students who will be satisfied with nothing short of high and solid attainments." [59] Had the colleges diversified their courses of study, they might still have realized no increase in enrollment.

But their defiance of the demands of the people and of the "spirit of the age" is somewhat intriguing. We have noted earlier that the colleges were willing accomplices to political squabbles before 1820. After that time the institutions seemed almost hostile to the "democratic" political temper of their states. They even refused to adapt to the rhetoric of the times. Of our four colleges, only Columbia in its appeal for city support in 1830 lauded the virtues of the people — perhaps Columbia was too small even for rhetoric to help. Despite this defiance, the colleges, particularly Yale and Harvard, still expected the states to support them and were disappointed when the assemblies refused. Did they not realize that they had made themselves rather unattractive institutions to aid?

The thesis of competition, criticism, and the response to that criticism tries to explain the estrangement by factors directly touching the colleges and states. But is it a sufficient argument? Does it neglect the influence of other forces in American society that may have indirectly affected the couples?

In their book, *Commonwealth: A Study of the Role of Government in the American Economy, Massachusetts, 1774–1861* (1947), Oscar and Mary Handlin have noted that business corporations, like colleges, were selectively chartered as wards of the state before 1820. Over the next four decades these corporations lost their state connection because of the multiplication and fragmentation of business units. Thus by 1860 incorporation had become a convenience of business

59. The "Yale Report of 1828," p. 287.

rather than an alliance with the state. The "private" business corporation had become the norm. The Handlins are quick to point out that this divorce or estrangement of business corporations and the state was the result of economic expansion rather than of any carefully articulated theory of the state's role in the economy: "The laissez-faire argument found no place in Massachusetts thinking; the transformation came from the internal development of the institutions themselves." [60]

Did a similar transformation affect the colleges? The Handlins seem to think that the forces of expansion and multiplication of units also had a significant impact on the colleges. First, in *Commonwealth,* they stated, "The agencies that administered academies and colleges, sustained by fees and endowments, broke away from state dominance and asserted their independence as private bodies." [61] Later, in their *The American College and American Culture* (1970), they have again noted:

> The century after 1770 saw some fundamental changes in the American college. Most visible was the vast increase in the number of institutions and of students. By 1870 some 500 institutions were awarding bachelor's degrees to aspiring scholars — a total larger than that in all of Europe. Almost as dramatic was the apparent multiplication in the types of institutions. The old colleges became private corporations. [62]

In both books the Handlins try to ascribe what I call the "estrangement of college and state" to the same phenomena that characterized the business world. But this was simply not what happened, and particularly not in Massachusetts. Although there was a vast multiplication of colleges nationwide, only one of our states, New York, experienced this

---

60. Oscar and Mary Handlin, *Commonwealth* (New York, 1947), p. 262.
61. Ibid., p. 249.
62. Oscar and Mary Handlin, *The American College and American Culture* (New York, 1970), p. 19.

multiplication — and New York was the one state of our four which continued to grant financial aid to colleges after 1830, though not to Columbia. Tewksbury has noted that six states were little affected by the college boom: Maine, Vermont, New Hampshire, Massachusetts, Connecticut, and Rhode Island — that is, three of our four.[63] There were three colleges in Massachusetts in 1800; there were three in 1850. In 1859, when there were four colleges in Massachusetts, the state decided to renew its aid to them. And in Connecticut, it was the presence of a competitor, Trinity, which opened the treasury for Yale in 1831 after more than a ten-year drought.

Allured by the multiplication of institutions nationwide and the absolute increase in student numbers, the Handlins failed to see that the most significant aspect of American higher education, and the one mentioned by observers at the time, was its stagnation in relation to population growth. This stagnation continued into the 1870s. Numbers, numbers, everywhere the cry was numbers — and the numbers were not in the colleges.

The alliance between business corporation and state waned because the atomic business units cut their link with the commonwealth, usually out of their own desire. In our states, nothing of this kind happened with the colleges. No college, with the exception of Dartmouth, asserted its independence before 1850. They wanted to maintain the alliance; they asked the states to hold onto them, not to give them the liberty to break away. Our states refused to aid the colleges not because the institutions had multiplied or were competing with each other but because they had not expanded and diversified. This failure to grow was interpreted as proof that the colleges were relics of a past unworthy of favor.[64]

63. Donald Tewksbury, *The Founding of American Colleges* (New York, 1932), p. 28.

64. The Handlins do note in *Commonwealth* that the state broadened its responsibility for education by increasing support for common schools and establishing a state board of agriculture. They even admit a dilemma ("If

The private college was not the twin to the private business corporation.

As a final attempt to bolster the argument that the estrangement of college and state occurred because of a combination of competition, criticism, and reactionary response, one more avenue of inquiry should be followed. Let us again survey the activities of other states and their efforts to found "state universities" after the Dartmouth College decision of 1819. In this somewhat indirect manner, it should be possible to see if the estrangement was a nationwide phenomenon or one limited to those states which had tried to transform older colleges.

In chapter 2 a survey of state universities founded before 1820 revealed that these institutions exhibited no particularly different relationships to their states than did their private counterparts. Many historians have argued that the Dartmouth College decision ended such quasi-public arrangements. As Merle Curti and Vernon Carstensen have stated, "Once and for all it [the Dartmouth College decision] made clear the futility of efforts to transform private colleges into state universities. In doing so, it opened wide the way for launching universities piloted by the states themselves." [65]

Indeed, a number of the most noted state universities of today were founded between 1820 and 1850 — Indiana (1820), Michigan (1837), Missouri (1839) and Wisconsin (1848). Were these institutions really "piloted" by the states?

If the western states launched new universities of their own, financial support was not a part of the newness. Wisconsin made no appropriation to its university until 1867 and did not establish a permanent income through taxation until 1876. The year 1867 also marked the beginning of

---

the agricultural college and the grammar schools were public, why not universities and academies?" p. 259), but continue to hold to the theory of multiplication in the *American College*.

65. Merle Curti and Vernon Carstensen, *The University of Wisconsin*, 2 vols. (Madison, 1949), 1:15.

state appropriations to the universities of Michigan, Missouri, and Indiana. How had these institutions survived before the Civil War? And what had the role of the state "pilot" been?

From their various founding dates until 1867 most of the midwestern universities operated on income from lands granted specifically for a university to the states by the federal government and from small tuition fees — $10 to $20 a year. The role of the state, in each case, had been to charter the university and to act as agent for the federal government in selling the lands, establishing a university fund, and turning over the proceeds of the fund to the institution. As in the older states, a provision in the western state constitutions authorized the legislature to establish a university and usually made it a public duty to protect the fund that would accumulate from the sale of federal lands.

In Wisconsin and Indiana, legislators seemed satisfied that the university money be applied to higher education. But in Michigan and Missouri, despite constitutional provisions, attempts were made to divert the fund to other purposes — as in the east, to the common schools. In the late 1830s the Missouri legislature petitioned the United States Congress to release the state from its obligation to apply the land revenues to higher education. Congress did not respond to this request and the legislators never renewed their appeal.[66]

A similar maneuver took place in the Michigan assembly. The committee in charge of managing the university lands asked the legislature to transfer the fund to common schools. The legislature replied that it could not authorize this transfer because the lands had been accepted as a trust from the federal government under specific obligations. And, according to Michigan historian Andrew Ten Brook, that federal obligation was the only restraint that preserved the fund for the university. "If the fund could have been legally

66. For more information on the founding of the University of Missouri, see Frank F. Stephens, *A History of the University of Missouri* (Columbia, 1962), pp. 4–10.

transferred to other purposes, and quite lost to the noble end for which it had been given," he explained, "many would have seen this without a sigh, not a few with great satisfaction, none with disappointment, few with regret." [67]

In both Michigan and Missouri, a university arose only because the legislatures were bound by a federal trust. If they sold the federal lands, and they were under popular pressure to do this, they were required to apply the proceeds to a university. To use the money for any other purpose would have constituted a challenge to federal authority. In effect, the universities of Missouri and Michigan were really federal, not state, institutions. The federal or national quality was reflected even in the tuition charge at Michigan. When the university opened, all students, regardless of home state, paid the same fee — ten dollars. It was not until 1863 that a distinction was made between the fee paid by state and out-of-state students.

Even in Wisconsin, the legislature assumed no responsibility for university support other than managing the land fund. And it charged the university for the expense of administering this operation! The state's only other service was to act as banker, making loans at interest for the construction of buildings.

Can the actions of these states be considered responses to the Dartmouth College decision? I find it difficult to discern any public attempt to "pilot" or to "launch" a university, particularly when two of the states did not want a university at all. As Andrew Ten Brook has remarked on the launching of the University of Michigan, "There was no definite consciousness of ownership in the university and responsibility for its management. This consciousness existed everywhere, nowhere. The men officially charged with this responsibility harbored all shades of doubt, especially the darker ones, in regard to the success of the enterprise." [68]

67. Andrew Ten Brook, *American State Universities* (Cincinnati, 1875), p. 185.

68. Ibid., p. 184.

Although state support was much the same in the West as in the East, only Indiana was goverend by a self-perpetuating board of trustees — and only until 1852. In Wisconsin, Missouri, and Michigan, and finally Indiana, the governing boards were appointed by the governor or the legislature. The western legislatures probably took this action after seeing that self-perpetuating boards at older institutions, state and nonstate, tended to be monopolized by one religious denomination, thus giving the colleges a sectarian stamp. The new states could protect their institutions from this undesirable situation by appointing the trustees directly. At least this appeared to be the case in Indiana, where the university was allegedly a Presbyterian institution.

As early as 1827 the state appointed a board of visitors to oversee the trustees because of a fear of denominational control. In 1834 Indiana Methodists petitioned the assembly to change the organization of the trustees from a close corporation to a state-appointed board. They claimed that "one common hue, one common religious creed characterized every member of the faculty." Finally, in 1852, an act of the assembly assigned the election of trustees to the legislature.[69]

While Indiana University moved closer to the legislature, the University of Michigan moved away from assembly control but closer to the people. In 1851 Michigan's new constitution provided that the regents, who were formerly appointed by the governor, be elected directly by the people — one member from each judicial district. The constitution also prohibited the assembly from making rules for the institution. Howard Peckham has noted that the change made the university "a co-ordinate branch of state government and unique among state universities."[70]

69. For a full discussion of sectarian problems at Indiana, see James Albert Woodburn, *History of Indiana University*, 2 vols. (Bloomington, 1940), 1: 111–16.

70. Howard Peckham, *The Making of the University of Michigan* (Ann Arbor, 1967), p. 31.

A branch of government it may have been, but the university still received no state support, and would receive none for the next sixteen years. And although some state universities eventually adopted Michigan's version of direct election, others, strangely enough, preferred to copy the form of trustee election instituted at Harvard in 1865, alumni election. In these states the governors or legislatures appointed a certain number of trustees while other members were elected by the alumni of the institution rather than by the population at large.[71] Thus, as a potential source of influence, the 1851 change at Michigan should not really be considered a step that would clearly delineate state from private institutions.

If the term *state university* did not necessarily connote a public responsibility for higher education before 1850, it should not then be assumed that no states supported higher education. There were two "maverick" institutions that were annually and liberally supported by their states — South Carolina College (1801) and the University of Virginia (1819).

South Carolina College had been founded for reasons slightly different from most other institutions. As South Carolina had no college as late as 1800, certain men in the state combined this need for higher education with political considerations. Low Country patricians, who feared that men from the Up Country Piedmont section would soon take over the state legislature, thought a college could unite the state and ameliorate the sectional controversy. Governor John Drayton explained, "the friendships of young men would then be promoted and strengthened throughout the State, and our political union be much advanced thereby." [72]

But it was not just "friendships" which the Low Country men sought to forge in the new college. They wanted the

71. For example, this mixture of state appointment and alumni election occurs at state universities in California, Indiana, New Hampshire, and Pennsylvania. See chapter 5 for more on alumni election.

72. Daniel Walker Hollis, *The University of South Carolina*, 2 vols. (Columbia, S.C., 1951–56), 1:18.

Piedmont men to become interested in the values of the older section. According to historian Daniel Hollis, "They began a program of assimilation of the stronger society that had sprung up in their rear. If ultimately the Piedmont were to play a dominant role in the state government, it had to be indoctrinated with an appreciation of the tidewater values." [73] In Trojan horse fashion, the coastal patricians agreed to locate the college in the Piedmont, at Columbia, the state capital.

To some extent the South Carolinians had foreseen and reacted to that "crisis in manners" which so concerned Josiah Quincy forty years later. The southerners even announced that socialization was a function of the college. The motto of the institution, "Emollit mores nec sinit esse feros," loosely translated means "Learning softens manners and does not permit men to be rude." Possibly this explains why they did not call their institution a university.

To launch this project in manners and state unity the legislature chartered South Carolina College in 1801 with a board of trustees consisting of a number of ex officio members and thirteen men elected by the legislature. Fortunately, a treasury surplus resulting from a federal refund for Revolutionary War expenses made funds readily available for this state undertaking. From 1801 to 1820 the college received annual appropriations which averaged $15,000. After that date, the institution, unlike our eastern colleges or midwestern universities, continued to receive an annual grant. In fact, the state contribution rose and reached a level of $26,000 a year in the 1840s. In addition to funds for operating expenses, the state made frequent grants for the construction of buildings. All state grants, both annual and special, between 1801 and 1860 totaled more than $1 million. Even in the years 1831–33 when Thomas Cooper, president of the college, aroused political and religious passions in the state, the annual grant never lapsed.

South Carolina was able to launch a state college because

73. Ibid., p. 16.

the men who promoted the college turned the issue of geographic rivalry to their advantage. The success of South Carolina stands in striking contrast to the failure of the University of the State of New York. Like the Low Country patricians, the New Yorkers (city) had tried to maintain a dominance in their state by controlling a state university located at the capital. But the southerners succeeded where the New Yorkers had failed. Possibly the fact that the Carolinians were establishing a new institution made them more flexible about its location. Because of the Low Country's unhealthy climate, the coastal men were accustomed to leaving their area at various times of the year; they noted that Columbia was a particularly healthy location for a college. So, somewhat facetiously, one might use Ulrich B. Phillips's classic phrase in explaining the development of the first state-controlled and state-supported institution, "Let us begin by discussing the weather."

The other maverick institution, the University of Virginia, was not founded because there were no colleges in the state at the time — there were three — or as an attempt to unify the state politically. It was chartered because Thomas Jefferson could not give up an idea he had first conceived in 1779 — to transform William and Mary College from an institution controlled by the Episcopalians to a nonsectarian university with a broad, elective curriculum rather than a prescribed course of instruction.

After Jefferson's educational bill of 1779 failed to be passed by the Virginia assembly, the sage's attention was absorbed by other interests. In 1809, after he had finished his second presidential term, Jefferson resumed his interest in founding a state university. However, he wanted to create a new institution, not transform William and Mary. Through a series of maneuvers in the Virginia assembly, Jefferson first persuaded the legislators to charter Central College in 1816, and then in January, 1819, to transform the college into the University of Virginia.

Indeed, the University of Virginia had been founded because of Jefferson's failure to transform William and Mary. But depending on whether one accepts the 1816 or 1819 date, this university was established three years to one week before Marshall's Dartmouth College decision. And there is no evidence to suggest that Jefferson devoted his attention to a new institution because he thought that either the United States or the Virginia constitutions prohibited him from tampering with William and Mary. It appears as if he simply lost interest in his old alma mater.

Like South Carolina College, Jefferson's new university also received annual state support and was controlled by a state-appointed board of visitors. While state support at South Carolina came from legislative appropriations, the University of Virginia received an annual grant of $15,000 from the state's Literary Fund. The state had created this fund in 1810 from the sale of lands and had augmented the principal with the refund granted by the United States for expenses incurred in the War of 1812.[74]

Why did these two institutions alone receive continual state support? Neither held a state monopoly of higher education. The University of Virginia was not the only college in the state. Though South Carolina College had competitors after 1850, support continued. Was there a peculiar interest in higher education in these two states which did not exist elsewhere? There may have been a number of reasons, but one stood out above all others; neither state actively supported common schools. South Carolina left the lower levels of schooling completely to local or charitable authorities. As a result, common schools presented no competition for the funds of the state. While Virginia definitely accepted a responsibility for common schools and had established the Literary Fund for all levels of education, the funds for primary education were distributed in a manner different from that of New England.

74. See Philip Alexander Bruce, *History of the University of Virginia 1819–1919*, 5 vols. (New York, 1920–22), 1:85–86, for a full description of the Virginia Literary Fund.

As Virginia assumed public responsibility only for the poor, a school could make a claim on the Literary Fund only if the parents of its pupils consented to list themselves as paupers. Many Virginians were too proud to admit this; regrettably they often chose to send their children to no school at all. As a result of this "pauper clause," demands on the Literary Fund for common schools did not increase over the years as they did in New England. Therefore no opposition to a university grant arose on the ground that the money was needed for primary education. So in Virginia and South Carolina state education became principally state higher education.

This tour of state universities from South Carolina to Wisconsin has taken us far afield — but not without purpose. The estrangement between college and state proved neither to be merely an eastern phenomenon nor to be peculiarly the result of the Dartmouth College decision. And the distinction between "state" and "private" institutions appeared to be no clearer after 1820 than it had been before. In regard to support and control, there was as broad a spectrum of alliances between university and state as between college and state. At mid-century, the spectra still overlapped each other at many points.

4 Renewed and New Interest in the Colleges: The States and the Philanthropists, 1850–1865

> The history of the private gifts crystallized about the various public gifts, and especially about that of 1862, shows that well-directed public bounty, like that of the general government in 1862, stimulates private bounty.
>
> Andrew D. White, 1874

If our colleges and states had become estranged by 1850, they had not yet separated. As we have noted, the alliance had changed in regard to support but not in regard to control. And as we shall see, the element of faith which had been so important to the alliance was still strong in 1850; that sense of mutual responsibility for each other's welfare which had characterized the alliance before 1820 had not died. Our states had announced that the colleges were "not useful," but not yet "useless." Massachusetts was still concerned with the welfare of Harvard — or at least what it conceived to be the college's welfare. It was George S. Boutwell, the legislator who had defeated the college aid bill in 1849, who eventually tried to transform Harvard into a "useful" institution in 1850. And despite his defiance of government, Nathan Lord could not break the faith of college for state at Dartmouth. In 1863 the college dismissed him because it still felt a sense of responsibility for the welfare of civil government — in this case, of the federal government.

The faith may have been kept, but could it sustain the alliance indefinitely? Colleges, like most other institutions, cannot live by faith alone; they need money. In the 1830s they had begun to rely on friends and alumni for financial support when the state failed — and often for the very objects, such as the observatory and library at Harvard, which they had first asked the state to aid. In the 1840s and 1850s the largess from private philanthropy increased. Like the states, many wealthy men demanded that the colleges become more useful — specifically that they offer technical and scientific instruction. These men, however, unlike the legislators, offered the cash the colleges needed to adapt to the demands of the age.

If men who had captained those private business corporations, which had separated from the state, acted where the state refused, what would this do to the alliance? Would the philanthropists demand that the colleges, like their own businesses, break away from the state? Would the colleges now have to choose between an alliance with the state and an alliance with the wealthy? Amazingly enough, the captains of industry did not object to the state. Often they helped bring college and state — and the federal government — closer together. Just as the estrangement seemed to have reached its limit and separation appeared imminent, a new set of alliances between college and state emerged.

Let us now return to our colleges and follow the story of old faith and new money.

"The opinion is general, that the college fails to accomplish what might reasonably be expected of it, from its early history, its great reputation, its central position, and, when compared with other American institutions, its unequalled resources." So began the report of the Massachusetts house of representatives in April, 1850, "To consider and report what legislation if any is necessary to render Harvard College more beneficial to all the people of the Commonwealth." Why, in 1850, was the General Court investigating the usefulness of Harvard? Had the the assembly not effectively renounced any responsibility for higher education by rejecting the memorial of Harvard, Williams, and Amherst for financial support in 1848 and again in 1849?

George Boutwell did not think so and had made plans as early as 1847 to increase Harvard's benefit to the commonwealth. Like Edward Everett, Boutwell felt that the General Court was bound by a constitutional duty to "cherish the University at Cambridge." But whereas Everett had intended that this duty be fulfilled by a grant of funds, the young legislator concluded that structural change rather than funds was the way to carry out this obligation. According to Boutwell, who chaired the committee that made the report of 1850, "The committee think it impossible to perform this duty faithfully without a change in one branch of the college government, namely, the corporation." [1]

Boutwell, a Democrat and a reform idealist, expressed much of the same Jeffersonian ideology which William Plumer had advocated thirty-five years earlier in his efforts to reshape Dartmouth. Boutwell thought Harvard had failed to attract "popular" interest because of the self-perpetuating nature of the corporation. "This system," he noted, "necessarily leads to the perpetuity of particular opinions, in education and religion." [2] Though he did not object to opinions, he was distressed that the Harvard Corporation reflected only one — Unitarian in religion and Whig in politics. To remedy this situation he proposed a plan almost identical to the one Plumer had introduced in 1816: the corporation would be expanded from seven to fifteen members (i.e. the president, treasurer, and thirteen fellows) and the fellows would be elected by the senate and the house of representatives. The fellows would be limited to six-year terms, and one-third would be elected every second year.[3]

1. *Report to consider and report what legislation if any is necessary to render Harvard more beneficial to all the people of the Commonwealth, April, 1850*, p. 5 (Massachusetts House Document no. 164, HUA).

2. Ibid., p. 4.

3. Samuel Eliot Morison suggests there were motives other than Boutwell's idealism behind this 1850 movement: "But the Calvinists were still hunting for Harvard's scalp, the Democrats regarded the College as the haven of a smug aristocracy, and the abolitionists and other reformers of the day were in a continual state of irritation because the University did not promote their pet theories" (*Three Centuries of Harvard*, pp. 286–87). However, Boutwell's later career was marked by many causes "to make the world a

This change in college government would benefit both Harvard and the state. The college would gain from the new trustees "a variety of taste, knowledge, and opinion corresponding to the sentiments of the people of different sections of the Commonwealth." And the people of the state would at last be able to cherish Harvard because "They will feel it is their institution." [4]

According to the young legislator, the constitutional duty that motivated him to advocate this change also gave the General Court the power to enact the necessary legislation, with or without the consent of the college. Since the colony had been the founder of the college, the Dartmouth College decision did not apply; there were no private property rights to protect. In fact, had Boutwell needed additional support for this position, he could have relied on a General Court document written in 1821 by none other than Dartmouth's defender, Daniel Webster. In his "Report upon the constitutional rights and privileges of Harvard College," Webster had announced:

> The Government of the Colony was the Founder of this Institution, not in consequence of having granted the charter but in consequence of having made the first endowment. As founder it was entirely competent to the Government to prescribe the terms of the Charter, to grant the property, subject to such limitations as it saw fit, and to vest the power of visitation and control wherever it judged most expedient. [5]

Boutwell's Jeffersonian scheme for institutional flexibility did not please the Harvard Corporation. Few members of

---

better place." He helped organize the Republican party in 1854, was influential in drafting the fourteenth and fifteenth amendments to the U.S. Constitution, joined the movement to impeach Andrew Johnson, and became a leader of the anti-imperial movement in 1892.

4. *Report to consider and report,* April, 1850, p. 5.

5. *Report Upon the Constitutional Rights and Privileges of Harvard College: and Upon the Donations that have been made to it by this Commonwealth* (Boston, 1821), p. 5.

that body had been followers of the Virginia sage when he was alive, and in the ensuing decades their views on the necessity for institutional stability had not changed. But to preserve Harvard as they knew it, they needed to find someone to reply to the legislator's plan.

Fortunately for the college, an alumnus of the class of 1839, S. E. Guild, sat on Boutwell's committee and issued a minority report. Although Guild did not deny that the colony had founded the college, he argued that times had changed:

> The legislature cannot now watch over the management of the details of the government of the college as it did in the first few years of its existence. It would now be unreasonable to attempt to provide that the legislature should be the body to direct, as it did in 1698, whether or not the president should reside in Cambridge, or to fix, as it did in 1695, the precise amount of his salary.[6]

Attempting a line of argument that would disassociate the interest of the state from Harvard, Guild contended that corporations, including the Harvard Corporation, were not agencies of the state: "The Commonwealth provides — it does not carry on the corporations which it creates." [7] Since the state did not control the manufacturing and railroad corporations it chartered, it need not increase its influence over Harvard to fulfill its duty as founder and charterer of the college.

Although Guild tried to link the Harvard Corporation with business corporations, he did not want to carry this analogy too far; he did not want to claim that the state had no legitimate interest in the college. So he pointed out that the state's interest was already represented through the board of overseers. The presence of this body, he thought, had induced the corporation to be responsible to the needs of the

6. *Report to consider and report,* April, 1850, p. 14.
7. Ibid.

people. As proof he noted the establishment of the divinity and medical schools and the acceptance of Abbot Lawrence's offer to endow a scientific school. Under the existing organization of the college, Guild claimed, "no important measure, for the increase of its usefulness can be brought to the knowledge of its government and remain long unheeded." [8] Thus it was unnecessary to alter the corporation.

The fellows did not have to depend solely on the support of a minority report. Sitting in the house of representatives in 1850 was one of the leading lawyers in Massachusetts and an alumnus of the class of 1802, Samuel Hoar. Speaking to defend Harvard, Hoar refuted the charge that the college "had failed to answer the just expectations of the public" and implored the Court not to tamper with the corporation. According to the *Boston Daily Atlas,* his argument "had a most overpowering effect upon the House." Although the house had been inclined to pass Boutwell's bill, Hoar's speech persuaded the legislators to postpone action for a year. Now the college had time to prepare a lengthy defense.[9]

The preparation of this defense presented an interesting problem to the trustees. Obviously their case would have to rest on the facts of the college history; the fellows would have to prove with references to the past that the state did not possess the authority to change the corporation. But in 1825 when the faculty had tried to gain control of the college, the fellows had announced that the corporation derived its authority solely from the legislature. And Everett's 1849 oration in the General Court had portrayed the colleges as a virtual ward of the state. How would the trustees handle these statements which they had already made or which had been made in their behalf?

The corporation was not daunted by these previous assertions. With their very survival at stake they appeared to have

8. Ibid., p. 15.
9. No written report of Hoar's speech exists. See George F. Hoar, *Autobiography of Seventy Years,* 2 vols. (New York, 1903), 1:29.

no qualms about revising Harvard's heritage to meet the present crisis. In their 1851 memorial to the General Court, the president and fellows wrote the state out of the history of Harvard. According to the trustees, the original grant of £400 made by the Court to the college in 1636 did not "found" the college because there was no party with whom the legislature could contract for such a purpose (i.e. the General Court could not make a contract with itself). The trustees claimed that the grant was "merely a legislative resolve of what was expedient to be done for the public good." Though constituting "an assurance of public favor and support, and thereby inducing private individuals to endow it," it still could not be construed as "an actual gift, by which the College acquired any absolute estate or fund, or means of subsistence." Since John Harvard, or rather the executor of his estate, was the first person or outside party to make a gift of "substance," he, not the state, was the founder.[10]

Possibly the fellows knew the legislature would find this argument tortuous. They went on to assert that even if the colony had founded the college, it had permanently given away its rights of visitation in 1650 when it chartered the college without expressly reserving the right to change the charter. In granting this charter, the trustees claimed:

> there arose an implied contract on the part of the Government with every benefactor, that if he would give his money, it should be deemed a charity protected by the charter, to be administered by the Corporation according to the general law of the land. As soon then, as an implied contract, springing up and founded on a

10. *Memorial to the House of Representatives from the President and Fellows of Harvard College, January, 1851,* p. 44 (Massachusetts House Document no. 10, HUA). It is interesting to note that when John Harvard's bequest was announced in 1638, the affairs of the college were still handled by a committee of the General Court. There was as yet no corporation to receive the gift. So the trustees in 1851 essentially said that an individual or his executors could make a gift to the General Court for the use of the college, but that the court could not make a gift to itself.

valuable consideration, that the State would not revoke or alter the charter, or change its administration, without the consent of the Corporation, the Government by thus inducing benefactors to endow the College have contracted to give perpetuity to their benevolence, in this form, and in this stipulated manner of exercising it. And they have private rights.[11]

Thus Harvard was a private, not a public, corporation.

So, in 1851, Harvard used for the first time the argument that had been made in the Dartmouth College case. Fortunately the college did not have to ask the United States Supreme Court, or any other court, to uphold the 1819 decision. The bill to change the corporation never reached the floor of the General Court in 1851. As Boutwell had been elected governor in the fall of 1850, he obviously could not chair the committee that was to reconsider the bill. A Harvard alumnus, Giles Whitney (1837), assumed leadership of the joint committee of 1851 and presented a bill placating the state and preserving the corporation.

Whitney displayed amazing tact in his report to the assembly. He in no way doubted the authority of the General Court to change the corporation and even agreed that the trustees were "highly conservative in spirit" and possessed a "systematic fixedness of character." But he felt that the exercise of legislative power to reform the corporation would be "inexpedient," as it would disregard the "tenderness due to all trust funds." This meant, in effect, that wealthy men might cease making donations to the college if the legislature tampered with the corporation.[12]

Whitney well understood that he could not use his admonition about the tenderness of trust funds as a justifica-

11. Ibid., p. 50.
12. *Report of the Senate Committee to whom was referred so much of the Address of the Governor as relates to Harvard College together with the Memorial of the President and Fellows of Harvard College, May, 1851* (Massachusetts Senate Document no. 102, HUA), p. 3.

tion for no action whatsoever. The state, and particularly its governor, demanded some kind of reform; the idealistic Boutwell could not accept the status quo as the best possible form of college government. The Harvard legislator was not unequal to the task of satisfying all parties. He claimed that the conservative qualities of the corporation could be accepted as long as another avenue existed for "infusing into the administration of the college, fresh blood, new ideas, movements, progress, without hazard of shaking the confidence of any portion of the community in the time-honored public faith of the Commonwealth of Massachusetts." [13] The board of overseers was the body to receive the transfusion.

According to Whitney's report, the presence of the senate on the board retarded its vigor because the annual election of the state representatives prevented any "continuity of thought and policy." This situation could be remedied by a simple reorganization of the board. Whitney proposed a new body consisting of seven ex officio members (governor, lieutenant governor, president of the senate, speaker of the house of representatives, secretary of the board of education, president and treasurer of the college) and thirty persons elected by the senate and house of representatives, but not members of either body at the time of election, for a term of six years. By this act, not only were the senators as a group removed from the board, but the ministers were also displaced. The board would now consist merely of "persons" rather than specific state or church groups.

The General Court passed this bill in May, 1851, and the corporation and overseers quickly gave their consent. The fellows had been saved, and the reformers in the legislature were momentarily satisfied that Harvard was still a flexible institution which could, in true Jeffersonian fashion, adapt its institutional form to meet the changing times. As an act of further good faith, the corporation conferred an honorary LL.D. degree on Boutwell at the 1851 commencement.

13. Ibid., p. 4.

For the purposes of the separation of college and state the events of 1851 have a significance beyond the simple reorganization of the overseers. For the first time in more than two hundred years the Harvard Corporation had announced that it was a private body; no longer would the college try to identify itself as the child of the state. Even so, to save the corporation from the General Court it had been necessary for Giles Whitney to divert the attention of the legislators from the fellows' defense of private rights.

Despite Whitney's heroic effort, Harvard again found itself a subject of legislative concern three years later. This time, however, it was an alleged friend rather than a critic who thrust Harvard into the turmoil of the state house. Like the 1810 Federalists who had tried to protect the college from the Republicans, George Washington Warren (Harvard, 1830), a Whig senator from Middlesex, thought he could save Harvard from the perils of politics. In 1854 he introduced a bill that would permanently dissolve any connection between Harvard and the state and place the election of the overseers in the hands of the alumni.

Although the only action the legislature had taken in regard to the college since 1851 had been the election of the new overseers in groups of ten every year, Warren feared "that the annual recurrence of the election of overseers by the legislature will have the tendency, at no distant period, to connect the college with party politics, and with causes of transient excitement, so as to endanger its stability and impair its means of usefulness." [14] He proposed that all ex officio members leave the board and that the thirty remaining positions be elected by the alumni. For some reason, which is not at all clear in his bill, the proper moment for separation would come when Harvard raised $200,000 from private sources to provide a hundred free scholarships for Massachusetts boys. In like fashion, Amherst could divest itself of

14. *Senate Report on the Separation of College and State, April, 1854* (Massachusetts Senate Document no. 134, HUA), p. 6.

the five state officials on its board of trustees by raising only $20,000 for scholarships. Finally, to maintain some form of state supervision, Warren's bill recommended a Board of Collegiate Examiners similar to the University of the State of New York.

This bill did not represent the consensus view of Harvard graduates in the General Court or even on the committee that proposed it. Thomas Russell (Harvard, 1845) issued a minority report strongly objecting to any separation. Russell noted that a parting of the state from the board of overseers would place Harvard solely in the hands of the Unitarians. He felt that far too many Massachusetts boys had been alienated from Harvard by this sectarian quality; Warren's proposal would only intensify this situation. As to the alumni, he could see no particular wisdom coming from their counsel. They were scattered over all parts of the country, and Russell concluded that in no short time any election by them would quickly fall into the hands of a "few graduates living just about the college." The legislature, not the alumni, was still the best protector of the public good.[15]

Russell was supported in his minority report by a young Yale graduate, William Barrett Washburn (Yale, 1844), who later became governor of Massachusetts (1871–74). Washburn successfully convinced the legislature to take no further action on the bill. The internal affairs of Harvard College, which had been thrust into the assembly by one of its own sons, had been rescued by a Yale graduate!

Though Warren's bill died in the legislature, certain of the assumptions on which it rested continued to vex the relations between Harvard and the state. Implicit in the 1854 bill was a lack of confidence in the ability of the men who composed the new board of overseers. The thirty men whom the legislature had chosen could easily dismiss the affront of a little-known state senator, but they could not overlook what

15. Ibid., pp. 20–31.

seemed to be a direct insult hurled at them by the corporation in 1855.[16]

Early that year the corporation had accepted the bequest of Miss Caroline Plumer to establish the Plumer Professorship of Divinity. Shortly thereafter the corporation determined the statutes by which the professorship would be governed, fixed the salary of the post, and named a man to fill it. The president presented these actions to the overseers in March, 1855, as an "accomplished fact."

The fellows had not circumvented the overseers without cause. In 1850 the appointment of Francis Bowen to the McLean Professorship of Ancient and Modern History had been rejected by the overseers. Bowen had incurred the wrath of Massachusetts Democrats and Free Soilers by supporting Webster's Compromise of 1850, and even more by criticizing Louis Kossuth and the Hungarian independence movement. The vote among the overseers for his rejection split clearly along party lines. Understandably, the corporation wanted to avoid any possibility that another of its appointments might be rejected. Possibly the fellows thought that if they did not solicit the approval of the overseers, the new body would assume that such a course was standard procedure and eventually would allow the corporation sole management of the college.

Irritated that its consent had not been asked in making this appointment, the new board was not inclined to let the oversight pass unnoticed. Since they thought they had rectified the transgressions of the previous board by installing Bowen in the Alford Professorship of Natural Religion,

---

16. The General Court placed distinguished men on the board of overseers. The group included Robert Winthrop, Speaker of the United States House of Representatives (1847–49), Caleb Cushing, Attorney General of the United States during the Pierce administration, and four former governors of Massachusetts: George Boutwell, George N. Briggs, Marcus Morton, and John H. Clifford. Twenty-three men were college graduates; thirteen were Harvard graduates.

Moral Philosophy, and Civil Polity in 1853, they felt no need to atone for the sins of their predecessors. Furthermore, the overseers pointed out that the principal reason the General Court had not abolished the corporation in 1850 was the assurance from the fellows that the overseers held the final right to confirm appointments to professorships, the amount of salaries, and the acceptance of donations for specific trusts. Had the corporation given false information to the General Court?

The overseers intended to find out the extent of their rights. A committee including Samuel Hoar examined the charter and the actions of the corporation for the past two hundred years. They concluded that the overseers indeed possessed the ultimate right to confirm or deny the acceptance of donations and the appointment of officers. Having gathered this information, they called a meeting with a committee from the corporation to establish rules of procedure for reporting actions of the fellows to the overseers. Committees from the two boards met in April, 1856, but came to no agreement because the corporation delegates announced that they would have to make some "investigations" of their own. As in earlier crises, the fellows were obliged to revise, and even ignore, some of their previous statements to answer the present challenge.

In December, 1856, the corporation presented a report claiming that the overseers had absolutely no right to demand confirmation on donations, salaries, or the appointment of officers of instruction; the overseers possessed the right of confirmation only in filling vacancies on the corporation and in "the enactment of *orders* and *by-laws,* embracing statutes and foundations of professorships and any new offices in the government or instruction of the institution." According to the corporation, to admit the right of confirmation to the overseers would transfer the whole control of the college to that board and reduce the corporation to "nothing more than mere trustees to hold the legal title of its estates with a power of nomination to its offices, and of suggesting measures for its government." [17]

The overseers were amazed at the corporation's reply. How could they now be charged with trying to transform the corporation into a nominating committee? Only five years earlier, in 1851, the fellows themselves had announced to the General Court, "The Corporation, has in effect, only a nominating power in the election of its own members as well as all other officers. No elections can be made, no degrees can be conferred without the concurrence of the two boards. In the exercise of power, the Corporation of Harvard College is under much heavier restraints than is customary in other similar institutions." [18] Also, if the overseers did not possess the right of confirmation, why had the corporation presented Bowen's appointment to them in 1850?

The corporation had presented what seemed to be a puzzling, changing conception of the government of Harvard College. Trying to make sense of the intent of the fellows, the overseers mused:

> If these positions taken by the committee of the part of the Corporation are well founded, or shall be acquiesced in, the Board of Overseers is a mere cypher, and may well be abolished. The assembling together five or six times a year in the Senate chamber or elsewhere, of His Excellency the Governor, His Honor the Lieutenant Governor, the Honorable Speaker of the House of Representatives, the Secretary of the Board of Education and some thirty other Reverend and Honorable Gentlemen, will not much be better than an idle and useless ceremony. [19]

17. *Report on the Rights and Duties of the President and Fellows of Harvard College in relation to the Board of Overseers* (Cambridge, 1856), p. 11.

18. *Report of the Committee of the Overseers of Harvard College Appointed to Confer with a Like Committee of the President and Fellows and Agree Upon Certain Joint Rules* (Boston, 1857), pp. 23–24.

19. Ibid., pp. 26–27.

More than likely, the president and fellows nodded in agreement when they read this statement.

The overseers, as a publicly appointed board, had accurately prophesied their demise; but they were not ready to resign in 1857. For the next five years the board continued to assert its rights; the corporation continued to deny them. As long as the corporation acted in this manner the overseers were powerless. They must either acquiesce or initiate legal or legislative action against the fellows. Though many people, including Harvard librarian J. L. Sibley,[20] feared a lawsuit would develop, the overseers resorted neither to a court nor to the legislature to demand their rights. The struggle for "home rule" remained within the confines of the college. Finally, in 1865, the deadlock was resolved when the public board resigned and the General Court made the alumni the electors of the overseers.[21]

While the fellows and overseers struggled over the question of home rule, private philanthropy when combined with the ingenuity of Louis Agassiz brought state support once again to Harvard in 1859. This renewed alliance of support developed quite independently of the question of state responsibility for Harvard as manifested first in Boutwell's attempts to transform the college and later in the dispute between the two governing boards.

In 1847, the year Boutwell first thought of modernizing Harvard, Abbot Lawrence offered $50,000 to establish the Lawrence Scientific School. About the same time that Lawrence made his gift, the Swiss Louis Agassiz first came to America; shortly thereafter the Harvard Corporation appointed him professor of geology and zoology in the new school. Though Lawrence had intended to establish an en-

20. Sibley's Private Journal, Jan. 29, 1857 (HUA): "There is a difficulty growing between the Corporation and the Overseers as to their respective rights. The modification made in the lower Board a few years since and acceded to by the upper is opening a way for difficulty which will produce serious consequences which will probably result in a law suit."

21. See chapter 5 for the 1865 change in the election of the overseers.

gineering school, Agassiz quickly monopolized the school and turned it into a center "for individual study and research in geology and zoology."

Among Agassiz's accomplishments was the founding of the Museum of Comparative Zoology, known today at Harvard as the University Museum. After the executors of the estate of Francis Gray offered $50,000 for this project, Agassiz convinced the General Court in 1859 to appropriate $100,000. This was as large a grant as the state had ever made to any college and one of the largest single gifts Harvard had received from any source — only the Gore bequest equaled it. The General Court made this grant with the proviso that Agassiz match the sum with private funds. The Swiss had no trouble convincing donors to mix their money with that of the commonwealth. After all, that had been the tradition of the Puritan fathers!

Technically, the General Court did not grant the money to the Harvard Corporation but to a separate organization created by Agassiz, the Trustees of the Museum of Comparative Zoology. The Harvard Corporation later absorbed this board and its property in 1876. Because of this technicality Morison has belittled the state's gift and noted, "Agassiz promptly fascinated the General Court of Massachusetts into granting the Museum a hundred thousand dollars at a time when they would not have given a penny to Harvard." [22]

This statement seems unfair. The same bill granted $25,000 to Amherst, $25,000 to Williams, and $50,000 to newly founded Tufts, and made similar provisions that these funds be matched with private gifts.[23] Clearly the assembly was not opposed to higher education. Was it discriminating against

22. Morison, *Three Centuries of Harvard*, p. 297.
23. "An Act to Increase the School Fund and to Grant Aid to the Museum of Comparative Zoology, Tufts, Williams and Amherst Colleges and the Wesleyan Academy at Wilbraham out of the Proceeds of the Sales of Back Bay Lands," *Massachusetts Resolves*, 1859. This bill granted 50% of the funds to the Common School Fund. The remainder was given to higher education, with the one exception of the Wesleyan Academy.

Harvard in granting the funds to a separate corporation? Possibly that was so. The General Court may have been concerned about the dispute between the fellows and the overseers, though no particular evidence exists to indicate this. But would the General Court have granted $100,000 to an activity of a Harvard professor if it had really been in a mood "not to give a penny to Harvard"?

The technicality of the separate corporation at Harvard is only a part of the mystery of the state's liberality in 1859. It is hard to tell what prompted this generosity. Though Agassiz had directly approached the General Court, the colleges had made no joint appeal. Williams historian Frederick Rudolph can find no petition from Williams to the legislature. Instead, he suggests that the grant may have been a spontaneous action by a nativist, anti-Catholic legislature; the College of Holy Cross was noticeably absent from the act of 1859. According to Rudolph, "More than one legislator, casting his vote for the appropriations of 1859, must have thought that he was making at least a small gesture toward preserving old Massachusetts from the ruin which Irish immigration seemed to foreshadow." [24]

Whatever the reasons for this grant of 1859, it has importance in answering our questions about the compatibility of state aid and private philanthropy. The state had required that its grant be matched; all four colleges succeeded in raising the necessary funds. At least in Massachusetts, it did not appear that a separation of college and state would be necessary if Harvard or any other college wanted to attract the donations of the wealthy. However, the grant did not necessarily indicate that the state had rewarded the colleges for becoming "useful." The Harvard grant went to the Museum of Comparative Zoology, not to the Lawrence Scientific School. The grants to the other three were not tied to technical education. In fact, if Rudolph's interpretation is correct, the

24. Frederick Rudolph, *Mark Hopkins and the Log* (New Haven, 1956), pp. 198–99.

grants were made because of the conservative rather than the progressive aspects of the colleges.

In the story of Harvard's affairs with the state in the 1850s it has been suggested that the issue of control existed quite independently of the issue of support. Does this sound strange? Or should one interpret the grant of 1859 as recompense from the state for meddling in the government of Harvard in the early 1850s? This would have been the case only if the state had considered control merely a contractual consideration received in exchange for financial support. But in mid-nineteenth-century America, Massachusetts and many other states saw their role as transcending that of a partner in a contract. The various legislatures viewed themselves as protectors of public interests even when they did not materially support those interests. The overseers, as the appointed delegates of the legislature, struggled with the fellows because they thought they held a public duty to "oversee." The state did not have to make a financial grant to retain this right.

This sense of protectorship existed in New York as well as in Massachusetts. Although New York had made no financial grant to Columbia since 1819, it responded to a call in 1854 to protect the college from the sectarianism and consequent religious intolerance of its trustees. The events that led the state to initiate an inquiry into the affairs of Columbia began in 1853 when James Renwick retired from the professorship of natural and experimental philosophy and chemistry. The filling of this vacancy aroused much concern among alumni, parents of undergraduates, the popular press, and the faction of the trustees who called themselves "progressives." These groups felt that the college had shown little appreciation for the teaching of physical science and concluded that the appointment of a young man well respected by American scientists would be the first step in raising the position of science at Columbia. Their choice was Wolcott Gibbs, an 1841 graduate of Columbia who was currently teaching at New York's Free Academy. So anxious were the alumni for this appointment that they made the unprecedented move of submitting a petition with two hundred signatures to the trustees.

Despite this overwhelming enthusiasm for Gibbs, the other faction of the trustees, whom the progressives called the "fogys" or the "Fossil party," opposed the appointment. Publicly the fogys claimed that they could not support Gibbs because "outside pressure," the petition by two hundred alumni and editorial endorsements by a number of New York newspapers, was being applied on them in favor of this appointment. However, two progressives, George Templeton Strong (Columbia, 1838) and Samuel B. Ruggles (Yale, 1814), recorded in their diaries that the real objection to Gibbs was his Unitarian religious affiliation. Strong wrote that four of the clerical members of the board, who formed a bloc against Gibbs's appointment, said they would vote for him if he were a member of Trinity Church or the Presbyterian Church.[25]

The "fossils" successfully rejected Gibbs's nomination in April, 1854, and appointed Richard McCulloh, a little-known scientist who later enraged the trustees in 1863 by accepting a commission in the Confederate army. The progressives and the alumni had no intention of allowing the issue to die, or of settling it within the confines of the board. Samuel Ruggles immediately published a pamphlet entitled, "The duty of Columbia College to the community and its right to exclude Unitarians from its professorship of science, considered by one of its trustees," which was printed in a number of newspapers. According to Ruggles, Columbia was a public institution. "Founded by a temporal sovereign [King George II]," he asserted, "it is solely a creature of the State, and to the State alone does it owe duty and obedience." The trustees

25. See Allan Nevins, ed., *The Diary of George Templeton Strong*, 4 vols. (New York, 1952), 2:146–57, for the details of the inner workings of the board of trustees in the Wolcott Gibbs rejection.

were merely agents entrusted with the interests of the community, "not a fraternity nor a religious order, set apart from and independent of the community." [26]

Emphasizing the public nature of the board, the "progressive" charged the trustees with gross dereliction of duty; the Gibbs rejection was just one instance of a general neglect. "Can Columbia College, with its little handful of graduates and professors, feel that it has accomplished the object of its creation?", Ruggles asked. Ruggles answered his own question in the negative and went on to claim that the college's stagnation had not been the result of a lack of material resources, but of a lack of human imagination: "We have wanted trustees — more truly and zealously to carry out the purposes defined by our charter. We have avowedly and perseveringly neglected, undervalued and disparaged the Liberal Arts and Sciences, and the world has avenged the neglect by neglecting us." [27]

Ruggles did not represent the only party that desired to keep the case open. The alumni of the college, who had hitherto met only for social purposes, formed a "general committee of alumni" which challenged the foundations of the board. This committee drafted a proposal whereby the board of trustees would be changed from a self-perpetuating body to a board elected by the alumni.

The progressives and the alumni doubted that they could reform the fossils by "moral suasion" alone. As a legislative act of 1810 amending Columbia's charter stated that the "ordinances" and "by-laws" of the college "shall not make the religious tenets of any person a condition of admission to any privilege or office in the said college," the pro-Gibbs faction turned to the state assembly for support. They asked the senate to investigate the college in order to ascertain whether the rejection of Gibbs constituted a violation of the

26. Samuel Ruggles, "The Duty of Columbia College to the Community . . . ," in Richard Hofstadter and Wilson Smith, *American Higher Education: A Documentary History*, 2 vols. (Chicago, 1961), 1:454.

27. Ibid., pp. 453–54.

charter. In addition, the alumni asked the senate to consider enacting their proposal to elect the trustees.[28]

As had been the case at Dartmouth forty years earlier, the legislature was asked—it did not decide on its own — to investigate the college and to protect it from its trustees. Whereas the president had made the appeal at Dartmouth, at Columbia a faction of trustees implored the legislature to protect the college from the abuses of another faction on the same board. In both cases the role of the legislature was the same — as grantor of the charter, the assembly was the protector of the college.[29]

The senate committee began its investigation in June, 1854. After a preliminary examination of the college's financial condition, the committee asked the trustees as a group, "Have the board of trustees at any time rejected a candidate for any professorship in the college, on account of his peculiar tenets in matters of religion?"[30] As a group, the trustees answered in the negative. Finding both this answer and the line of questioning that elicited it unsatisfactory, the committee addressed the following question to each individual trustee, "Did you, or did you not, vote for any candidate for the above office with reference to the religious views or tenets of such candidates?"[31] Only three trustees answered this question; the others felt the state could not require them to betray the secrecy of the ballot.[32]

28. The alumni request was introduced in the senate in "An act to amend an act entitled an act relating to the different colleges within this State, passed April 9, 1813," May, 1854 (New York Senate Document no. 114).

29. The king of Great Britain granted the charters both of Dartmouth and of Columbia. After the Revolution the assemblies succeeded to the rights of the king.

30. *Report of the select committee appointed to examine into the affairs of Columbia College, March, 1855*, p. 4 (New York Senate Document no. 67).

31. Ibid., pp. 94–101.

32. No doubt a number of the trustees would have taken this stand on their own, but it should be mentioned that the board of trustees had passed a resolution on June 6, 1854: "We think therefore that inquiries are not to be expected of the votes or the discussions of personal character or fitness which led to them."

The committee did not challenge their refusal but posed two additional questions to each trustee:

> Have the affairs of the college been so conducted as to persons, appointments, and course of study, as best to promote the government and education of the students belonging thereto?

> Have you any knowledge that the trustees have in any respect violated the terms and conditions of the charter of the college? [33]

After collating the responses to these questions, which were answered in varying degrees of detail, the committee concluded that the trustees had indeed never passed a "resolution" or a "by-law" excluding a man from a position on religious grounds. However, if a majority of the trustees had voted against Gibbs on these grounds, the committee thought the board would have violated the intent of the charter. But even Ruggles could not attribute all the votes against Gibbs to religious grievances — though he thought the decisive votes were cast by those opposed to Unitarianism. Unless the majority had voted on this ground, the senate concluded that the charter had not been violated. According to the committee,

> The State must deal with the corporation, and not the individual trustee; and the motives, objects, and intentions, or even the acts, of the individual trustee, are not always the actions of the corporation. The individual trustee may be guilty of a breach of trust, but can hardly be said guilty of a violation of the charter, so as to warrant a dissolution of the corporation.[34]

The senate then announced that since no charter violation had occurred, it could not amend the charter and alter the

33. *Report of the select committee . . . Columbia College,* pp. 131–60.
34. Ibid., p. 10.

board as the alumni had suggested without the consent of the old trustees. The senate concluded that the Dartmouth College decision controlled their action in this matter. Strangely enough, the state, not the college, appealed to the 1819 ruling.

Though the fossils stayed, the senate report was not a complete defeat for the progressives. The committee agreed that Columbia was a static institution and seconded Ruggles's assertion that the college was not performing its duty:

> It is a fact that our colleges, universities and seats of learning in this country do not occupy the position they ought. The college under consideration has existed for a century, is possessed of productive property of over $1,000,000 in value — is situated in the great American metropolis — and yet is employing but seven professors, and educating but 129 students in all the classes. Surely there must be a cause for this, and it should be diligently sought for, and when discovered, removed.[35]

So the state allowed the trustees to retain their power. But acting as the conscience of the college, it clearly announced that it was displeased with the board's use of that power. Though the assembly proposed no legislation either for support or structural change, it, in effect, gave the progressives a mandate to pursue their plans to elevate Columbia to university status.

Some progress had been made in this direction even before the Gibbs case. In 1852 the trustees had appointed a committee to "consider and report upon the expediency of engrafting upon the foundation of this college a scheme of University Professorships and Lectures in the higher Departments of Letters and Science." And in November, 1853, only a few months before the Gibbs nomination came to a vote, the trustees had made an unusual statement that seemed to reconcile "excellence" with the "spirit of the age":

35. Ibid., p. 13.

The public generally unaccustomed to look upon the mind except in connection with the body and used to regard it as a machine for promoting the pleasures, the convenience, or the comforts of the latter, will not be satisfied with a system of education in which they are unable to perceive the direct connection between the knowledge imparted and the bodily advantages to be gained. For this reason, to preserve in some degree high and pure education and strict mental discipline and to draw as many as possible within its influence, we must partially yield to those sentiments which we should be wholly unable to resist. Your committee therefore think that while they would retain the system, having in view the most perfect intellectual training, they might devise parallel courses having this design at their foundation, but still adapted to meet the popular demand.[36]

Were not some of the old conservatives at least mellowing in their positions?

Just as the state investigation began in May, 1854, the trustees altered the collegiate course; a student would now pursue the prescribed classical curriculum for three years and in his senior year elect studies in one of three faculties: a school or faculty of philosophy, a school of jurisprudence and history, or a school of mathematical and physical science. Three months later the board followed its plan to devise parallel courses by authorizing a scientific program. Students in this course would join their classical brothers for a common senior year of elective studies. The committee which proposed this reform again stated that the college had a duty not only to provide as good an education as possible but also "to extend the benefits of that education to as large a number as possible." [37]

While proposing and resolving to expand the course of

36. CCT Minutes, November, 1853.
37. CCT Minutes, July 10, 1854.

instruction, the trustees also voted in 1854 to remove the college to a site in the Botanical Garden. The state investigation did not alter this plan, and Columbia occupied its uptown campus in 1857. Originally the trustees had retained an architect, Richard Upjohn, to draw plans for an entire new complex of buildings. But in 1856 the New York Asylum for the Deaf and Dumb offered to sell Columbia its buildings, which were near the Botanical Garden (49th Street and Madison Avenue) for $65,000. Figuring that the cost of the asylum plus repairs of $18–20,000 would be much less than the estimated $210,000 that Upjohn's buildings would cost, the trustees accepted the Deaf and Dumb offer, gave the architect a final compensation of $1,000, and dropped plans for any new buildings.[38] In addition to providing the college with a new campus, the 1857 move augmented the college treasury, because some of the vacated property at Park Place was sold for $596,350.

Despite the mandate from the state and the move to a new campus, George Templeton Strong was still convinced that the trustees were a body of mummies and that their desire, much less their sense of public duty, to raise the college to university level would never advance beyond the stage of resolutions. In 1857 no professional schools or university professorships had as yet been established, and Strong even worried about the upcoming appointments the trustees would make to seven professorships in the college faculty. Thinking about these positions as he surveyed one of the buildings on the new campus, the young trustee mused: "The building has been very thoroughly overhauled and is rapidly being got into decent order swept and garnished; the old deaf and dumb spirit that possessed it so long being cast out. It remains to be seen whether seven other worse spirits, deafer and dumber, have not taken its place. All depends on the appointments we're on the eve of making." [39]

38. CCT Minutes, Nov. 3, 1856.
39. Nevins, ed., *Diary of George Templeton Strong*, 2:335.

A few months later Strong confessed that he was pleased with the appointments to the college faculty, which included Francis Lieber, but he still doubted that university studies would ever materialize. He found fault not only with the trustees but with American youth. "This people," he claimed, "is not yet ripe for higher education. The ingenuous youth of Fifth Avenue wouldn't take it as a gift without money and without price." [40] Strong thought the only way to begin a program of university studies would be to lure young men into a school of law or a school of applied science, and

> Having caught them, liberalize both schools by additional courses of study, optional or imperative, gradually expanding and improving them, and in effect saying: We will furnish you with all the armory of the mere lawyer, on condition that you become accomplished in kindred but higher pursuits. We will qualify you to construct railroads and superintend mines better than anyone else if you will consent to go a little faster and submit to a thorough education in liberal science.

The trustees, he feared, would never consent to such a program of "indirection" but would insist upon "establishing at once and in vacuo, something like the skeleton of a complete "University" system, with all its parts harmonious on paper; which will be about as sensible and hopeful an undertaking as the attempt to produce an oak tree by constructing it instead of planting the acorn and letting it grow." [41]

All of the progressives were not as cynical as Strong. Samuel Ruggles never ceased agitating for university expansion and served on many committees to achieve this goal. He had been actively pushing for the establishment of graduate and professional departments since 1854, but a vote on his resolutions had usually been postponed. In March, 1858, he was appointed to still another committee to consider new schools.

40. Ibid., p. 388.
41. Ibid.

This group desired action and in June, 1858 presented for a vote eight resolutions, which included the recommendation that the services of four professors who were named be immediately secured for postgraduate instruction. The trustees voted positively, and Ruggles proceeded to contact the men he had recommended.[42]

James Dwight Dana, Arnold Guyot, and George P. Marsh agreed to give lectures in the postgraduate departments; Theodore W. Dwight accepted the professorship of municipal law. Unfortunately, Dana was unable to deliver his lectures because of poor health, and Guyot and Marsh remained only two years. Dwight's appointment, however, proved permanent and laid the foundation for the Columbia Law School. The school opened in the fall of 1858 with thirty-five students. Only three years later the school enrolled 117 young men, a larger number than the law schools of either Yale or Harvard could command; Columbia was to maintain this lead throughout the 1860s and 1870s.

Columbia's complement of professional schools grew in 1860 when the College of Physicians and Surgeons secured an enabling act from the regents which allowed it to become the medical school of Columbia College. The addition of the medical school convinced even Strong that Columbia was at last making progress. In 1860 he recorded in his diary, "So we have our medical school now as well as our law school and begin to look like a real University." [43]

In this expansion toward university status Columbia thought the state, after acting as a conscience, might want to be a partner. In 1857 the trustees petitioned for a direct subsidy to buy the Deaf and Dumb asylum. When this appeal failed, the board decided to ask for tax exemption on the college's rental property. With the Botanical Garden valued at more than $1 million in 1858–59, tax exemption on the

42. For Ruggles's efforts to raise Columbia to university status, see Daniel G. Brinton Thompson, *Ruggles of New York* (New York, 1946), pp. 90-100.
43. Nevins, ed., 3:31.

property would have the same effect as a substantial subsidy. Even though the trustees resolved to use the remitted taxes for free scholarships to "meritorious students," the legislature refused to approve this request in 1858 and again in 1861.[44]

While Columbia attempted to secure legislative patronage on its own, the regents sought to persuade the assembly to aid all of New York's colleges. Annually from 1858 to 1862, the regents tried to arouse interest in the legislature for the colleges and used Columbia's university plans as an example of the progressive character of higher education in the state. Failing in these attempts, the regents organized a University Convocation in 1863 "to exert a direct influence upon the people and the legislature of the State, personally and through the press so as to secure an appreciation of a thorough system of education together with such pecuniary aid and legislative enactments as will place the institutions represented here in a position worthy of the population and resources of the state." [45] This united appeal was equally unsuccessful in securing public aid.

So it appeared in the early 1860s that even though New York had admonished Columbia in 1855 to make better use of its resources, state-granted privileges or subsidies would not be among the tools the college could apply to the task. The unlikelihood of state support helped compound the trustees' fears that Columbia's future might still be precarious. Despite a rise in undergraduate enrollment from 111 in 1850 to 203 in 1860, and the addition of two professional schools, the trustees still wondered if the college could successfully compete for patronage by both students and wealthy benefactors in New York City.

In 1854 a third competitor, the College of the City of New York, had been chartered. City College, an outgrowth of the Free Academy that had been established by the New

44. CCT Minutes, Mar. 23, 1857; Jan. 4, 1858; May 6, 1861.
45. *Report of the Regents of the University of the State of New York, 1864* (Albany, 1865), p. 326.

York City Board of Education in 1848, charged no tuition fee and by 1857 attracted 331 students. Columbia's trustees debated abolishing tuition to meet this competition but decided against such a plan. However, they did lower the fee from a hundred to fifty dollars.[46]

Columbia's concern with attracting students was matched by its desire to secure the wealth of the rich. Unless the college was to finance its expansion solely on the revenues generated by wise property management, it would have to receive substantial donations from wealthy men. In the late 1840s and in the 1850s a number of philanthropists had emerged in New York, but they had not viewed Columbia as an object of their charity. John Jacob Astor had given $400,000 in 1848 to construct and to endow a great library for the city. In 1857 Peter Cooper had established the Cooper Union to advance scientific education, with a gift of $300,000. Even though Cooper was a close friend of Samuel Ruggles, all attempts to merge Cooper's interests and wealth with Columbia's expansion had failed.

The competition of a free college and the seeming disinterest of the wealthy when coupled with the failure to secure state appropriations left the trustees in 1860 with almost as many doubts about the place and purpose of Columbia in New York City as they had possessed a decade earlier. The college was still questing for its identity.

While Columbia was investigated and Harvard reorganized by the state in the 1850s, Dartmouth and Yale profited — or suffered — from a period of benign neglect. New Hampshire did not challenge Lord's theocracy, and the senators on the Yale Corporation displayed little if any concern with the affairs of the Connecticut college. But like Harvard, both colleges received substantial gifts from philanthropists for technical education. With these gifts Dartmouth and Yale

46. CCT Minutes, June 1, 1857; June 15, 1857.

prepared themselves for a new state alliance that would develop after the passage of the Morrill Act in 1862.

Though Benjamin Silliman had been appointed professor of chemistry at Yale in 1802 and had given lectures to undergraduates since that time, no "scientific course" or school where a student could pursue a nonclassical course had developed at Yale until the late 1840s. As mentioned in a previous chapter, Yale had established professorships of agricultural chemistry and of practical chemistry in 1846, and had created a department of philosophy and the arts to house these new activities the next year. It was from this department that the Yale Scientific School, later the Sheffield Scientific School, emerged.

The original plans for this department envisioned much more than a scientific division. The corporation committee that recommended its creation noted:

> From time to time, new branches of study are called for by the public which if introduced into our undergraduate course would greatly crowd it and interfere with its object as a course of training for the mind.[47]

To meet these demands, the new department was to embrace philosophy, literature, history, and modern languages as well as the natural sciences. In fact, this new department would really offer everything except the classical course.

The catholic conception for the department of philosophy and the arts was more than just a pipe dream. Eventually it was to serve as the channel through which both graduate and undergraduate instruction in such modern-day humanities as English literature and modern history would enter Yale. But in the 1850s the growth of the department was connected mainly with the natural and applied sciences. It was this aspect of education which attracted the philanthropists, and later the state.

47. YC Minutes, August, 1847.

In 1852 William A. Norton was named professor of engineering. Like those of the professors of applied science appointed before him, Norton's salary was to be paid by student fees until an adequate endowment could be raised. The financial resources of the college were not available for science. In fact, to secure Norton's appointment, Benjamin Silliman, Jr., had to assure President Woolsey that the new professor would not compete with the college in soliciting funds. The corporation would not allow a scientist, much less an engineer, to interfere with its plan to raise $100,000 from alumni and friends.[48] The college successfully netted its $100,000 in 1854 and made no objection two years later when the scientists proposed a financial appeal to the general public.

Before soliciting funds, the scientific faculty thought it should bring some order to what appeared to be a band of disparate professors, each a school unto himself. A few steps had already been made in this direction. In 1852 the corporation had authorized the granting of a Ph.B. degree to students who pursued a systematic course of study for three years. Two years later the "schools" of engineering and of applied chemistry had been combined to form the Yale Scientific School, and a professor of metallurgy had been added in 1855.

The most ambitious "system" emerged in 1856 when the faculty drafted "A Plan for a Complete Organization of the Scientific School connected with Yale College." The plan announced that the school would offer practical training in mining, engineering, agriculture, and manufacturing, as well as graduate work in the natural sciences. For practical training either of two degrees could be obtained, a Ph.B. (three years) or a B.S. (two years). Graduate degrees still lay in the future, but the not too distant future. Yale authorized the

48. See Russell H. Chittenden, *A History of the Sheffield Scientific School*, 2 vols. (New Haven, 1928), 1:56.

Ph.D. degree in 1860 and granted it for the first time, both at Yale and in the United States, in 1861.

With such a noble plan the scientists felt prepared to ask for financial support. Although they had appealed to the legislature in 1846 for a chair of agricultural chemistry, now they disregarded the assembly and turned to the public at large — anyone interested in science or technology could contribute. To help the Scientific School secure the permanent and ongoing interest of potential donors, the corporation even allowed a new or adjunct system of control for the school. The trustees declared in 1856:

> Any persons contributing $5,000 or upwards to the funds of the school or to any special fund for the use of same may constitute a board of visitors with power to attend examinations, see that the terms of subscriptions are carried out and report and recommend to the President and Fellows any regulations which they may think best.[49]

The fund-raisers desired $150,000; in the first year, 1856, they garnered about $25,000. Of that sum, $10,000 came from Joseph Sheffield, a New Haven railroad promoter who had never attended any college but who was the father-in-law of John A. Porter, professor of agricultural chemistry. Out of an interest to promote technical education, and no doubt out of loyalty to his family connection, Sheffield continued to support the school. In 1859 he provided a site and building for the school and contributed $50,000 to endow three professorships in chemistry, metallurgy, and engineering.

The corporation was duly impressed with Sheffield's munificence, which totaled over $100,000 in 1861, and decided in that year to rename the school the Sheffield Scientific School. This proved a wise move; Sheffield eventually contributed more than $1 million. In little more than a decade

49. YC Minutes, 1856.

Yale had developed what was recognized as the leading scientific school in the United States. Could this development have come from the same college which had issued the conservative Report of 1828? Had Yale changed?

It would be safe to say that the corporation allowed New Haven to change, but not Yale College. A school of science could exist in the same locality as the college, but it could not depend upon the financial resources of the college or even the fees of college students. Instruction in the school was open only "to graduates and others not members of the undergraduate classes." Yale College students could not even attend classes in the Sheffield School until 1888.

By establishing a separate and distinct scientific school the corporation could maintain the conservative, classically oriented college course, satisfy the demands made by advocates of science, and receive the donations of wealthy industrialists. It would have been difficult to resist the claims of science and technology in the 1850s without resorting to neanderthal conservatism. And could Yale have afforded to put itself in the position of turning away donors who wished to support this kind of instruction? With a scientific school Yale was able to satisfy all parties. For example, when a donor offered $20,000 to endow a chair of botany in 1864, the corporation announced that such instruction had no place in the course of liberal arts, but accepted the gift for the Sheffield School.[50] Possibly the philanthropists of science might one day understand the values and claims of the classics.

The reluctance of college trustees to refuse a substantial gift or bequest also led to the establishment of a scientific school at Dartmouth. Although Nathan Lord had announced in 1828 that a college should teach only the liberal arts and should not "commingle" students of different interests, Abiel Chandler, a Harvard graduate who had resided in Walpole, New Hampshire, bequeathed $50,000 to Dartmouth in 1852

50. See Chittenden, *History of Sheffield Scientific School*, 1:96.

for the foundation of a scientific department. As if to irritate Lord even more, the will specified, "No other or higher preparatory studies are to be required in order to enter said department or school than are pursued in the common schools of New England." [51] Chandler's will further stipulated that a board of visitors for the school be appointed with a veto power over the college trustees to insure that the older board did not violate the provisions of the gift. In this request for such an adjunct board, Chandler had asked for the same degree of control which the college had granted the state in 1807.

Lord presented the offer of the bequest to the trustees in 1851 with no recommendation that they accept it. Despite the stipulations of the will, the trustees could not bring themselves to refuse $50,000, the largest gift that had ever been offered the college, and established the Chandler School of Science and Arts. The school opened in the fall of 1852 with seventeen students.

Unlike the scientific school at Yale, instruction at the Chandler School was given by the existing college faculty. But Chandler students and college students did not attend joint classes. Interestingly enough, the separation of students resulted as much from the request of the men in the Chandler School as from Lord's ideas of education. The Chandler students knew they were considered inferior by the collegians and rejected any proposal for joint classes:

> As the unity of classes among themselves [college students] and the want of sympathy for all others makes our position extremely unpleasant, that the inconvenience we cause them tends to create prejudice and renders difficulty very probable; and that there is sacrifice of feeling attending it which cannot but lessen our progress in study.[52]

51. Leon Burr Richardson, *History of Dartmouth College*, 2 vols. (Hanover, 1932), 1:423.
52. Ibid., p. 424.

The hostility of the collegians for the Chandler students remained a constant theme in the history of Dartmouth in the second half of the nineteenth century.

By accepting Chandler's gift, and consequently compromising Lord's ideal of collegiate purity, the trustees indicated that regardless of a desire to be independent and aloof from the popular pressures of society, a college could not completely resist the "spirit of the age" — particularly when that spirit offered $50,000. In addition to remaining aloof from the "spirit," Lord wanted Dartmouth to be independent of the state, or any other government, lest his college become a "panderer to despotism." But there was also a limit, at least in the 1860s, beyond which a college could not maintain this type of independence. It was reached at Dartmouth in 1863, not because of any measure of repression on the part of a government, but because of a sense of responsibility to the state and to the nation held both by the trustees and by society at large as represented by the churches. And this responsibility existed above and beyond any financial consideration made by a public body.

Nathan Lord caused this college-government responsibility to become an issue in 1863 because of his peculiar orthodoxy; the president continued to sanction slavery as justified by the Bible during the first years of the Civil War. Lord had even written newspaper articles denouncing abolitionists as late as 1862. After the implementation of the Emancipation Proclamation in 1863, which did not free slaves in Union states, both the New Hampshire clergy who supported the college and leading members of the board of trustees decided that Lord's deviance had exceeded the limits they could tolerate.

In late June, 1863, the Merrimac Confederation of Congregational Churches addressed a resolution to the trustees, in which they warned that the welfare of the college "is greatly imperilled by the existence of popular prejudice against it arising from the publication and use of some of his [Lord's] peculiar views touching public affairs — tending to embarrass our Government in its present fearful struggle and to encourage and strengthen the resistance of its enemies." [53] The churches advised that a change in the presidency might be called for.

The trustees met in July and summarily dismissed Lord from his position. In justifying their act they announced, "it is the duty of literary institutions and the men who conduct them to stand in no doubtful position when the government of the country struggles for existence." [54] The board declared that their dismissal of Lord definitely indicated their support for Dartmouth men in the war and their abhorrence of slavery. Like John Wheelock, Nathan Lord challenged the jurisdiction of the trustees and claimed that they possessed no charter right to impose a religious or political test on any officer of the college. Since he probably thought there was no legislature or court that would support his claim, however, he resigned.

Even if the trustees now stood in "no doubtful position" to the federal government, Lord's dismissal may seem unrelated to our story of philanthropy or of Dartmouth's connection with the state of New Hampshire. Though it was indeed the national government for whom the trustees made a direct stand, the dismissal of Lord now allowed the board to pursue actively a possible new alliance with New Hampshire. For while Lord had shown no interest in the state during the last years of his administration, New Hampshire had become attracted to the college and its new scientific school. And the recently passed Morrill Act (1862) provided largess that brought the two even closer together.

As early as 1858 New Hampshire governor William Haile had suggested to the legislature that the interests of agriculture could be promoted by "establishing a department in Dartmouth College or in connection with some other insti-

---

53. DCT Minutes, July 23, 1863.
54. Ibid., July 24, 1863.

tution of the state, for the instruction of young men in science and practical agriculture." [55] A year later Governor Ichabod Goodwin had announced that a plan was in progress "to connect with Dartmouth an agricultural department where our young men preparing to be farmers can get a scientific education, fitting them not only to be accomplished agriculturists, but wise legislators." [56]

Even before Haile had spoken in 1858, a wealthy New Hampshire farmer had proposed a plan to unite private, state, and federal support for an agricultural college. In 1856 Benjamin Thompson of Durham had drafted a will bequeathing his entire estate to the state of New Hampshire provided the agricultural college be located on his farm in Durham. The will stipulated a number of other provisions to insure the success of the school.[57]

First, the state had to guarantee a 5 percent annual interest rate on the estate for twenty years and hold both the principal and the interest intact to form a fund for the support of the school. Also, the state itself had to appropriate $3,000 a year for twenty years, guarantee an annual interest of 5 percent, and hold both the principal and the interest intact to supplement the fund from Thompson's bequest. The donor did specify that the twenty-year period of accumulation could be waived at any time if the state appropriated "such sums of money as will make said funds equal in amount to what said funds would become if accumulated during twenty years according to terms."

Thompson's school would admit no one under sixteen years of age and would teach "theories" of agriculture by experiment. The results of all experiments were to be pub-

55. *Journal of the Honorable Senate of the State of New Hampshire, June, 1858* (Concord, 1858), p. 25.

56. *Journal of the Honorable Senate of the State of New Hampshire, June, 1859* (Concord, 1859), p. 25.

57. The details of Thompson's will can be found in *By-laws of the Trustees of the New Hampshire College of Agricultural and Mechanical Arts* (Durham, 1893), p. 50.

lished and sold to citizens of New Hampshire and the nation at cost. Possibly foreseeing the eventual passage of the Morrill Act, Thompson suggested that the state also apply to the federal government for a grant of land to support the school. Here in 1856 was a plan for private, state, and federal support of an agricultural school. Though Thompson did not die until 1890, his final will offered New Hampshire much the same proposal he had drafted in 1856. The state accepted his $400,000 estate in compliance with the stipulations and established an agricultural college, eventually to become the University of New Hampshire.

Fortunately, Dartmouth did not have to wait until 1890 to participate in a plan similar to Thompson's. Only a year after the Durham man had drafted his will, United States Representative Justin Morrill first introduced a bill in the United States Congress to set aside federal lands for the endowment of an institution in each state to offer instruction in the agricultural and mechanical arts. This bill was defeated in 1857 and again in 1859 because of opposition both from states' rights southerners, who claimed a New England-style school system would be forced upon them, and from westerners who feared eastern ownership of scrip for lands in the West.[58]

In 1862, with the southern representatives out of the Congress, Morrill reintroduced his earlier bills. At the same time Senator Benjamin Wade of Ohio presented a similar bill in the upper house, increasing the acreage to be given by the governor. The Congress passed the latter bill and Lincoln signed it in July, 1862.

The act of 1862, which is nevertheless known as the Morrill Act, authorized each state to receive federal land scrip amounting to 30,000 acres for each senator and representative. The revenue resulting from the sales of the land was to become a fund with a state-guaranteed annual yield of 5

58. See Paul Gates, "Western Opposition to the Agricultural College Act," *Indiana Magazine of History* 37: 103–36.

percent for the support of a college, not an academy or a common school, which, without excluding the classics, would offer instruction in the agricultural and mechanical arts. Military instruction was also to be provided. The act further stipulated that the fund and its income could be applied only for instruction, not for the acquisition of a site or for the construction of buildings. As the sole exception to this rule, 10 percent of the fund could be used to purchase an experimental farm. Finally, to prod the states to action, the act required each state to accept or to decline the offer within two years and to have a college in operation within five years of its acceptance of the grant.

The Morrill Act in no way specified what type of college any state should establish, or that it necessarily had to establish a new institution. The legislatures were allowed to allocate the fund to any institution that suited them; the public bodies could mix the federal money with their own funds or those of an individual. In fact, the act was so vague on the point of institutional organization that five years after its passage Daniel Coit Gilman feared that the purpose of the bill, which he considered to be the creation of a system of national schools of science, would soon be lost in a hodgepodge of different institutions with no central direction or plan.[59]

The bill seemed less concerned with the organization of the colleges than with the class of people who should attend them. As if responding to the "professional" criticism hurled at the colleges for years, the act specified that the land-grant institutions were "to promote the liberal and practical education of the industrial classes in the several pursuits and professions of life."

Interestingly enough, in many states the Morrill Act aided the industrial classes by bringing them in contact with the old liberal arts college. Thus the act did not necessarily have the effect of returning students to their own social classes.

59. Daniel Coit Gilman, "National Schools of Science," *North American Review*, October, 1867.

Often farmers became engineers, and the atmosphere of the liberal arts even diverted some potential farmers and engineers to the "learned professions." Eventually farmers were to become distressed that many of their sons never returned to the farm once they had been exposed to a liberal arts college, particularly if the college was in a city. In Connecticut as well as in New Hampshire this distress led to demands in the 1890s for separate, independent agricultural colleges, and forced those states to sever their land-grant connections with Yale and Dartmouth. But before these connections were severed, let us first see how the alliances were formed.

While Dartmouth was still embroiled in the ousting of Lord, Yale allied with Connecticut as a land-grant college, thus setting an example for the New Hampshire college to emulate. When news of the Morrill Act reached Yale, the faculty of the Sheffield Scientific School proposed to the legislature that the grant be applied to Yale. Since the assembly had no desire to appropriate any of its own funds to build a new college, it quickly voted in 1863 to favor the Sheffield Scientific School: no other college in Connecticut had made a competing offer. The agreement between Yale and Connecticut indicated that, as in the days of Ezra Stiles, private and public funds could be mixed for the benefit of both the college and the community. Neither Yale, its philanthropists such as Sheffield, nor the assembly posed any objection to this joint venture.

The Connecticut fund amounted to $135,000. The state actually retained possession of the fund and turned the interest over to Yale. In exchange, the Sheffield Scientific School offered forty free scholarships for Connecticut students. The income from the fund, $6,750 per annum, greatly augmented the operating revenue of the school. Although Sheffield's largess had provided facilities for the school, the private endowment from which operating revenue could be drawn amounted to less than $100,000. Hence, the state money doubled the annual income of the school. The only additional expense incurred from accepting the grant was a provision for agricultural instruction; William H. Brewer was appointed professor of agriculture in 1864.

Although the governor, lieutenant governor, and six senators sat on the Yale Corporation, a new state board of visitors, including the governor, lieutenant governor, three senators, and the secretary of the board of education, was created to oversee the expenditure of the state fund. No further alterations in either the Yale Corporation or the Sheffield Scientific School were required to make Yale Connecticut's land-grant college.

Yale and Connecticut maintained this relationship until 1893. In that year the Connecticut Grange forced the legislature to sever its connection with Yale and to devote the federal funds to the Storrs Agricultural College, later the University of Connecticut. On the ground of breach of contract, Yale sued the state and received a cash settlement of $154,604 — the largest grant ever given by the state to Yale!

From our position of hindsight the state land grant appears insignificant in the development of the Sheffield Scientific School, and even more so of Yale University. Sheffield and other donors continued their gifts to the school, but the state never made a single appropriation to augment the federal funds. However, this could not have been foreseen in 1863. At that time the $135,000 which the state held as an endowment matched the gifts of private philanthropists. As Michigan, Wisconsin, and even Massachusetts were to do, Connecticut might have appropriated its own funds for the institution to which it had awarded federal funds. In 1863 the future of college and state was indefinite. At that time it appeared as if the public and the private sectors were advancing together.

After Nathan Lord's dismissal in 1863, Dartmouth was eager for some kind of union such as Yale had acquired, and volunteered to be the land-grant college for New Hampshire. President Asa Smith noted that a connection between Dartmouth and the state would be particularly easy to negotiate because state representatives were already allied with the trustees to oversee state funds by the agreement of 1807.[60]

Despite Dartmouth's offer, a union of college and state was delayed because animosity toward the college existed in the legislature. Republicans resented the college because it had retained Lord during the war years. The Democrats were angered that Dartmouth had so peremptorily dismissed him. There were even groups in the New Hampshire assembly who delayed the union because they thought the Morrill Act was too restrictive; they wished to grant the money to an academy.

By 1866 the forces antagonistic to Dartmouth had prevented the fund from being used at all. In that year the governor reminded the legislators that the agricultural college must be organized by July, 1867, or the state would lose the grant. He pointed out that the funds could not be applied to an academy, only to a college. "As to which college," he added, "there can fortunately be no question, since we have but one, deservedly the pride of New Hampshire, both in its past renown and its present excellent and energetic management." [61]

The governor acknowledged the fact that some farmers did not want to send their sons to Dartmouth "where they may be subjected to unfavorable comparisons with the students in the classical department." He tried to soothe the farmers with the assurance that a connection with the college would be mutually beneficial. "It would have the happiest effect," he exclaimed, "in endearing that whole institution to the hearts of the people, infusing the vigor and lifeblood of the sons of the hills into its ancient veins while from it, in return, something of the learning and grace of the schools will be carried into the homes of the farmers and mechanics of the state." [62]

60. Richardson, *History of Dartmouth College*, 2:533.

61. *Journal of the House of Representatives of the State of New Hampshire, June, 1866* (Concord, 1866), p. 36.

62. Ibid.

Finally in 1866 the college and the state reached an agreement. Unlike the arrangement at Yale, the grant was not directly given to the trustees nor did the existing scientific school become the division for instruction. Instead, a legally independent body, the New Hampshire College of Agriculture, was created. The new "college" would have nine trustees; four appointed by the trustees of Dartmouth College and five by the governor.

The New Hampshire College of Agriculture was independent in name only. All the facilities of Dartmouth College were placed at its disposal, and only one faculty member was not a member of the Dartmouth staff. The laws of Dartmouth also applied to the agricultural students and the president of Dartmouth was also its president.

Even with a supposedly independent body as the recipient of the land grant, the state was still wary of its connection. The agreement of 1866 stipulated that the union could be terminated after fourteen years. In 1867 an additional provision allowed either party to terminate the agreement with one year's notice after 1874.

Under this arrangement Dartmouth and the state were united until 1893. In that year the New Hampshire College of Agriculture dissolved its tie with Dartmouth and moved to Durham, where it later became the University of New Hampshire. New Hampshire farmers convinced the legislature to add Benjamin Thompson's bequest to the federal funds and to make the New Hampshire College of Agriculture completely independent of Dartmouth.

So Dartmouth and Yale, the two colleges whose development in the 1850s had been marked by the rise of private philanthropy to the applied sciences and an almost complete lack of state interest, became the land-grant colleges of their respective states. But what of our other two colleges? Massachusetts had been endeavoring to make Harvard more responsive to the needs of all the people; New York, in the investigation of 1855, had advised Columbia to diversify its offerings. Would not the land grant make it possible for the state to prod the colleges in this direction?

In Massachusetts early signs indicated that the state might very well use the land grant to continue its plan to reshape Harvard. Governor John A. Andrew (Bowdoin, 1837) announced to the legislature in 1863 that the grant should be used to unite Harvard, the Bussey Institution, and the newly chartered Massachusetts Institute of Technology (1861) into one system of higher education for the state. Harvard was not averse to this plan, but others were.[63]

William Barton Rogers, president of the Massachusetts Institute of Technology, informed the governor that he would never accept a grant from the state or any other source if the institute must become part of an organization dominated by Harvard College. Rogers was not hostile to Harvard, nor was Harvard hostile to the new institution; John A. Lowell, senior member of the Harvard Corporation, was a vice-president of the technological school. But Rogers felt that first-rate scientific instruction could be offered only in an institution independent from a classical college. It was the classical college, he thought, which had always viewed applied science as inferior education. How could such instruction flourish within an institution where it was considered to be only peripherally important?[64]

Rogers had held this view for some time. As early as 1846, while he was still professor of natural philosophy at the University of Virginia, he had developed a plan for an independent Polytechnic School in Boston. When the Lawrence Scientific School opened in 1847, he had concluded, "It can only as now organized draw a small number of the body of students aside from the usual college routine. It should be in reality a school of applied science, embracing at least four

63. *Address of His Excellency John A. Andrew to the Legislature of Massachusetts* (Boston, 1863; Massachusetts Senate Document no. 1), pp. 46–58.

64. Rogers's position on the land grant is stated in a letter to Dr. W. J. Walker, May 4, 1863, in Emma Rogers, ed., *The Life and Letters of William Barton Rogers*, 2 vols. (Boston, 1896), 2:163–64.

professorships, and it ought to be in great measure independent of the other departments of Harvard." [65] Rogers
had found no reason to amend this view in the ensuing
years.

While the Massachusetts Institute of Technology tried to
attract the land grant for mechanical instruction, a bevy of
men and institutions lobbied for a portion of the fund for
agriculture. Amherst and Williams offered a course of lectures in agricultural science. Members of the State Board of
Agriculture appealed for an independent agricultural college.
Harvard itself was not silent. President Thomas Hill and
Louis Agassiz supported Governor Andrew's plan to unite
the land grant with Harvard and the Bussey Institution. [66]

To unite the competing voices into one plan, the legislature appointed a commission headed by Erastus Haven, a
Wesleyan graduate who currently served on the Harvard
Board of Overseers. [67] After a number of hearings the committee came to share the philosophy of William Rogers that
technical and agricultural instruction would flourish best
in colleges independent of older institutions. In March, 1863
Haven reported that two completely independent colleges
should be aided. He suggested that 3/10 of the land grant
be applied to Massachusetts Institute of Technology; the remainder would be used for the support of a new institution,
the Massachusetts College of Agriculture.

Haven's committee advocated both private and public
support for the new college. Governor Andrew still hoped

65. Ibid., 1:274.
66. In 1835 Benjamin Bussey (Harvard, 1803) bequeathed his 200-acre
estate and his personal property to Harvard. One half of the fund from the
bequest was to be used to establish a school of agriculture and horticulture.
Bussey died in 1842 but Harvard did not receive the trust until 1861, at
which time it amounted to $413,000—the largest grant the college had ever
received.
67. Haven left Massachusetts soon after he made his report, to become
president of the University of Michigan. It was during his administration
that the state first made annual appropriations to the institution. Haven
was also president of Northwestern University (1869–72) and chancellor of
the University of Syracuse (1874–80).

the new college would ally with the Bussey Institution and use the latter's $200,000 fund earmarked for agricultural education. But the trustees elected in 1864 to accept an offer of $75,000 made jointly by individual donors and the town of Amherst. In the twentieth century, the Massachusetts College of Agriculture became the University of Massachusetts.

Although Massachusetts had hoped to obtain $450,000 from the sale of its land scrip, the state realized only $236,307. To oversee the expenditure of the fund, the chief justice, the secretary of the state board of education, and the governor were made ex officio members of the board of trustees of the Massachusetts Institute of Technology. Strangely enough, though the legislature appointed the trustees of the agricultural college in 1863, it surrendered its right to fill vacancies on that body in 1871; thus the trustees became a self-perpetuating body.[68]

The disposition of the Morrill grant to two independent institutions did not completely end the plan to make Harvard the hub of a comprehensive educational system. In 1870 President Charles Eliot of Harvard, who had been professor of chemistry at MIT from 1865 to 1868, tried to induce the technological institution to merge with Harvard. But William Rogers was steadfast in his beliefs. Though a sick man in 1870, he rose to protest any merger with Harvard. Rogers prevailed; Eliot failed, as had Governor Andrew, to create a grand university in Cambridge by a union of institutions.[69]

In New York, the failure of Columbia to receive the land grant is not difficult to explain. Though the Columbia trustees recorded an interest in securing the grant,[70] they had little influence in the state legislature. And unlike Connec-

---

68. A full description of the land-grant negotiations in Massachusetts can be found in Harold W. Cary, *The University of Massachusetts* (Amherst, 1962), pp. 17–29.

69. For Rogers's stand against Eliot, see Samuel C. Prescott, *When M.I.T. Was Boston Tech.* (Cambridge, 1954), p. 70.

70. CCT Minutes, Apr. 6, 1863.

ticut and New Hampshire, where only one college existed
or offered to accept the grant, some twenty colleges in New
York wanted the federal largess — principally the People's
College at Havana and the Agricultural College at Ovid.

However, it was no existing college that successfully captured the favor of the state. An educational reformer and
state legislator, Andrew Dickson White (Yale, 1853), persuaded the legislature to charter a completely new institution — an "American university" that would unite the New
York land grant with the $500,000 gift of Ezra Cornell.

Persuasion was not exactly the technique White used to
win the grant. Opposition from the existing colleges to a
new institution was considerable, but White simply bought
them out. He secured the vote of the representative from
Ovid by arranging to build a new state insane asylum in his
district. The representatives from Genesee County were
silenced after White persuaded Cornell to make a cash payment of $25,000 to Genesee College for a department of
agricultural chemistry; the *Ithaca Journal* called this an endowment for the "Blackmail Professorship." Blackmail it
may have been, but White secured the votes of these representatives. The bill to incorporate the Cornell University was
approved by the New York assembly on April 22, 1865, and
signed by Governor Fenton five days later. The new university opened in 1868 with White as president.[71]

The new Cornell University was truly a hybrid; its initial
endowment came from a combination of public and private
funds, and its governing board united seven ex officio state
officials with a body of self-perpetuating trustees. But there
was another hybrid quality of public and private cooperation
at Cornell that was not immediately evident in 1865.

The New York land grant amounted to 989,920 scrip acres,
which the state imagined would net about $600,000. With
the hope of raising the value of the grant, Ezra Cornell

71. White's efforts to secure the land grant are well recorded in Carl
Becker, *Cornell University: Founders and the Founding* (Ithaca, 1943), pp.
90–110.

bought the scrip from the state and gradually sold it over a long period of time. By 1905 Cornell's shrewd management, and that of his agents who managed the land sales after his death in 1874, had yielded his university $5,765,000 — a sum almost ten times as large as either Cornell's original benefaction or the sum the state thought the land grant would yield. Thus a large portion of the endowment of Cornell, like that of Columbia, was secured not from a combination of public and private funds but from the application of individual or private management to a state-granted resource — the Morrill land grant for Cornell and the Botanical Garden for Columbia.

So a completely new "university" rather than New York's oldest "college" became the land-grant institution for the state. Though Columbia had been unsuccessful in this venture, it proceeded on its own to offer the kind of instruction contemplated by the Morrill Act. In 1864 Columbia opened the School of Mines to provide training in applied science and engineering.

The disposition of the federal land grant in our four states took varying forms, but one common theme emerged in all cases. There was no aversion or hostility on the part of our colleges or of our states toward a combination of state funds with the gifts of private benefactors. Dartmouth and Yale volunteered for and received the state fund. Columbia and Harvard failed to gain the land grant not because they did not want the money but because they faced competitors. Ironically, they had to compete with other dreams and ideas rather than with other institutions. Columbia lost to Andrew Dickson White's dream of an "American university." Harvard was defeated by William Barton Rogers's dream of an independent technological institution.

Harvard and Columbia were not the only colleges to be defeated by the dreams for new institutions. The state universities of Michigan and Indiana also failed to become land-grant colleges because the legislatures of their states preferred to erect new institutions. Michigan established the Michigan State University of Agriculture and Applied Science at East Lansing. And in Indiana the new institution was one which a private benefactor, John Purdue, agreed to endow with $100,000.

So the old faith and the new money were compatible. The colleges did not have to abandon their alliances with the states to accept the gifts of the wealthy. The states gave their federal windfalls to schools recently endowed by philanthropists, and millionaires like Sheffield did not forsake the institutions they had launched once state aid had been granted. In 1865 it appeared as if Ezra Stiles's theory that all universities should consist of endowments by individuals and states would hold true in the future.

5 The Separation of College and State, 1865–1876

> The best and most truly democratic mode in which the universal cultivation of all the faculties of the inhabitants of the State and their physical prosperity could be secured, would be for the government itself to provide, at the common expense, all those schools, colleges, and seminaries of every description which are necessary, in order best to provide for the physical, intellectual, and moral wants that are felt throughout the community.
>
> Samuel Eliot, 1848

> Now the habit of being helped by the government, even if it be to things good in themselves — to churches, universities, and railroads — is a most insidious and irresistible enemy of republicanism; for the very essence of republicanism is self-reliance. With the continental nations of Europe it is an axiom that the government is to do everything, and is responsible for everything. . . . This abject dependence on the government is an accursed inheritance from the days of the divine right of kings.
>
> Charles Eliot, 1873

From 1850 to 1865 it appeared as if our colleges and states might have decided to be partners once again in promoting higher education. Massachusetts had rediscovered its "duty" to Harvard and had appropriated substantial funds for higher education. Yale and Dartmouth had joined with their states as land-grant colleges. And Columbia had continued to appeal to the state for support even though the rents from the Botanical Garden had brought the college close to a position of financial independence.

Yet, strangely enough, just as the new alliances seemed to be gaining strength, the "private" college reared its head. Although state representatives had continued to sit on governing boards in the days when no aid came at all, just as public funds began to appear, the legislators yielded their seats to the alumni. By 1876 some form of alumni representation was to emerge at Harvard, Yale, and Dartmouth.

Once the visible, legal connection between college and state disappeared, some men announced that the colleges and the states had never been allied at all — a position which the alumni had never really voiced and which the states had in no way envisioned when they yielded their seats. Unlike the philanthropists, these men were eager to reject that bond of faith which had held college and state together. As we shall see, the man who became the chief spokesman for the private university, Charles William Eliot of Harvard, was the son of the man who had once fought to keep college and state together.

But what of the alumni? When did they first demand representation on the college governing boards? And why?

The first call for alumni election had come at Harvard in 1854 when George Washington Warren had tried to separate Harvard and the commonwealth by transferring the election of the overseers from the General Court to the alumni. There is no evidence to indicate that the alumni had expressed any desire to manage the affairs of the college; it appears that Warren proposed the substitution of alumni merely as a method to displace the state.

In the same year the alumni at Columbia had asked that they be allowed to elect all the members of the board of trustees. Unlike the alumni at Harvard, Columbia's graduates were dissatisfied with the trustees' management of the college. The alumni were not trying to protect the college from the state; they had solicited the aid of the state to investigate the college and to support their proposal. Thus the "alumni movement" to elect college trustees originated from two separate and distinct intentions — one to remove state-elected representatives, and the other to change the composition of self-perpetuating trustees, regardless of any state connection.

It is important to remember the dual origin of the alumni movement in tracing its rise at other colleges. At Dartmouth the Columbia plan was dominant. It was dissatisfaction with the self-perpetuating trustees, not the ex officio presence of the governor or the contract between Dartmouth and the New Hampshire College of Agriculture, which led the Dartmouth alumni to demand the election of trustees in 1869.

A blending of the two strains of alumni action was evident at Yale. The graduates of the college definitely desired a voice in the management of the college. They achieved their goal in 1871 by displacing the six state senators who had shown little interest in the affairs of the college. But the movement at Yale was not as markedly antistate as the venture at Harvard. All vestiges of state interest were dissolved at Harvard in 1865; the election of the overseers was placed in the hands of the alumni, and all ex officio state officials were removed. At Yale the governor and lieutenant governor remained on the corporation; they still hold seats a century later.

Ironically, Harvard, the college whose alumni had shown the least desire to manage the college, was the first institution to allow alumni election. Columbia, whose graduates had been the first to criticize college management, was the last college in our group to elect trustees. The "vote" did not come to Columbia until 1908.

The call for alumni election was not the sudden, spontaneous outburst of an ad hoc committee of graduates. The alliance between colleges and their sons had been developing through organized alumni associations for years — more than four decades in the case of Yale. The beginning of these alumni organizations offers another case of dual origins; graduates often formed associations simply for the purpose of camaraderie, but they also created organizations at specific times to meet specific needs of the colleges.

None of our colleges can claim the original organization. The first alumni society in the United States began in 1821 at Williams. A crisis in the college was the immediate cause. For many years the president had attempted to move the location of the institution in opposition to the desires of the trustees. This controversy had so demoralized the college that upon the resignation of President Moore, the sons of Williams joined together as the Society of Alumni to help "rebuild" the college. As part of their effort they raised $25,000. Such was the foundation of the first formal organization of alumni in the United States, and for that matter at any college or university in England or in Europe.[1]

Of our colleges Yale was the first to form a general alumni society. Drafted at the 1827 commencement, the constitution of the Society of Alumni of Yale College stated that the purpose of the group "shall be to sustain and advance the interests of Yale College." [2] The "interests" of Yale had been brought to the attention of its alumni, among other reasons, by a financial crisis in the affairs of the college. In 1825 the Eagle Bank, a leading New Haven financial institution, had failed. Only three years before, friends and alumni, but not an organized society of alumni, had contributed $27,612 for the Dwight Professorship of Didactic Theology. Of that sum, $9,200 was lost in the bank failure.

Though the new society did not specifically state in its constitution that it had been organized to counteract this financial distress, a subscription book was opened at the first 1827 meeting — and anyone, graduate of Yale or not, could become a "Director for life" for $50 and an "Honorary Vice-President for life" for $250. Though $3,814 had been raised by 1831, this was not sufficient to rescue Yale's finances from the Eagle Bank disaster. In that year the Society of Alumni

1. See Frederick Rudolph, *Mark Hopkins and the Log* (New Haven, 1956), pp. 201–14, for the complete story of alumni activities at Williams.
2. The 1827 constitution of the Society of Alumni of Yale College appears in Ebenezer Baldwin, *Annals of Yale College,* 2d ed. (New Haven, 1838), pp. 320–21.

announced that it would solicit $100,000 as a permanent fund for the college. By 1838 the Centum Milia Fund had received pledges of $105,938, most of which had been collected. This campaign was indeed an "alumni fund." Of those people donating more than $100, 65 percent were graduates.[3] In 1854 the society successfully repeated this $100,000 drive, and also presented a building to the college — Alumni Hall.

Finance provided the impulse that led to the formal organization of the Society of Alumni; but there had been informal alumni groups before 1827. Class records at Yale date to 1792 and alumni reunions at commencement had long been a common practice. In fact, it was probably the regularity of informal associations which facilitated the founding of the society. Also it appears that local alumni societies existed even before the general organization. In 1825 the subscription list for the Gibbs Mineralogical Cabinet listed an $800 contribution from the Alumni of Yale College in South Carolina.[4] Later, in the 1860s, formal alumni associations in various cities as subdivisions of the general society became quite common.

At Columbia an alumni organization had been formed in 1837 to commemorate the fiftieth anniversary of the restoration of the college charter.[5] This group met mainly for literary and social purposes until 1854, when the controversy surrounding the Wolcott Gibbs incident moved the alumni

---

3. The complete subscription list for the Centum Milia Fund appears in Baldwin, *Annals of Yale College*, pp. 328–42. Of the 616 givers, 133 — or 22% — gave more than $100 apiece and contributed 72% of the fund. The percentage of alumni among these large givers was:

Over $1,000	4/6	67%
$1,000	13/19	68%
$500	22/35	63%
$101–$499	48/73	65%

4. Baldwin, p. 319.

5. Most sources, including Walter Schultz Stover, *Alumni Stimulation by the American College President* (New York, 1930), cite 1854 as the date of alumni organization at Columbia. Though the alumni may have formed a new organization at that time, Strong records that he was elected treasurer of the Alumni Association in 1839.

to make their first effort on behalf of the college — the request for a charter change to allow them to elect the trustees. Still, in 1854 no alumnus or body of alumni had made a single financial contribution to the college. In 1857 Columbia, the college so closely connected with Trinity Church, received its first alumni gift from Sampson Simson, a Jew.[6]

The impulse of camaraderie rather than crisis led to the organization of the Harvard Alumni Association in 1840. The graduates intended that the association benefit themselves more than the college. The stated purpose of the asssociation was to induce alumni to make a "periodical return to her [Harvard's] sacred groves," not for fund-raising but for moral improvement. "They believe," a committee reported, "that the causes of Christian morals, and intelligent patriotism, as well as that of good letters, might be essentially advanced by public addresses to be pronounced by the distinguished statesmen and scholars whose names crowd her catalogue."[7] This report admitted that the Society of Phi Beta Kappa already performed such a function but possessed an exclusive character which "exerts an unhappy and extensive influence in alienating numbers of the Alumni from attending at the annual festival of the college, who would gladly throng her halls, if they could come to meet their classmates and friends upon equal terms, in communion upon the topics of learning and patriotism."[8] The founding of the alumni association at Harvard is particularly interesting, for it points out that although small groups of graduates such as Phi Beta Kappa had long been in existence, a need was felt for a general, inclusive organization to unite men whose only common bond was loyalty to one institution.

Dartmouth was the last of our colleges to found an alumni organization. Unlike the other colleges, the organization in New Hampshire seems to have been the plan of the president,

6. Columbia had received the $20,000 bequest of Frederic Gebhard in 1846, but Gebhard was not a Columbia graduate.
7. John Hays Gardiner, *Harvard* (New York, 1914), p. 313.
8. Ibid., p. 314.

Nathan Lord, rather than a spontaneous act on the part of the alumni. In 1854 the Dartmouth trustees decided to raise $100,000. In previous appeals for $50,000 in 1829, 1834, and 1848, Lord had tried to raise the funds by using the Congregational clergy as agents. These early campaigns had met with varying degrees of success; the 1834 drive had failed altogether and the other two had yielded less than $30,000 apiece. Often the clergy failed to collect the pledges they had solicited, and it became necessary to hire agents to complete this task. Finally, Lord decided to forsake the clergy and asked the alumni to organize the appeal. In 1855 The Association of Alumni met at Hanover for the first time; three years later they agreed to undertake the $100,000 drive. Like the clergy, they failed; by June, 1859, they had raised only $16,572. But they were organized! Soon, like their counterparts at Columbia, they began to take an interest in the management of the college, despite their failure as fundraisers.

The interest in the affairs of the colleges which formal associations generated was reflected in a diversity of criticisms aimed at the governing boards. All of these objections ultimately led to a demand for alumni election of trustees. At Dartmouth this demand was quite intense because the trustees were both old and not predominantly graduates of the college. In 1869 only four of the nine trustees were Dartmouth alumni; the average age of the group was sixty-seven, the youngest was fifty-six.[9] Although Columbia's alumni criticized their trustees for being "unprogressive," eighteen of the twenty-four men were graduates of the college. At least the fogys were not a band of aliens. And Samuel Ruggles, the leader of the progressives, was one of the older trustees and a graduate of Yale.

The successor trustees at Yale were nearly all alumni, but they were all ministers. Thus the barbs of the Young Yale movement were aimed at the homogeneity of the body. And

9. Leon Burr Richardson, *History of Dartmouth College*, 2 vols. (Hanover, 1932), 2:579.

at Harvard there was little criticism at all of either governing board. The corporation was solely composed of graduates; even the board of overseers, which was elected by the legislature, contained substantial alumni representation. Of the original thirty men elected by the General Court between 1852 and 1854, thirteen were alumni. This proportion held for the next ten years.[10] Also, over this ten years the legislature moved in the direction that usually pleased the alumni — it elected younger men. In 1854 only one of the thirteen Harvard alumni was a graduate of less than twenty-five years. Over the next ten years twenty-one new alumni were elected to the overseers; ten were graduates of less than twenty-five years at the time of election, and three were graduates of less than fifteen years.

Only at Dartmouth, then, did the Association of Alumni aim for the placement on the board of trustees of a certain category of men — graduates of the college — who had previously lacked what they considered to be adequate representation. But at all four colleges the alumni advocated, or in the case of Harvard merely supported, the principles of election by an outside body and of rotation in office for the governing boards. Of course, these principles, which were essentially checks on self-perpetuation, were not inventions of the alumni but of the state. William Plumer had espoused them in 1816. And it was the General Court of Massachusetts which first passed legislation in 1851 to bring election and rotation in office to the Harvard Board of Overseers.

It seems, then, that the alumni began to demand a share of control in their colleges when as a group they assumed

10. The General Court elected the first thirty overseers in lots of ten in 1852, 1853, and 1854. The ratio of alumni to the total from 1854 to 1865 was:

1854	13/30	1860	11/30
1855	12/29a	1861	10/30
1856	11/29a	1862	11/30
1857	10/30	1863	12/29a
1858	8/30	1864	14/28a
1859	10/30	1865	13/25a

a Unfilled vacancies in these years.

that sense of protectorship which had once been reserved to the state. Why the alumni felt this sense of responsibility in the years after the Civil War is a question social historians will probably discuss for years to come. Were the alumni accepting a task the state had neglected or were they trying to transfer that task to themselves as part of a quest for some form of group identity? Whatever the reasons, it is not difficult to discern from their rhetoric that the alumni voiced many of the same ideas governors and legislators had been advocating for years.

With these introductory remarks in mind, let us follow the drama of the alumni movement in each of our colleges.

The first college that allowed its alumni to elect members of a governing board was Harvard. The reasons for Harvard's lead are not at all clear. The alumni seemed satisfied with the management of the college and no outrageous act on the part of the General Court had marked the overseers' election since the Act of 1851. However, George Boutwell did mention in his autobiography, written in 1902, that the "immediate results" of the election of overseers by the legislature were "not favorable to the college." According to the former governor, "The lobby became influential in the selection of overseers and unemployed clergymen of various denominations were active in lobbying for themselves." [11] Still, few people voiced dissatisfaction with the composition of the board, and Boutwell commented that the 1851 change in the board eventually "gave a popular character to the institution, and it was one of the elements in its recent prosperity." [12]

Yet some strain of dissatisfaction must have prompted the move for alumni election. Change for change's sake had never been a Harvard characteristic! Although the politicking of unemployed ministers may have irritated some people, the

11. George Sewell Boutwell, *Sixty Years of Public Service*, 2 vols. (New York, 1902), 2:95.
12. Ibid., p. 96.

internal struggle between the board of overseers and the corporation for control of finances and appointments provides a better point of departure for our story.

The corporation-overseers struggle, which was mentioned in the previous chapter, did not abate after the corporation told the overseers in 1857 that they held virtually no rights. And in 1862 the opportunity arrived for the overseers to exercise the one right of confirmation the corporation had conceded — the election of a new president.

In April, 1862, the corporation presented the name of Thomas Hill (1843) to the overseers for confirmation. Hill, a Unitarian minister and a mathematician, was at that time president of Antioch College in Ohio, a position he had held for three years. The corporation thought he would be a force of quiet progress in the college. As a clergyman and as a Republican he would placate the political and religious elements outside the university; his desire to expand scientific and graduate instruction would add strength inside the institution. However, the overseers were unimpressed with this balance of virtues and rejected the nomination 16 to 9.

The objections to Hill were varied; he was at once too modern and too traditional. Some claimed they did not want a clergyman and that Hill was the choice of the orthodox. Others said a scientist would upset the classical traditions of the college. And there were some who felt Hill's manners were unpolished. But Harvard librarian J. L. Sibley thought the weight of the opposition stemmed from the struggle between the two boards:

> Perhaps, however, the result was owing very much to the antagonistic feelings of the Overseers against the Corporation, the Overseers endeavoring to control the funds and consequently the college by insisting that all salaries shall be submitted to them for approval and, if possible, annually.[13]

13. Sibley's Private Journal as quoted in William G. Land, *Thomas Hill, Twentieth President of Harvard* (Cambridge, 1933), p. 125.

The corporation was determined to elect Hill and resubmitted his name to the overseers in September, 1862. At their October meeting the board decided to confirm the nomination 15 to 8. Despite this confirmation, many members of the board were not willing to give the new president a vote of confidence; Hill's character and qualifications for the office became a subject for much oratory after the vote had been taken. According to one report of the meeting:

> Mr. Bassett made a speech against Mr. Hill accusing him of eccentricity and the members who had changed their votes of bribery and corruption. Mr. Bassett ended by saying that the orthodox had put Mr. Hill in, contrary to the wish of leading Unitarians, and now he hoped they would say no more against Unitarianism. Mr. Sears made a speech setting forth his views upon the importance of the classics and the dangerous tendencies of the physical sciences. Hon. Edw. Everett, horrified that there should be any non-concurrence between the two boards . . . confessed his slight acquaintance with Mr. Hill, but from the partial insight he had obtained relevant to his principles, he was reluctantly obliged to admit that he did not consider him the man for the place. Judge Abbott spoke warmly in Mr. Hill's favor, also Judge Russell who read Mr. Quincy's letter. Rev. Mr. Muzzey spoke against and Rev. Mr. Manning in favor of him. The other four opponents we do not know.[14]

Even though most of the participants, for and against Hill, in this postelection oratory were alumni (Francis Bassett, 1810; Philip Sears, 1844; Edward Everett, 1811; Thomas Russell, 1845; Josiah Abbott, 1832; Artemas Muzzey, 1824; and Jacob Manning, Amherst, 1850), it appeared to many that something must be done to end the struggle between the

14. A letter from Mrs. Arthur Lyman to her sister, in Land, *Thomas Hill,* p. 133. (Mrs. Lyman was the daughter of J. A. Lowell, senior fellow of the corporation.)

two boards. The controversy had leaked into the public press, and literally the ability of Harvard "to keep its house in order" had been called into question. Commenting on the Hill debate, Theodore Dwight Woolsey, president of Yale, noted in 1866:

> We have seldom been more disgusted than when the debates of this body on the qualifications of a gentleman elected as president of the University by the corporation were spread through the world by the newspapers, when the opinion of men like Mr. Everett, given no doubt with the greatest unwillingness that they should be made public, became a sort of public condemnation of one who needed all support at this entrance upon a most responsible office.[15]

Thus the debate over Hill's election should be considered, I think, the event that sparked the 1865 change in the overseers. This change came not because of any act on the part of the state, but because the corporation needed to find a way to tame the overseers.

Ironically, the overseers proved to have been right in their opposition to Hill. Within a year of his appointment, the president lost the respect of the corporation. And in 1865, when his failure to create a position for Charles Eliot resulted in Eliot's departure to M.I.T., Hill alienated most of his supporters among Boston's prominent families.[16]

If the corporation was to tame the overseers, a very good plan seemed to be the one suggested by George Washington Warren in 1854 — transfer the election of the board to the alumni. The Alumni Association, which would, no doubt, have an influence in nominating the candidates for whom all graduates would vote, was definitely not hostile to the corporation. From its inception in 1840 the association had been

---

15. Theodore Dwight Woolsey, "Dr. Hedge's Address to the Alumni of Harvard," *New Englander* 97 (October, 1866): 699.

16. For Hill's later problems with the corporation and Eliot's friends, see Morison, *Three Centuries of Harvard*, pp. 305–06, and Land, pp. 135, 158–59.

closely allied with the fellows. A member of the corporation, Charles G. Loring, had been one of the five men who first proposed the organization. Two of the original officers of the association, Joseph Story (vice-president), and Lemuel Shaw (director) were members of the corporation at that time. The original secretary, Benjamin R. Curtis, became a fellow in 1846. And a later president of the association, Ebenezer R. Hoar, joined the corporation in 1858. Thus, of the eleven fellows who sat on the corporation between 1840 and 1865, five had either been officers of the association or been instrumental in organizing it.

Though the corporation would not necessarily control the election of the overseers, it was at least logical to think that even if the same men were chosen by the alumni as would have been chosen by the General Court, they might view their relationship to the corporation somewhat differently. The simple fact that the constituency which the overseers represented would change from the public at large to the alumni might lessen the struggle over finance and appointments. If both boards were composed of "insiders," the natural antagonism between an "inside" and an "outside" party might not be as tense. Of course, all of this was not certain or preordained, but it was clearly a sensible alternative to try.

The leader of the movement to exchange the state for the alumni was Ebenezer Rockwood Hoar (1835), son of Samuel Hoar, the man who had preserved the corporation from the legislature in 1850.[17] Hoar's career as a governor of Harvard had begun in 1857 when the legislature elected him to the overseers. Well aware of the struggle between the two boards, Hoar decided to make a public statement in favor of the

17. Two references in Land lead me to think Hoar was the leader: "Hoar placed the utmost confidence in President Hill by asking him to draw up and present the Corporation view before the legislative hearing of April 20, 1864 on the proposed separation of Harvard from the state" (p. 159); and "in 1865 Judge Hoar and William A. Richardson were prime movers in securing the separation of Harvard from legislative control and in establishing alumni election of overseers" (p. 169).

overseers almost immediately after his election. On March 13, 1857, the *Boston Daily Advertiser* reported Hoar's proposition:

> There are two classes of functions which the corporation discharges. One is the possession and control of the property of the college as property, providing for its security, its investment, its care. The other is the application of this property to the work of the college, applying it to the purpose for which the college was founded, the education of the youth of the state. With the first function, in my judgment, the Board of Overseers have very little to do by the charter of the college, unless in the exercise of the visitational power to guard against its abuse, which does not appear likely to occur, but with which for the satisfaction of the community, the less this Board interferes the better; the other is the application of all the means and powers at the disposal of the Corporation to the practical work of educating youth. With that it seems to me to be the intention of the charter to entrust powers to the Board of Overseers of supervision, of concurrence, and of action co-extensive with the duties of the Corporation.[18]

The next year, however, Hoar resigned as an overseer to take a seat on the corporation, which he held until 1868. It is entirely possible that he transferred his allegiance as well as his presence to the corporation. And the Hill turmoil of 1862 probably convinced him that even if right, the intractibility of the overseers might be harmful to the college.

With the aid of William A. Richardson, a newly elected overseer, and President Hill, Hoar presented a bill to the senate in 1864 which called for both the removal of all ex officio members from the board and the transfer of the election of the other thirty members to the alumni.[19] This bill

18. *Boston Daily Advertiser,* March 13, 1857, quoted in Moorfield Story, *Ebenezer Rockwood Hoar* (Boston, 1911), pp. 118–19.

19. I am unsure exactly how the bill entered the senate. Hoar was not a member of the General Court.

was deferred to the 1865 session and was passed on April 28 of that year. There was an attempt in the house of representatives to retain the governor as an ex officio member,[20] but the final version of "An Act in Relation to the Board of Overseers of Harvard College" provided that only the president and treasurer of the college be ex officio members.

The Act of 1865 contains a clause worthy of special attention for the separation of college and state. Though the state mounted little opposition to the change in the overseers, it did not want to sever its relation with Harvard forever. The last article of the act stated, "this act shall not be construed as in the nature of a contract, or a charter, but may at any time be repealed at the pleasure of the legislature." [21] The General Court had asserted for many years that the Dartmouth College case did not apply to Harvard; it did not want any chance piece of legislation to overturn what it considered to be the historic relation between college and state.

The separation of college and state that occurred at Harvard may seem somewhat bizarre if viewed only as an isolated event in 1865; the alumni had not petitioned for a change in the overseers and the state had not directly interfered with the college. But in the context of Harvard's history for the preceding forty years, the separation is not difficult to understand. It has previously been noted that the struggle between the corporation and the overseers which began in 1855 probably sparked the movement for alumni election; the origins of the Act of 1865 really extend as far back as the faculty revolt of 1825. The corporation had been engaged for almost half a century in a struggle to retain control of the college. It had defeated the faculty only to be challenged by the overseers.

Throughout the years, the corporation had always tried to find some way to establish its right to absolute control.

20. *Journal of the House of Representatives of the Commonwealth of Massachusetts* (Boston, 1865), p. 241.

21. *Acts and Resolves Passed by the General Court of Massachusetts in the year 1865* (Boston, 1865), p. 567.

Often the fellows had resorted to novel interpretations of Harvard's history. But in 1864–65 a better way appeared — a legislative act. As Morison has noted, "The moment was propitious; the war, in which sons of Harvard had rendered distinguished service, was over; both state government and college government were overwhelmingly Republican." [22] The corporation capitalized on the moment.

The Act of 1865, the legislature's gift to Harvard, provided many safeguards to prevent the overseers from falling into the hands of alumni who might be hostile to the corporation. The act specified that "no officer of government or instruction in said college shall be eligible as an overseer or entitled to vote in the election." The overseers would be immune from faculty domination. Also, only alumni who were graduates of five years or who held masters or honorary degrees could vote or be elected. This provision prevented any possibility that the overseers might fall into the hands of very young graduates who might represent the "student interest." Finally, the vote was extended only to alumni who were Massachusetts residents; hence, men who were not closely in contact with the college could not organize from a distance to control the overseers.[23] In effect, the franchise was extended only to selected alumni. As long as the fellows could exercise influence over this group, they might be spared the struggle for home rule which had been waged for years.[24]

There was, no doubt, some motive on the part of Hoar to sever the state connection; why else would he have advocated the removal of all ex officio officials? If not deleterious, the state connection had often been irritating, and the complete removal of all outside threats was obviously another

22. Morison, p. 309.

23. Admittedly, the requirement for Massachusetts residency may have been for the benefit of the state more than of the college. However, in 1854, Thomas Russell opposed alumni election precisely because of the danger involved in allowing widely scattered graduates who convened only at commencement to elect overseers. The residency requirement was removed in 1880.

24. Further extension of the franchise occurred between 1902 and 1916 to include alumni of all graduate and professional schools at Harvard.

gain for the corporation. Still, the Act of 1865 did not so much concern a problem of external state interference in the affairs of the college as of internal struggle. The state really acted as an outside referee in a "house dispute," not as a party in a separation or divorce. This was the same role New York had performed in 1854 in its investigation of the Wolcott Gibbs case. In 1865 the Harvard trustees secured the legislative act that New York had failed to grant — alumni election.

The state of Massachusetts would gain by this 1865 legislation, even though it lost representation. It could settle a dispute and reward Harvard for the service of its sons in the Civil War. The General Court could retract the act at any time, and the legislators were probably just as happy to be freed from the lobbying of "unemployed ministers." After all, the legislature had succeeded fourteen years earlier in engrafting the principles of election and rotation in office on the government of Harvard. In 1865 it merely transferred the vote to the alumni; it might even be said that the franchise had really been widened and returned directly to at least a segment of the people. No legislator seemed to fear that the virtue of republican government was being violated. Even Boutwell approved of the change.

The Act of 1865 proved to be the "shot heard 'round the world" for the revolution in college government. But at different colleges, different men or groups of men heard the shot and acted upon it in different ways. In some cases the alumni acted spontaneously; in others the president called the alumni to assert themselves.

The Society of Alumni at Williams was the first group to join the Harvard movement. At their July, 1866, meeting they requested that the trustees ask the General Court to create a board of overseers for Williams, "the members of which shall be elected by the graduates of the college." [25]

25. See Rudolph, *Mark Hopkins,* pp. 206–07, for details of the alumni request at Williams.

Evidently, the allure of dual boards and the need for legislation waned during the year, because the society changed
its request in 1867. Rather than a new board, the alumni
wanted the present trustees, who were equally Williams and
non-Williams men, to elect into their own body five alumni,
one to be chosen each year for a five-year term, who would
be nominated at each commencement by alumni ballots. The
society also asked in 1867 that the trustees authorize a board
of six alumni visitors to report annually on the course of
instruction and discipline of the college.

None of these requests required a charter change; merely
the consent of the trustees was needed, and this was granted
in 1868. Thus the second college to allow alumni election
did so without any interaction with the state. This method
of alumni representation, a right granted purely by the
trustees without state legislation, came to be known as the
Williams Plan.

Though the state did not grant the Williams alumni their
power, it decided to encourage them to accept their responsibility. In 1868 the Massachusetts legislature gave Williams
$75,000 with the proviso that the college raise an equal
amount.[26] According to Frederick Rudolph, "The General
Court in 1859 and 1868 passed legislation designed to test
their [the alumni's] manliness." [27] The same Act of 1868 also
granted $75,000 with a matching provision to Harvard's
Museum of Comparative Zoology.[28] Was there now a new
rule for state support of higher education? Would the state
grant money to an institution if it did not have to be bothered with supervising it?

At Yale it was President Theodore Dwight Woolsey who
first reacted to the events at Harvard. In an October, 1866,

---

26. *Massachusetts Resolves,* 1868, chap. 64.

27. Rudolph, p. 207.

28. The state must have been fascinated with Agassiz and his museum. In
addition to the 1859 grant of $100,000 and the 1868 grant of $75,000, the
General Court also authorized $20,000 in 1861, $10,000 in 1864, and $50,000
in 1874 — in all, a total of $255,000.

article in the *New Englander,* Woolsey commented that the change in the overseers was for the better, but he really did not know why. On the one hand, he claimed that the old board had been tied to political and religious interests, which sometimes conflicted with the good of the college. On the other had, he saw no necessary benefit coming from the election of alumni: "What is there, again, under the altered charter to prevent party tickets among the graduates with the necessary excitements before and the ill feeling after the election? Nor is it certain the jealousies of former times between corporation and the overseers may not yet be removed." [29] To Woolsey the very number of overseers, regardless of how they were chosen, was a "radical vice" susceptible to polarization.

The structure and size of the Yale Corporation, thought the president, was inherently better, and the body might even be improved by alumni election. The alumni could enhance the efficiency of the corporation not by increasing its size with additional members but by replacing the state officials. Woolsey announced:

> Let that part of the Board now elected from the Senate of the State, and with them, if thought best, as at Harvard, the two highest magistrates of the Commonwealth, give place to graduates, who shall hold their offices for at least six or eight years, and be reeligible when their term expires; let the elections be held not every year, but every other year, or even less frequently; will not the result be greater interest, punctuality, knowledge, sense of responsibility, and devotion to the welfare of the institution on the part of the new members; will they not, if well elected, be a new strength of their Alma Mater? [30]

So the president of Yale had proposed that the alumni replace the state senators, and possibly even the governor

29. Woolsey, "Dr. Hedge's Address," pp. 700–01.
30. Ibid.

and lieutenant governor. Why? The alumni had yet to advocate such a move and they had given generously to the college in their unenfranchised state. Woolsey himself had never demonstrated any particular aversion to the state presence. In his 1850 *Historical Discourse* he had called the public alliance beneficial; little change had occurred in the nature of this alliance since that time.

Of course, the president may well have thought that the prospect of alumni representation was a good plan which he should promote. On the other hand, Woolsey may have acted out of a desire to protect the clerical trustees from any potential assault by the alumni. Eventually, Yale graduates, like their Williams brothers, might want to follow Harvard's lead. By inviting the alumni to assume the state seats before they formulated proposals of their own, Woolsey could divert their attention from the positions held by the clergy. Years later, in 1890, when the alumni indeed tried to sever the ten successor trusteeships from the clergy, Daniel Cady Eaton, an art historian on the faculty, announced that this latter theory had been the intent of the corporation in Woolsey's time. Accusing the clerics of nothing short of conspiracy, Eaton explained:

> The device they excogitated was so clever that graduates are still admiring the astuteness of the clerical intellect when pushed. It consisted in substituting graduates for the "assistant" state members, leaving the Governor and Lieutenant Governor. The clericals knew that state members would be glad to be shorn of power; and they thought the graduates would be so puffed up with their new honor that it would be quite a time before they discovered its emptiness.[31]

Whatever Woolsey's reasons for summoning the graduates to new duties, he was initially unable to persuade the alumni

31. Daniel Cady Eaton, *Yale College in 1890, Reflections on its Charter* (New Haven, 1890), p. 40.

to accept the challenge. It took the sons of Eli three years to pick up the torch.

The success of the Williams alumni in 1868 may have motivated Yale's graduates to action. In 1869 a committee of the Associated Alumni issued a report with the proposal "to substitute for the six senators, six other persons to be in some way designated or chosen by the graduates." The report suggested that those alumni eligible for a seat on the corporation be "any person who has received from Yale College the degree of Master of Arts in course, or any honorary, and shall have attained the age of 35 years . . . provided that he is not an officer of instruction in Yale College, or in any similar institution." [32] To be a voter an alumnus must be a graduate of five years. As at Harvard, only selected alumni would replace the state.

This report of 1869 was hardly an expression of force and desire on the part of the alumni. The committee found that the present relation with the state "has been generally regarded as a wise and beneficial arrangement." Although the committee proposed a change, it did not recommend that change: "As to the more important question whether the proposed change or any change is desirable, the Committee express no opinion, for the reasons that they are not agreed in opinion." [33]

The basis for this disagreement became known in 1870 when the Reverend Noah Porter, professor of moral philosophy and metaphysics, and one of the five members of the alumni committee, published his *American Colleges and the American Public*.[34] The professor was definitely opposed to alumni representation. According to Porter, the clergy was the only truly cultured class in America; laymen as college

32. *Report of the Committee Appointed by the Associated Alumni to Consider Whether Changes were Desirable in the Corporation, 1869*, Beinecke Library, Yale University.

33. Ibid.

34. *American Colleges and the American Public* orginally appeared as a series of six articles in the *New Englander*, January–October, 1869.

trustees were inherently dangerous because "many college graduates are not aware of the extent of the advantages which they have derived from their education." [35] Though he welcomed the advice and counsel of lay alumni, he feared that "the chance nomination and election of one or more representatives by a body which is organized for an hour, and changes its members very considerably every year, might open the way to constant dissatisfaction and personal discussion, and should not be resorted to except after grave deliberation." [36] So there was danger in alumni election and, as Porter went on to point out, no particular gain from their presence. "A self-perpetuating board of trustees," he explained, "resting on some historic basis, with a traditional spirit acting in relations of confidence and free communication with the board of instructors, cannot be ignorant of the wishes and feelings of the alumni, and cannot, if they would, refuse to be affected by them." [37] Let well enough alone!

What was Woolsey to do now? He had finally persuaded the alumni to follow his plan for representation only to find opposition within the ranks of the faculty. He could not abandon the alumni plan merely to conciliate Porter. Though Woolsey's 1866 suggestion had drawn a negative response from Porter and other conservatives, it had sparked some of the younger alumni to form a group known as Young Yale. The Young Yale movement, which had as its representative on the alumni committee of 1869 William M. Evarts of New York, demanded lay representation on the corporation and even thought the time had come for the clerics to abandon their monopoly of the successor trusteeships.[38] In 1870 their ideas spread beyond the confines of alumni gatherings and received public attention in a series of articles in the *College Courant* and *The Nation*.

35. Noah Porter, *American Colleges and the American Public* (New Haven, 1870), p. 33.

36. Ibid., p. 248.

37. Ibid., pp. 247–48.

38. See Harris E. Starr, *William Graham Sumner* (New York, 1925), pp. 80–95, for a full description of the Young Yale movement.

At the same time the Young Yale movement started among the alumni; a faculty group led by James Dwight Dana and Timothy Dwight advocated that the college progress to the level of a full-fledged university, with graduate and professional studies holding equal importance with the collegiate life.[39] There was even talk among some alumni and faculty that the presidency should be offered to a layman. Daniel Coit Gilman, formerly librarian of Yale College and at that time secretary of the Sheffield Scientific School, was suggested as the man to succeed Woolsey, who had indicated a desire to step down.

Of course, there was an old Yale as well as a young Yale. The conservatives among the alumni liked the ideas of Noah Porter and supported him for the presidency. The possibility that the president of Yale College might come from the Sheffield Scientific School was unthinkable. Porter, who cringed at the word *university,* would be the best guardian for Yale.

So in 1870 the forces of progress and tradition were warring at Yale — or at least they were confronting one another. The guardians of the Sheffield Scientific School were probably not convinced that the "progressives" would triumph; in February, 1871, they formed a separate corporation, the Trustees of the Sheffield Scientific School, to relieve the Yale Corporation of the duty of managing the school's property.

While the Sheff men were retreating, Woolsey seemed to be effecting a compromise to keep everyone loyal to Yale. Eighty years earlier Ezra Stiles had reconciled the college and the state. Could Woolsey reconcile the young and the old?

Evidently, Woolsey had influence with both the legislature and Governor Marshall Jewell, ex officio a member of the corporation. In his opening address to the May, 1871 session of the General Assembly, Jewell announced that it

39. See James Dwight Dana, *The New Haven University: What It Is and What It Requires* (New Haven, 1871), and Timothy Dwight, "Yale College: Some Thoughts Respecting Its Future," *New Englander,* July, 1870.

would be "well for the state, the college, and the alumni at large to surrender one-half of the state representation in its Board of Corporation — the new members to be elected by the alumni to serve for four years, one to go out each year." [40] The governor's plan proved conservative; the bill that finally emerged from the judiciary committee surrendered 3/4 of the state representation — the alumni could elect all six positions formerly held by the senators; only the governor and lieutenant governor would remain.

With virtually no opposition the assembly passed the bill on July 6, 1871. More than likely the corporation had been informed of the probable action of the legislature; on that same day Woolsey resigned and the trustees elected Porter to replace him. Twenty-five years earlier Woolsey had accepted ordination in order to become president. Porter accepted the alumni for the same privilege. Which man had made the greater sacrifice?

The compromise of 1871 placated most of the factions. The conservatives won the presidency and the progressives secured six seats on the corporation. The clerics still held the original trusteeships and the presidency, at least for a few more decades. [41]

While peace was being made within the Yale household, few noticed — or really cared — that a separation of college and state had come about. As at Harvard, the separation at Yale had largely resulted from an internal struggle over the control of the college rather than from a contest between legislators and trustees. By surrendering a major portion of its control, the state acted as a referee to settle an argument within the college. In 1871 no trumpets announced the emancipation of the "private" or "independent" college from state control. That simply was not what happened.

40. *Journal of the House of Representatives of the State of Connecticut* (Hartford, 1871), p. 58.

41. Payson Merrill was the first layman elected among the successor trustees, June 27, 1905.

Dartmouth's alumni had failed to raise $100,000 in 1859, but ten years later the excitement of the college's centennial celebration led a convocation of alumni to claim they could raise $200,000 — if the trustees would allow some form of alumni election on the board. Specifically, the alumni proposed that a minority of trustees be elected from alumni nominations for a limited period of time and that the self-perpetuating trustees agree to limited terms in office. Thus the principle of rotation in office and a modified form of election would come to Dartmouth. As the alumni were scattered over the various states, they also requested legislative action to decrease the number of trustees who by charter stipulation must be New Hampshire residents. Only this latter request would require an act of the state.

Whether the trustees were really alarmed at the thought of legislation or simply wanted an excuse to offer the alumni, the board replied in July, 1870 that nothing but the gravest consequences could result from a change in the charter. Summoning visions of the Dartmouth College case, the board warned:

> We may well hesitate to undo, or even seem to undo what was so thoroughly and so nobly done. We may well be fearful of the perilous uncertainties even of the best legislation. We may well think, especially in times like these, from putting the college afloat on the troubled, and turbid sea of party politics.[42]

Since the only alumni proposal that required legislation was the New Hampshire quota, the trustees could easily have accepted alumni election and merely rejected the quota change. This was not their desire; they would allow no form of election or change in the board. According to the trustees, it would be dangerous to submit "a question involving points of great delicacy . . . to any form of popular election."

42. DCT Minutes, July 4, 1870.

Alumni election would bring "the constant liability to party and perhaps partisan action, to jealousies and feuds to annoying disappointments and to permanent and damaging alienations." [43] Despite this blanket rejection, the trustees invited the alumni to appoint a committee to make suggestions, and they encouraged the graduates to go forward with the $200,-000 campaign!

The alumni were unimpressed by this offer. They abandoned all plans for the financial drive and, in rhetoric similar to that of William Plumer fifty years earlier, accused the college of monarchical principles. One impassioned alumnus exclaimed, "Some concession must be made to the spirit of liberty. Autocratic colleges built on European models savor of royalty. The American demands a college without an oligarchy, an oligarchy without a despot." [44]

Still, Dartmouth needed money. Before submitting to the alumni, President Asa Smith tried in 1872 to raise $100,000 through the Congregational churches of New Hampshire.[45] Predictably, the clergy and their churches failed to respond. When the alumni, led by the New York Association, renewed their demands for representation in 1875, the trustees were less bold in their response.

The board was still hesitant to permit direct election by the alumni; instead the members proposed an indirect method of alumni nomination. As the next three vacancies on the board opened, the alumni would nominate four men for each post. The trustees agreed "that ordinarily and in all probability, invariably some one of the persons nominated will be selected to the vacant place." [46] When any of these three positions became vacant again, the alumni would have the right to fill them in the same manner. Neither the prin-

43. Ibid.

44. Richardson, *History of Dartmouth College*, 2:581.

45. Richardson does not record this appeal to the clergy, but Richard T. Ely, a student at that time, records it in *Ground Under My Feet* (New York, 1938), p. 29.

46. DCT Minutes, Aug. 12, 1875.

ciple of direct election nor of rotation in office was achieved by this plan, but the alumni accepted it in 1876. They had achieved at least a modified version of the Williams Plan.

Finally, in 1892, the alumni secured the right from the trustees — but without a legislative act — to elect directly five members of the board, with the tacit understanding that the elected members would serve only a five-year term.[47]

Unlike the alumni movements at Yale and Harvard, the Dartmouth effort involved no trace of a separation of college and state. The position of the governor as an ex officio board member was never challenged. The charter which the trustees were so anxious to keep out of the legislature sealed the governor to the board. However, at Dartmouth more than at any other college, the alumni voiced the demands the state had once made. In their desire to infuse new blood into the college, their demands to the trustees and their accusations about the composition of the old board were remarkably similar to Governor Plumer's desires in 1816. Without the power of a legislature behind them, it took the alumni over twenty years of constant debate and negotiation with the conservative guardians to achieve what Plumer had attempted in one year through one piece of legislation.

By 1876 the alumni at Dartmouth, Yale, and Harvard had secured some form of direct or indirect election of trustees, but Columbia, the college whose alumni had first challenged the trustees in 1854, still retained the same form of corporate organization it had possessed since 1787. Not until 1908 did alumni election appear at Columbia. Though Columbia's graduates made attempts to emulate the other colleges, they failed time and again. The explanation for this lack of success is not difficult to understand — money.

47. In the interim, the alumni as a group again failed to raise any substantial funds. Though the endowment rose from $486,000 to $1,029,000 between 1869 and 1892, the gifts were from individuals, many of whom were not alumni. By 1895 nonalumni gifts were $1,375,000 and alumni gifts totaled $363,367 (gifts of $5,000 or more).

At Yale, Harvard, and Dartmouth either the promise of alumni giving or the fear that alumni might cease giving had been a major factor in persuading the trustees to enfranchise the graduates. But Columbia in 1866 was the richest institution of higher education in the United States. In that year the college, which had survived for the first half of the nineteenth century on borrowed money, reported productive endowments of $2,227,541, and for the first time surpassed Harvard's endowed wealth, which amounted to $1,999,505. The gap in Columbia's favor widened over the next ten years. In 1871 Columbia reported $3,785,470, Harvard, $2,425,711. Five years later Columbia could boast $4,677,644 to Harvard's $3,406,653.[48]

While a chart of Harvard's endowments revealed the gifts and bequests of scores of friends and alumni, Columbia owed its wealth to no man. The land grants of Trinity Church in colonial times and of the state's Botanical Garden in 1814 constituted Columbia's wealth.[49] Thus Columbia's income, unlike Harvard's, was virtually unrestricted; only the Gebhard Fund was tied to a particular department or professor-

---

48. There was a difference between the endowment of the two colleges. Whereas Harvard's endowment consisted largely of bonds, mortgages, and securities that had a certain money value in any given year, Columbia's endowment was all in land that produced annual rents. Thus Columbia's treasurer annually announced that the value of the land was figured at a 5% capitalization of the rents.

49. A few notes on Columbia's wealth: 1) In 1865 the only items listed among Columbia's endowment other than land were $12,100 in bonds and the $20,000 Gebhard Fund; 2) Note the changes in the value of Columbia's two land grants, the Lower Estate at Park Place, and the Upper Estate at the Botanic Garden:

	1865	*1866*	*1868*
Lower	$913,181	$1,063,181	$1,076,681
Upper	$777,300	$1,194,360	$2,051,773
	1871	*1872*	*1874*
Lower	$1,548,618	$1,908,933	$2,056,000
Upper	$2,051,778	$2,041,773	$2,041,773

Source: Annual Report of the University of the State of New York (Albany, 1865–76).

ship. And with endowment doubling and income tripling between 1865 and 1876, the decade of the alumni movement, Columbia's trustees could easily afford to ignore the graduates.[50] A promise to raise $100,000 — though it was never made — would probably have made little impact on the trustees; in 1876 they reported that income had exceeded expenses for the year by $92,342.[51]

According to men who were Columbia undergraduates at the time, the trustees seemed well pleased with this operating surplus. Economist Richard T. Ely, who arrived in 1873 as a sophomore, reported, "At that time Columbia laid aside each year a surplus of $90,000. The trustees thought this was an admirable policy." [52] Nicholas Murray Butler, Columbia's future president, later recorded that Columbia's treasurer, Gouverneur M. Ogden, viewed the college as a business enterprise. "He was able, devoted, and most conscientious," Butler remarked, "but his whole conception of the college was a property-owning and property-developing corporation. To spend money for the precise purpose for which it had been given to the trustees seemed to him most reprehensible. His every instinct was to save, to acquire, and to what he described as "plow in." [53]

While "plowing in" this surplus, which by 1876 amounted to $441,722, the trustees did not slight the "insiders" — the faculty. Though Columbia's president and professors were

---

50. Income of Columbia College: 1865, $94,061; 1866, $126,322; 1876, $311,594.

51. Note the rise of Columbia's "profit" from 1865 to 1876:

Year ending September 30

1865	−$16,489	1871	+$22,518
1866	−$ 3,940	1872	+$68,165
1867	+$12,369	1873	+$92,902
1868	+$17,521	1874	+$84,070
1869	+$35,745	1875	+$92,981
1870	+$34,442	1876	+$92,342

52. Ely, *Ground Under My Feet*, p. 33.

53. Nicholas Murray Butler, *Across the Busy Years*, 2 vols. (New York, 1939), 1:81.

already the most highly paid academic men in America in 1865 (professors received $4,000 v. $2,400 at Harvard; the president received $4,500 v. $3,000 at Harvard), the trustees decided to raise the salaries. In 1866 the president's income rose to $6,000; the following year the professors' salaries netted $7,500; the president, $8,000. The treasurer received $7,125.

"Outsiders," however, were shocked at the arrogance of Columbia's trustees. Visiting the campus in 1873, Cornell's Andrew D. White recommended that the trustees spend the $90,000 surplus plus an additional $90,000 to be raised by the alumni. White had enfranchised Cornell alumni in 1872, the year the first class graduated, with the precise understanding that they were to raise money in return for this privilege.

White's advice went unheeded. The trustees had never appreciated outsiders, and they even extended the term *outsider* to include the alumni. George T. Strong recorded in 1865, "Our alumni give us a cold shoulder, and small blame to them. Their poor little 'alumni association' has, from time to time, appointed its committee to attend the College examination and has once or twice ventured to send us their reports. They have been received with alarm and studiously suppressed on our minutes, because it was so dangerous to concede to outsiders any privilege of criticizing our operations." [54]

Despite these rebuffs, the alumni had tried to "influence" the election of trustees, and there was a time between 1868 and 1876 when it appeared that alumni election might come to Columbia.

In 1868 the alumni were angered, according to Strong, at the election of a nonalumnus, New York lawyer Stephen P. Nash, to the board of trustees. [55] There was also concern within the board over this election. Hamilton Fish, chairman of the trustees, believed that the election of Nash "was man-

54. Allan Nevins, ed., *Diary of George Templeton Strong*, 4 vols. (New York, 1952), 3:550.
55. Ibid., 4:185.

aged with reference to its effect upon the approaching election of a professor." [56] The soon-to-be secretary of state was convinced that "danger" lay inherently in the closed, self-perpetuating nature of the board. "There is a point," he wrote president F. A. P. Barnard, "at which, in an institution like a college free from visitation and without guardians superior to its own trustees, a trustee should cease to be a mere resistant of evil tendencies and should become a denouncing remonstrant and perhaps even should place himself outside of the Board to expose the dangers of an institution which he can no longer aid by protecting within it." [57]

Fish decided to remain on the board, even though he did offer his resignation in 1869 when he was appointed secretary of state. However, his remaining did not indicate a concession. He was resolute in his determination that the college needed a thorough "shaking-up." In 1873 Fish and other members of the board began to investigate the possibility of alumni election. George T. Strong was asked to be chairman of a committee to consult with the alumni. He declined the position but commented, "Any change in the college government can hardly fail to be an improvement." [58]

Fish pursued the possibility of alumni election and enlisted the aid of Seth Low for the cause in 1874. Two years later a committee of the trustees was appointed to meet with the alumni about a change in college government.[59] Nothing came of these meetings; the "insiders" prevailed. As long as Columbia's coffers were overflowing with surplus treasure, the trustees hardly needed to concede their "corporate dignity" to any form of election or visitation.

The attempts by the alumni to secure election at Columbia in no way involved the displacement of state officials on the board of trustees — there were none to displace — or of the

56. Hamilton Fish to F. A. P. Barnard, Feb. 5, 1868, Hamilton Fish Papers, Columbia University Library.
57. Ibid.
58. Nevins, ed., 4:498.
59. CCT Minutes, Dec. 4, 1876.

supervisory control of the University of the State of New York. However, it seems that in asserting their independence from the alumni, the trustees were emboldened to defy another group of "outsiders" — the regents.

Around the year 1876[60] the regents notified the trustees that they desired to make an official visitation of the college. When the regents' committee, led by Chancellor John V. L. Pruyn, arrived at Columbia's 49th Street gates, they were met by Hamilton Fish, Samuel Ruggles, and Gouverneur Ogden. Fish received the state officials by saying:

> Mr. Chancellor, we are most happy to welcome you here this morning. It is my duty to say to you, however, that if you come as Regents to make an official visitation to Columbia College, as a matter of right, then the gates behind me are closed. If, on the other hand, you come as citizens of the State of New York interested in education, to see our work and our equipment, then everything that we have is freely at your service.[61]

The chancellor decided not to press the issue, accepted Fish's "citizens' invitation," and toured the college.

So while Yale and Harvard exchanged state officials for alumni and Dartmouth allowed alumni nominations for its governing board, Columbia announced its independence from all entangling alliances. In 1876 Columbia was sui generis — the "independent university"; its income was absolutely unrestricted; its trustees were absolutely self-perpetuating and, it appeared from their rebuff to the regents, absolutely free from visitation. Evidently the state could intervene only if the trustees flagrantly violated the charter. Since the senate had decided in 1854 that Gibbs's rejection did not constitute a charter violation, the trustees would

60. It is difficult to pinpoint the exact date. Butler says in *Across the Busy Years,* "Shortly before I arrived at Columbia," which was 1878.
61. Butler, 1:82.

probably have to close the college and vote themselves the funds before the state intervened.

Ironically, if Columbia was the "independent" university, it was also the ideal form of the "state" university as contemplated in the first half of the nineteenth century. A substantial portion of Columbia's income came from a state land grant; this state fund was perpetual, requiring no annual appropriation or approval. The sole function of the state assembly through the charter was to protect the funds from being fraudulently misused. Was not this the "independence" which the early state universities in Georgia and Vermont had desired, which the midwestern state universities had hoped their land grants would yield, which Harvard, Williams, and Amherst had requested from the General Court in 1848, and which the Morrill Act had contemplated for the land-grant colleges?

This concept of the state university continued even after the Civil War. In 1867 the Regents of the University of Wisconsin convinced the state for the first time to grant the university support, not because of an obligation to the "state university," but because the state had been irresponsible in its duty to protect the university fund derived from the first federal land grant of the 1840s. According to Merle Curti and Vernon Carstensen:

> Acknowledgement of the obligation of the state to give financial support to the University thus derived primarily from the charge that the state had not fulfilled its responsibility to protect the property of the University. Although many argued then, and some had argued since the 1850's, that the state had the obligation to support the University because it was head of the public school system, this factor was less weighty than the charge of maladministration of the trust.[62]

62. Merle Curti and Vernon Carstensen, *The University of Wisconsin*, 2 vols. (Madison, 1949), 1:305.

In Wisconsin the idea that the state must appropriate the funds it had failed to protect persisted into the 1870s. The "state university idea" of John Bascom and Charles R. Van Hise was still to come.

It could be said that the origins of state support for the late nineteenth century "state university" arose out of the failure of those institutions to become state universities on the antebellum model, which only Columbia successfully achieved. Columbia was truly the only college or university to prosper on the basis of an early land grant.

Clearly such a thesis would be a broad generalization, but an intriguing one. After all, Columbia was the college that had changed the least in the century of our study. No alteration in Columbia's governing structure had taken place after 1787. And no change had occurred in Columbia's sources of income after the state land grant of 1814 and the cash grant of 1819. In 1876, as in 1819, rents and tuition fees were the sources of revenue.

In the 1820s, 1830s, 1840s and 1850s, Columbia's relation to the state had appeared to be similar to that of Yale and Harvard, and of the so-called state universities. Yet in 1876 Columbia differed from the other institutions in its independence from both the state and the alumni, who, I have suggested, constituted a substitute for the state. But it was the other colleges and the "state universities," not Columbia, which had changed. Through its singular success with an early land grant, Columbia, the "independent university" of 1876, had survived the century in a form which the authors of the Northwest Ordinance, the drafters of many state constitutions, and the casual observer of 1800 would have called a "state university."

Thus Columbia had become an independent, a "private" institution by standing still. Oddly enough, the college had never wanted to stand still; Columbia had been forced into this position of independence because so many potential partners — the city, the church, the navy, the wealthy, and even the state — had rejected it so many times. Columbia had become "free" by 1876 because in its quest for identity it had been unable to give its liberty away.

The year 1876 marks the close of our narrative of the separation of college and state. By that year our four colleges had assumed the corporate form and had developed the sources of income which, with only minor variations, they would carry into the twentieth century — a time when the most casual observer of higher education could point out that there were two types of institutions, "state" and "private."

It is understandable, at this point in our story, if the reader feels somewhat confused. He may think that he has missed something. When did the "separation" occur? When did the colleges assert their independence from the states? If the Dartmouth College case was not the watershed, not the point at which the colleges girded themselves to defend learning against the encroachment of the state, then when did the colleges and the states part ways?

Our story has traced a waning of interest on the part of the states for the colleges in the 1830s, 1840s and 1850s, but a waning which the colleges continually countered with reminders to the states of their "duty" to support higher education. In the late 1850s and 1860s it appeared that financial grants from states such as Massachusetts and state-administered federal land grants from the Morrill Act could combine with the largess of the wealthy to bring college and state back to the kind of alliance they had held at the turn of the century. And in the final act of our drama, the election of trustees by alumni, it looked as if the states of Massachusetts and Connecticut were really acting as referees to settle internal college disputes rather than as parties in a "separation": if Harvard and Massachusetts had separated in 1865, why did the General Court vote the Museum of Comparative Zoology matching grants of $75,000 in 1868 and $50,000 in 1874?

After a century of debates over public duty and responsibility, after periods of estrangement and renewed interest, was the relation between college and state still just as hazy and ill-defined, still just as "quasi" as it had been when the nation declared its independence? Is the most we can say about the "transformation from quasi-public to private institutions," that Columbia was leading the way — and a way it had not particularly wanted to lead — by standing still? Had anything changed during the century? But if nothing had changed, how did the differentiation between "private" and "state" become so marked by 1898 that a conference to discuss the difference was assembled at Johns Hopkins University?

The dilemma is not completely inexplicable. Although the changes or variations that occurred in our colleges up until 1876 did not signify a dramatic separation of college and state, they blurred the alliance to the point that men and groups who wanted to separate — or protect — the colleges from any state connection could pull the institutions away from their old moorings with little resistance.

Throughout the nineteenth century, and even back in the eighteenth, there had always been men who wanted their institutions to be independent and autonomous: Thomas Clap, the trustees of Dartmouth in 1816, Nathan Lord, and the fellows of the Harvard Corporation in the 1850s. Often this desire for autonomy arose as much from a sort of corporate arrogance or personal stubbornness as from any issue of learning or scholarship. But before the final departure of state officials and the arrival of the alumni in the 1860s and 1870s, there had always been some counterweight to maintain the alliance with the state, particularly at Harvard and Yale.

If the Harvard Corporation really wanted to be autonomous in the 1850s, it could not readily circumvent the fact that by law the General Court elected the overseers. With the legal basis of the college-state alliance dissolved after 1865, it became easier for a man to assert Harvard's independence. Now only reminders of the college's history could stand in the way. This posed no obstacle; Harvard's guardians were skilled at bending the past to fit their purposes. We will soon see that this is exactly what Charles William Eliot did.

What we have really traced over the course of a century has not been a separation or a transformation but the preconditions for such. The ships' anchors were raised, but it was necessary for someone to give the vessels a tug. They might not have drifted into the "private sea" on their own. Almost as soon as these preconditions were set, men appeared to begin the towing. Strangely enough, the first whistles came from the Midwest, not the East.

The presidents of small denominational colleges, most of which were in the Midwest, were the first men to announce that there should be no alliance between college and state — at their institutions or any others. Ostensibly, they claimed that religion could not exist at state-supported universities. In reality, they opposed the state institutions because they feared their colleges could not compete for students with the large state campuses they thought the Morrill Act would create.

These men had not always advocated privacy in college affairs. When Julian M. Sturtevant (Yale, 1823), president of Illinois College in Jacksonville, first heard that the state might launch a new university with the proceeds from the land grant, his reaction was to advocate a merger of his college with the new institution. In December, 1866, he stated:

> I am therefore satisfied that the system of education in this great state will culminate in a state university and all colleges which are in competition with that university will be insignificant. I therefore think it clearly our duty to cooperate in the founding of that university and to exert all the influence to mold it right. The best thing then which we can do is to ally it with Illinois College or rather engraft it upon Illinois College.[63]

63. Charles Rammelkamp, *Illinois College* (New Haven, 1929), p. 231.

But when Sturtevant's efforts at merger failed, the president soon became a champion of the "private" college.[64]

Sturtevant's voice from the Midwest reached the East as an appeal for the riches of the wealthy. This channel had been developed even before the land grant was authorized. In January, 1862, six months before the Morrill Act was passed, Sturtevant had written an article for the *New Englander* entitled "The Claims of Higher Seminaries of Learning on the Liberality of the Wealthy." In this piece Sturtevant had argued that higher education could survive only if supported by the rich; he felt there was no hope for support from the state, though he did not necessarily oppose such support. Eleven years later, after Sturtevant had failed to secure that state aid which he could not even imagine in 1862, he wrote another article in the *New Englander*, "Colleges and State Universities." Again the Illinois president appealed to the wealthy, not because they alone could support "seminaries of learning," but because he feared the state would take over higher education if the wealthy did not mount an opposition. Danger loomed ahead if the rich did not answer his call: "The tendency therefore is to exclude religion more and more from that portion of our system of education which is under the control of the state." [65] He implored easterners to endow small colleges such as his own. "One hundred thousand," he exclaimed, "on one of these colleges will do more for the cause than a million drawn by a university from some state treasury." [66]

So denominational colleges in the Midwest, fearful of encroaching state universities, spread a theory in the East that

64. Sturtevant was not the only man who attempted to ally a denominational college with the land grant. In California, Henry Durant successfully merged his College of California with the land grant to create the University of California. Two denominational colleges in Wisconsin — Lawrence and Ripon — tried unsuccessfully to secure the federal lands.

65. Julian M. Sturtevant, "Colleges and State Universities," *New Englander* 124 (July, 1873): 455.

66. Ibid., p. 466.

private wealth, not state or federal treasure, was the proper foundation for higher education.[67] It would be difficult to assess the impact in the East of this "private college" movement from the West. There were no growing state universities on the seaboard; and Columbia, Yale, and Harvard were not trying to remain small colleges — they aspired to university status. Though Dartmouth continued to be a small college, it had no need to advocate a "private" theory of education. The state had made no encroaching gestures in almost half a century, and Dartmouth had secured the land grant.

The "message from the prairies" may have influenced some college men in the East, but there were others in our recently emancipated colleges who needed no help from afar. It may be an exaggeration to attribute any movement to a single individual, but to a very large extent the idea of the private eastern university was the creation of one man, Charles William Eliot.

Both by his family and by his contact with educators and institutions of the day, Eliot (Harvard, 1853) had been nurtured in the theory of state support for higher education. During his undergraduate days at Harvard, he had heard his father Samuel Eliot proclaim in the public press that it was the duty of the commonwealth to support Harvard College. He had remained at Harvard for a decade after graduation as a tutor and assistant professor, but when he failed to win the Rumford Chair of Chemistry in 1863, he departed for Europe. While abroad the future president investigated European universities, the best of which (the German) were state supported. When Eliot returned in 1865, he accepted the

---

67. In addition to Sturtevant's articles on the "private" college, the annual reports of the Society for the Promotion of Collegiate and Theological Education at the West, an association of denominational colleges, made similar statements of the dangers of state support in regard to religion and morals.

chair of chemistry at M.I.T., the independent scientific school that had been founded with a combination of state and private aid.

While at M.I.T., Eliot no doubt maintained an interest in Harvard and surely heard Professor Frederic Hedge's 1866 commencement address, which implored Harvard to aspire to university status and to emulate the state-supported University of Michigan. Hedge proclaimed, "unless the State of Massachusetts shall see fit to adopt us, and to foster our interest with something of the zeal and liberality which the State of Michigan bestows on her academic masterpiece, Harvard cannot hope to compete with this precocious child of the West." [68] And Eliot must have known that in 1868 the General Court had granted $75,000 to the Museum of Comparative Zoology.

Would Eliot carry the idea of state support, which he had known all his life, with him as president of Harvard, a post he attained in October, 1869? Only a few months before his election, he had stated some of his views in a series of articles in the *Atlantic Monthly* entitled "The New Education." In these articles Eliot had called for university studies and also for one of the principles on which M.I.T. had been founded, the independence of a technological institution from a college. Indeed, it looked as if Eliot was echoing the voices he had heard around him. But what of state support? The *Atlantic* articles were silent on the subject.

In his 1868 inaugural speech Eliot again made no mention of the state. But he did call for the overseers to assert "an attitude of suspicious vigilance" over the corporation. "Without the Overseers," Eliot pointed out, "the President and Fellows would be a board of private trustees, self-perpetuating and self-controlled. Provided as it is with two governing boards, the university enjoys that principal safeguard of all

68. Frederic Hedge, "University Reform, An Address to the Alumni of Harvard, at Their Triennial Festival," *Atlantic Monthly* 18 (July, 1866): 299. (Hedge was somewhat misinformed. The state of Michigan did not make an annual appropriation to the university until 1867.)

American governments — the natural antagonism between two bodies of different constitution, powers and privileges." [69] Harvard was not to be Columbia; Eliot did not announce himself as the protector of the corporate and independent power of the president and fellows.

So Eliot was installed; Caesar had entered Rome. Now that he held the throne, the new president appeared to be reversing himself and to be fashioning a new empire. Though Eliot had proclaimed in early 1869 the need for independent technical schools, he attempted in early 1870 to amalgamate M.I.T. with Harvard. As has been previously mentioned, President Rogers opposed this move in order to preserve that independence which the Harvard president had advocated only a year before. Eliot did not allow this defeat to stop him, however; in 1873 he reversed the history of both Massachusetts and Harvard and became the champion of the private university.

A proposal by the National Education Association to establish a national university supported largely by a federal endowment of $20 million triggered Eliot's stand. Like the presidents of midwestern colleges who feared the competition of state universities, some presidents of universities, both in the Midwest and the East, feared a national competitor.[70] But Eliot's invective against the national university delivered in an 1873 address before the NEA was so sweeping that it effectively negated any government support, federal or state, for higher education. Harvard's president exclaimed:

> Let us cling fast to the genuine American method — the old Massachusetts method — in the matter of public instruction. The essential features of that system are local taxes for elementary education, voted by the citizens themselves; local elective boards to spend the money raised by taxation and control the local schools; and, for

69. Charles William Eliot, *Educational Reform: Essays and Addresses* (New York, 1898), p. 28.

70. See David Madsen, *The National University* (Detroit, 1966), p. 67, for more on the 1873 proposal and Eliot's part in it.

the higher grades of instruction, permanent endowments administered by incorporated boards of trustees. This is the American voluntary system, in sharp contrast with the military, despotic organization of public instruction which prevails in Prussia and most other states of continental Europe. Both systems have peculiar advantages, the crowning advantage of the American method being that it breeds freemen.[71]

According to Eliot, the land-grant act of 1862 had been an unwise piece of legislation. "The fatal objection to this subsidizing process," he explained, "is that it saps the foundations of public liberty." [72] State support was inimical to the spirit of American freedom! Unlike his predecessors at Harvard, Eliot wanted to be in step with the "spirit of the age."

The president offered some practical considerations for opposing the university besides his appeal to the spirit of freedom. Frankly, he was suspicious of the ability of the federal government to administer any enterprise competently. Eliot explained:

> The president is to have the same salary as the Chief Justice of the United States, and the heads of the faculties are to have the salary of a Judge of the District Court of the United States. The places are desirable so far as pay, patronage and conspicuousness go, they would be desired by a great number of incompetent people, the more so because these eleven officers would never be brought, like a professor, to any public test of their capacity. There is no reason whatever to suppose that the appointments would be made on any better method than that which now prevails in the United States custom-houses and post-offices. We are disgracefully habituated to custom-house "rings," and post-office "rings"; last winter the papers talked of an agricultural college "ring." The

71. Charles William Eliot, "A National University," *Addresses and Proceedings of the National Education Association 1873* (Peoria, Ill., 1873), p. 119.
72. Ibid.

spectacle of a national university "ring" would be even less edifying.[73]

Rather than praise the largess of the proposed $1 million annual revenue for the university, Eliot commented:

> One million dollars is not a large estimate of the annual cost of the proposed university, considering the extreme wastefulness which characterizes most government expenditures. The private incorporated colleges and universities use their scanty reserves with the greatest possible thrift. Their example is a wholesome one. I fear that the example of a university which had one hand in the national treasury would not be salutary.[74]

Eliot was not alone in his distrust of the administrative abilities of government. Such a feeling had become prevalent during the Civil War and Reconstruction among men of Eliot's social and intellectual class. Disgusted at the inability of the army medical staff to care for the wounded during the war, prominent New Yorkers and Bostonians had formed the U.S. Sanitary Commission, a private organization that assumed the medical task at which the government had failed. Columbia's outspoken trustee George Templeton Strong was treasurer of this organization throughout the war. Harvard graduates dotted the membership roles.[75]

After the war, the record of the federal government in administering Indian agencies and the Freedmen's Bureau only helped to confirm the doubts about government which had arisen from the war. And this negative view of the federal government extended to state governments. According to Martin Anderson, president of the University of Rochester, "the literary managers of state institutions have been in a state of chronic trepidation lest their best efforts should be rendered nugatory by the caprices of unintelligent legisla-

73. Ibid., p. 111.
74. Ibid., p. 116.
75. See George M. Frederickson, *The Inner Civil War* (New York, 1965), pp. 98–112, for more on the U.S. Sanitary Commission.

tion." [76] Incompetent legislation was to be avoided as much as incompetent administration.

Despite these admonitions of governmental incompetence, many Americans of Eliot's day were stunned at the president's opposition to public support. At the 1874 session of the National Education Association (NEA) a series of rebuttals to Eliot's paper were delivered. Andrew D. White pointed out that the principle of private aid without state coordination had resulted in a hopeless scattering of resources and a bevy of mediocre sectarian colleges. He even doubted if a true university could arise without some form of public support. And far from alienating private support, public aid encouraged it: "The history of the private gifts to education crystallized about the various public gifts, and especially about that of 1862, shows that well-directed public bounty, like that of the general government in 1862, stimulates private bounty." [77] He cited his own Cornell as the prime example of this philosophy.

Eliot did not even attend the meeting at which White made his rebuttal. In a letter to the president of the NEA, Eliot wrote:

> I am afraid that my paper on a National University will have to take care of itself at Detroit. Most of the criticisms upon it which I have seen have been directed against my supposed opinions upon other subjects more or less remotely connected with the subject of a national university. My critics have inferred from my opinions that I must hold certain opinions obnoxious to them about compulsory education, or public schools, or State superintendency, or some other educational subject, upon which I have not expressed my opinions at all.[78]

76. Martin B. Anderson, "Voluntaryism in Higher Education," *Annual Report of the University of the State of New York 1875–1876* (Albany, 1877), p. 634.

77. Andrew D. White, "A National University," *Addresses and Proceedings of the National Education Association 1874* (Worcester, Mass., 1874), p. 69.

78. Ibid., p. 76.

If Eliot thought others had misinterpreted him, there was also reason to believe that he did not understand what *they* meant by public support. At the 1873 meeting, Eliot had announced that there were no state universities in the country. When asked about Wisconsin and Illinois, the president responded that to him "a real state university" was one "managed directly by the state and not through a close corporation provided by the state." [79] Possibly, Eliot had Germany too much on his mind and could not appreciate the existing American models.

Whether from unknowing, misunderstanding, or possibly complete comprehension, Eliot was as unimpressed with White's advice to combine public and private support as Columbia's trustees had been with the Cornell president's suggestion that they stimulate alumni giving. He had decided to build a university from private endowments, and he tenaciously clung to this idea.

So Eliot moved toward his goal with singleness of purpose. It is possible that the history of the college and state before the Civil War influenced such a straightforward course of action. Public aid had always come in erratic spurts. Often years of fruitless appeals were needed before a legislature suddenly showed a new interest in higher education. Such had clearly been the case in Massachusetts. In building his university, Eliot may well have thought it a waste of time to cajole and to persuade the legislature. Instead of mixing private and public aid, Eliot may have decided to gamble and to concentrate his appeals to one sector. The newly emerging fortunes of the industrial Northeast might well be easier to obtain than legislative appropriations. Possibly such singleness of purpose might induce the wealthy to contribute to an institution whose leader appeared to know what he wanted. [80]

---

79. *Addresses and Proceedings of the National Education Association 1873*, p. 131.

80. For the record, it is interesting to note the rise of Harvard's endowment. The first year after the Act of 1851 (1851–52) the endowment stood

Whatever his reasons, Eliot's achievement by 1898 was clear. With an endowment of $11,767,458, annual income totaling $1,396,109, 3,912 students (Harvard College 1,851; science 415; others 1,646), and a faculty composed of 466 members (134 professional grade, 277 other teachers and research fellows, and 55 other officers), Harvard was a major, if not the leading, university in the United States. Eliot had done what no one had imagined possible twenty-five years earlier. He had built a university, not a sectarian college, on the basis of private gifts. He had coordinated and concentrated wealth in one institution — a task that educators from Ezra Stiles to Andrew White had thought only the state could perform. Eliot had taken the place of the state.

In building Harvard and in turn creating the private university, it could be said that Eliot added a new dimension, a duality, to American higher education. Private as well as public support could produce a university. Eliot's position was given even more support by the foundation of Johns Hopkins, Clark, Stanford, and Chicago — all universities created by the largess of one individual. Would not the competition between the two kinds of institutions, state and private, for students and faculty produce a better educational system?

This may have been true. But there were disadvantages as well. In fostering the concept of dual institutions Eliot had polarized American higher education. Whereas a mixture of private and public money had not been unusual, Eliot had created a situation in which the two could no longer mix. And as the leading spokesman for private education, Eliot

---

at $888,611. By the year before alumni election (1864–65) it had risen to $1,898,618 — an absolute increase of $1,010,000 and a percentage increase of 113% over a thirteen-year period. In absolute terms, the endowment did not gain $1,010,000 for another ten years — 1874–75, $3,139,217. In percentage terms the endowment did not rise 113% for another fourteen years — 1879–80, $3,959,556. Thus the endowment did not grow more dramatically after alumni election than it had when the senate elected the overseers (*Harvard University Treasurer's Report[s]*).

pulled nearly all the institutions, particularly in the East, that were supported by large endowments into the private side — a position they might not have taken on their own. Ezra Cornell certainly had no objection to mixed institutions, and in 1898 Herbert Baxter Adams, professor of history at Johns Hopkins University, thought the state of Maryland should support the university that the gift of Johns Hopkins had launched. Such a proposition for a mixed institution would have sounded quite sensible in 1800, 1850, or 1865; by 1898 it was almost an impossibility. Cornell, not at all an unusual university when it was founded, was becoming an oddity by the turn of the century.

If Eliot's conception of the private university rejected the traditional idea of mixed support, it also rejected the eighteenth- and nineteenth-century theory of a necessary connection, a bond of faith, between college and state. It was necessary, educators had thought, "to cement a seat of learning with the public" in order both to gain public confidence in the college or university and to act as a constant reminder to the state of its need for educated leaders. If the government was not in some way connected with the institutions that produced educated leaders, the state as well as the college would deteriorate. Ezra Stiles had wanted Yale to retain its ecclesiastical character and had even thought that private endowments might provide sufficient income, but he had always recognized a mutual need for an alliance between college and state. Stiles might have cringed at Eliot's Harvard.

Could a university exist completely independent of the state? Would this not be the equivalent of pretending that the state and all civil government did not exist? Could a "private" university in any way fulfill its duty to the community, to the world? Eliot was confident that it could. And in his confidence the old Massachusetts method, the old American way, had been new made.

In following the rise of the private university, Eliot's new Rome, we have strayed from our story that ended in 1876, but not without purpose. The "private" way that was a well-known reality by 1898 had been only a newly voiced proposition as our story ended — a proposition espoused by the rearguard of American education, the denominational colleges, but also by the new president of America's oldest university. If one realizes that the "private" way, as *opposed* to the "public" or "quasi-public" way, was only a budding idea in 1876, then it should be easier to understand why a distinction between "private" and "public" did not exist in the century between 1776 and 1876. Few people perceived such a distinction or even considered that there was a necessity to conceive it.

With hindsight we can say that our "private" colleges were quasi-public institutions. But at the time, the two poles between which they took a "quasi" position did not really exist. It was assumed that all institutions would be connected in some way with both the state and private individuals. Yet the precise way in which the connection was made was not very important. Hence there was a variety of alliances, and a variety of changing alliances, between college and state. Before 1876 there were differences between the organization of the University of Michigan and of Harvard, but there were also differences between Harvard and Dartmouth. And the differences between Harvard and Dartmouth were probably as great as those between Harvard and Michigan. That all American colleges were not alike did not mean that they were basically different.

As long as the idea remained implicit that some bond between college and community should exist, the differences in the alliances were really insignificant. When Eliot turned a variety of alliances into two distinct categories, he also broke that bond of faith between college and state, a bond which many educators of the preceding century had thought was the underpinning of the institution's right to exist.

If the distinction between "private" and "public" was not clear before Eliot's ascension, I would also suggest that the sequence of events ending with the substitution of alumni for state officials at Yale and Harvard and with the momentary arrogance of Columbia's trustees did not necessarily herald the beginning of the "private way." This final chapter in college-state relations was really just another of the changing alliances between college and state. The state could have renewed its interest once again; the election of alumni did not signify the end of the alliance. Alumni also elected members of the governing boards of state universities.[81] As I have mentioned, this final form of the college-state alliance was a particularly useful foundation on which Eliot could base his private university. Still, it would be very difficult to assert that the emergence of the private university after 1876 was the logical outcome of the history of the preceding century.

In fact, toward the end of the nineteenth century, when the private way seemed secure, when both Dartmouth and Yale severed their land-grant connections, the old idea of a mixed college-state alliance came forward again. In 1893 the legislature of New Hampshire, upon the urging of Dartmouth President William Jewett Tucker, began financial grants to the college that continued until 1921. And in 1896 Columbia's trustees inscribed on the new Low Library that the college had been founded by the king and perpetuated by the people of the state of New York. Some of the strands of the private way were unraveling.

Though Eliot's way was not necessarily the logical outcome of the preceding history, there was nothing particularly illogical about this. Eliot had defied history. And that may well be the true American way. Goethe once mused in his poem "Den Vereinigten Staaten":

> Amerika, du hast est besser
> Als unser Kontinent, das alte,
> Hast keine verfallene Schlösser
> Und keine Basalte.
> Dich stort nich im Innern

---

81. Alumni elect trustees or regents at California, Indiana, New Hampshire, and Pennsylvania State.

Zu lebendiger Zeit
Unnützes Errinern
Und vergeblicher Streit.[82]

Cherishing their supposed freedom from a European past, Americans have also tried to free themselves from their own American past; they have always seem compelled, however, to create interpretations of history with which to defy that same history. If an outstanding part of the American tradition has been a defiance of tradition, then possibly that was the "old Massachusetts method" to which Eliot wanted to cling. And possibly the private university was just another example of the variety of alliances between college and state — no alliance at all.

82. Loosely translated:
America, you have it better
Than our continent, the old,
You have no ruined castles
And no basalt.
You do not disturb yourself inside
In this vital time
With unnecessary memories
And past strife.

An Essay on the Problem of Sources

Since I have made ample use of footnotes to direct the reader to sources on specific issues and have frequently devoted sections of the text to a discussion of bibliography, particularly with regard to the Dartmouth College decision, I will not attempt to repeat here what has already been said about sources. Rather, I would like to discuss some of the problems involved in compiling a list of references for the subject of the separation of college and state. First I will cover the colleges, and then the states.

Secondary Sources — Colleges

Although the literature on American educational history is vast (anyone interested in the full scope of it should consult Frederick Rudolph's excellent bibliography in *The American College and University* [New York, 1962]), there are particular problems in finding sources with extensive, or even reliable, information on the connection between institutions of higher education and state governments before 1876. At least two major problems bring about this situation:

1. Most secondary works were written after 1876 and tend to emphasize the college-state relationship which emerged after that date, to the point of reading such emphasis back into the pre-1876 history or overstating the importance of the roots for the future relationship. For example, historians of our "private" colleges often dwell on the lack of any state connection or on the inevitability of the separation of college and state. This obviously results in a belittling both of the role of the state before 1876 and of the colleges' desire for a state connection. Samuel Eliot Morison, *Three Centuries of Harvard* (Cambridge, 1936) is a notable example of this treat-

ment. One might almost think that Charles Eliot had commissioned this work!

On the other hand, historians of state institutions usually emphasize the abiding concern of the state and try to devalue the lack of public interest before the Civil War. For instance, one should compare the differing treatments of the role of the state of Michigan in Howard Peckham, *The Making of the University of Michigan* (Ann Arbor, 1967) and Andrew Ten Brook, *American State Universities* (Cincinnati, 1875). Ten Brook's work is particularly valuable because it is one of the few interpretative histories of American higher education written before the time that the distinction between "private" and "state" became clearly delineated. Thus he fully emphasizes the vague connection between many states and their supposed state universities.

The first chapter of Merle Curti and Vernon Carstensen, *The University of Wisconsin,* 2 vols. (Madison, 1949), "The Origins of the State University Idea," is an attempt to distinguish private from state institutions before the Civil War. The authors are careful to observe that the elements of the "state university idea," which they identify as "secularism, democracy, utilitarianism, and the imperatives of science in agriculture and industry," had not been fully realized in the western institutions by 1860. Yet they do not adequately discuss the fact that these same elements were also influencing the eastern institutions. Though these elements achieved fuller expression in the West after the Civil War, the paths of the private and the state institutions had not really divided as much in the 1840s and 1850s as Curti and Carstensen would have us believe.

There are some exceptions to my indictment of the modern historians' treatment of college-state relations. Both E. Merton Coulter, *College Life in the Old South,* 2d. ed. (Athens, 1951) and Daniel Walker Hollis, *The University of South Carolina,* 2 vols. (Columbia, 1951–56) have excellent chapters on the role of the state. I know of only one history of a private college in which the state is well-treated: Frederick Rudolph,

Mark Hopkins and the Log (New Haven, 1956). In this history of Williams College, chapter 12, "The Hand of the Commonwealth," provides a thorough analysis of the importance of state aid and attempts to explain why this aid ended.

2. Historians of higher education, and particularly of our colleges, tend to be uninterested in the antebellum history of the colleges, as opposed to their later university development. And if they do show an interest in the old college, their concern is usually with the internal affairs of the institution, such as curriculum and student life, rather than with the external affairs, such as a state connection.

George W. Pierson ably records the growth of Yale after 1871 in *Yale: College and University, 1871–1937*, 2 vols. (New Haven, 1952–55). Yale's history before 1871 has yet to be served by a modern chronicler. However, two forthcoming volumes, Brooks M. Kelley, *Yale: A History* (New Haven, 1974) and Richard Warch, *School of the Prophets: Yale College, 1701–1740* (New Haven, 1973), will soon fill this gap. The same holds true for Columbia. *The Bicentennial History of Columbia University*, 19 vols. (New York, 1954) includes a volume on Columbia College, Dwight C. Miner, ed. *Columbia College on Morningside* (New York, 1954), but only the history of the college after its move to Morningside Heights in the 1890s is treated there. Two earlier volumes by Frederick Keppel, *The History of Columbia* (New York, 1904) and *Columbia* (New York, 1914), also give only skimpy histories of the college before the Civil War. Even a sketch written in the 1840s by a president of the college, Nathaniel F. Moore, *The Origins and Early History of Columbia College* (New York, 1846), is of little value. Occasional articles in the *Columbia University Quarterly*, such as "The Riotous Commencement of 1811," vol. 2 (June 1901), are useful. But the *Quarterly* devotes most of its attention to Columbia as a university.

Harvard fares somewhat better than either Yale or Columbia. Samuel Eliot Morison does record the nineteenth-century history of Harvard in his *Three Centuries of Harvard* (Cambridge, 1936). However, only about one-third of the book is devoted to this era. Harvard is also served by two accounts written in the antebellum period. Josiah Quincy, *History of Harvard,* 2 vols. (Boston, 1840) is an excellent work, but the narrative ends with President Kirkland's retirement in 1826. Quincy did not choose to discuss his own administration. This is unfortunate and somewhat curious, as Quincy showed no reluctance to write about his term as mayor of Boston — along with his achievements and virtues — in his *A Municipal History of the Town and City of Boston* (Boston, 1852). Benjamin Pierce, *History of Harvard* (Boston, 1833) stops its record of Harvard with the American Revolution. Thus Morison's volume is the principal account of Harvard in the second and third quarters of the nineteenth century.

Dartmouth is the one college of our four whose history is thoroughly recorded: Leon Burr Richardson, *History of Dartmouth College,* 2 vols. (Hanover, 1932). Possibly the fact that Dartmouth never aspired to university status did not distract the author from the college's earlier history.

On a more general level, Richard Hofstadter's section, "The Age of the College," in Richard Hofstadter and Walter Metzger, *The Development of Academic Freedom in the United States* (New York, 1955) offers an excellent survey of many of the internal problems of the antebellum college but rarely touches the state relation. Only state intervention or interference with the internal affairs attracts Hofstadter's attention.

Primary Sources — Colleges
Trustees' Minutes

If the college-state relation has been overlooked or given the wrong emphasis in the general secondary literature, one would naturally resort to primary sources, particularly the minutes of the trustees of each college. Obviously, the trustees were most directly concerned with the problems of support and control. These sources vary in quality from college to college. The frequency of trustees' meetings and the details of those meetings which the men chose to record were not uniform.

The minutes of the Columbia trustees are the most informative. The trustees met at least twice a month and often weekly. They recorded seemingly all of their discussions, even those concerning resolutions and proposals they did not enact. Fortunately for the scholar who wants to use these minutes, a typed copy has been prepared and is housed in the Columbiana Library in Low Library.

In contrast to the Columbia documents, the minutes of the Yale Corporation are much less valuable. The trustees met only two or three times a year and seem to have recorded only those resolutions or actions they decided to put into effect. Moreover, the minutes include very little of the discussion that surrounded the proposals. At Yale the original minutes are available in Beinecke Library, and a microfilm copy is housed in the Historical Manuscripts Room of Sterling Library; a typescript of the minutes can be consulted in the Office of the Secretary.

The Harvard trustees (corporation) met frequently — about once a month. Though the corporation minutes often include discussions of the fellows' actions, the pages are amazingly silent on some issues. For instance, all that is mentioned about the reorganization of the board of overseers in 1851 or in 1865 is that the General Court passed legislation and that the corporation and the board of overseers accepted it. Though one has the double protection of having the minutes of both the corporation and the board of overseers, most of the actions of one board are recorded in the minutes of the other. Thus a double check rarely reveals additional information. The minutes of both the corporation and the board of overseers are housed in the University Archives in Widener library.

Though the Dartmouth trustees, like their Yale counterparts, met only a few times during the year, their minutes are very thorough, particularly during the years of the Dartmouth College case. The minutes can be found in the Dartmouth College Archives in Baker Library.

Diaries and Letter Collections

When the minutes fail to convey the intent and thinking of the trustees, diaries and letter collections of prominent members of the boards can often fill in the gaps. There are a number of such sources — some are published and others are still in manuscript form.

Columbia is best served in this respect. The diary of trustee George Templeton Strong is an invaluable guide to the motives and thinking of the Columbia trustees from 1850 until Strong's death in 1875. The complete manuscript version can be found in the Columbiana Library; an edited version appears as Allan Nevins, ed. *The Diary of George Templeton Strong,* 4 vols. (New York, 1952). The Hamilton Fish papers in Butler Library contain a number of letters touching on Fish's activities as a Columbia trustee in the 1850s and 1860s. The DeWitt Clinton papers, also in Butler Library, provide some information on Columbia in the 1810s. In addition to their diaries and letters, much information can be gleaned from the *Annual Report(s) of the University of the State of New York.* These have been published since 1828, and the Columbiana Library has a typed volume, "Extracts from the Reports of the University of the State of New York Relating to Columbia, 1788–1827," to supplement the published volumes. For the early years of the state university (1784–87), its minutes are identical to those of Columbia College. Franklin B. Hough, *Historical and Statistical Record of the University of the State of New York* (Albany, 1885) provides much information on the early years of Columbia.

The minutes of the Yale Corporation are ably complemented from 1775 to 1795 by Franklin B. Dexter, ed. *The Literary Diary of Ezra Stiles,* 3 vols. (New York, 1901). Unfortunately, I can find no comparable diary or letter collection of a Yale president or trustee for the nineteenth century. The most valuable source is Ebenezer Baldwin, *Annals of Yale College,* 2d ed. (New Haven, 1838).

Harvard is aided by the yet unpublished "Sibley's Private Journal," which can be found in the University Archives in Widener Library. John L. Sibley was the librarian of Harvard College and his diary covers the period from 1840 to 1880.

During the years of the Dartmouth College case, the Dartmouth minutes are complemented by a vast letter collection between trustees and their friends. Much advice was given! The collection is well indexed in the Dartmouth College Archives. Also, two valuable published works — John M. Shirley, *The Dartmouth College Causes* (St. Louis, 1879) and John K. Lord, *History of Dartmouth College* (Cambridge, 1913) — reprint much of this correspondence.

SECONDARY SOURCES — STATES

If the sources for college-state relations from the college view are sketchy, the view from the state level is even more so. Secondary material on state history is extremely poor, and particularly for our four states. I could not find a history of any of our states that could be considered an up-to-date general survey of state history. Occasionally a volume on a particular aspect of a state's history proved valuable. Maria Louise Green, *The Development of Religious Toleration in Connecticut* (Boston, 1905) provides a good survey of Yale and Connecticut from the 1790s to 1818. Otherwise one is limited to multivolume, encyclopedic histories of Connecticut. Works such as Harold J. Bingham, *History of Connecticut,* 4 vols. (New York, 1962) or N. G. Osborn, *History of Connecticut,* 6 vols. (New York, 1925) merely list the educational institutions in the state and give little interpretative history.

Oscar and Mary Handlin, *Commonwealth* (New York, 1947) is a valuable study of the role of state government in the economy of Massachusetts and touches on the history of education. I have already discussed its limitations in the latter respect.

Despite the lack or weakness of a general "state survey" literature, there is a series of volumes which treats the institutional development of higher education in our states. These works were published from 1887 to 1903 by the U.S. Bureau of Education as *Circulars of Information* under the general editorship of Herbert Baxter Adams. Notable volumes for our study are: B. C. Steiner, *History of Education in Connecticut* (Washington, 1893); Sidney Sherwood, *The University of the State of New York* (Washington, 1900); G. C. Bush, *History of Education in New Hampshire* (Washington, 1898); and G. C. Bush, *History of Higher Education in Massachusetts* (Washington, 1891). In addition to these specific state studies, Frank W. Blackmar, *The History of Federal and State Aid to Higher Education* (Washington, 1890) is valuable. Though all of these histories are informative as sources for facts and statistics — no small blessing — they tend to lack any interpretative perspective. Thus in Blackmar one finds that all four of our colleges received aid and how much, but not why the aid stopped or why it came at irregular intervals.

Three volumes in *Teachers College, Columbia University Contributions to Education* (New York, 1905–51) bear on our study: Lester William Bartlett, *State Control of Private Incorporated Institutions* (New York, 1926); Donald G. Tewksbury, *The Founding of American Colleges Before the Civil War* (New York, 1932); and William G. Stover, *Alumni Stimulation by the American College President* (New York, 1930). Tewksbury makes an attempt to discuss the public and private character of our colleges and of the state universities in his chapter 3, "The Founding of State Universities Before the Civil War," but he enforces a definition that a state university must have a state-appointed board of trustees. Hence, control becomes the principal distinction between private and public.

PRIMARY SOURCES — STATES
Governors' Messages

As with the colleges, one is driven to primary sources for state history because the secondary works are unsatisfactory. I found the one source of uniform quality for all the states to be the annual addresses of the governors to the legislatures. In these "state of the state" messages, higher education is usually mentioned. The governors were often quite specific in referring to particular institutions and the relation the state held to them. The governor's recommendations are much more informative than the legislative journals of the assemblies. These volumes tend to record only whether or not a particular bill affecting a college was passed.

The gubernatorial messages can be found in varying forms of publication. The messages of New York's governors, beginning with George Clinton, have been collected and published in a multivolume series, Charles Z. Lincoln, ed., *Messages from the Governors of New York,* 11 vols. (Albany, 1909). For Connecticut and New Hampshire the messages can be found as part of the published legislative journals. The messages for Massachusetts' governors have been published as individual pamphlets bearing the title (varying from governor to governor) *Address of His Excellency (name) to Both Branches of the Legislature (date).* These messages have not been collected in any series of volumes.

Committee Reports

Other valuable sources for the state view of higher education are the reports of legislative committees assigned to study the petitions and requests of colleges. Often these documents are very thorough and begin with a review of the history of the relations between a particular college and the state. Some of these documents were published for general distribution while others appear to have been printed for the convenience of the legislature.

A few of the more informative reports for our colleges are:

COLUMBIA

Report of the Select Committee Appointed to Examine into the Affairs of Columbia College (1855)

HARVARD

Report upon the Constitutional Rights and Privileges of Harvard College: and Upon the Donations that have been Made to it by this Commonwealth (1821)
Report on State Aid to Colleges (1848)
Report of the Joint Standing Committee on Education (1849)
Report to Consider and Report what Legislation if any is Necessary to Render Harvard more Beneficial to all the People of the Commonwealth (1850)
Senate Report on the Separation of College and State (1854)

YALE

Report of the Committee to whom was referred the Memorial of the President and Fellows of Yale College (1822)

DARTMOUTH

Documents Relative to Dartmouth College Published by the Legislature (1816).

Copies of these pamphlets can be found under the above titles in the archives of the respective colleges.

Thus the job of compiling a body of sources for college-state relations is a complex task. The body of standard secondary works is either nonexistent or tends to give the wrong emphasis to the relationship because of its later development. The primary sources lack uniformity of quality and of coverage from year to year and from college to college. Hence, one is forced to piece together snippets of information from diverse sources. Like the task of reconstructing a dinosaur when many of the bones are missing, often a certain amount of guessing is involved. For example, if the history of Williams has been more ably recorded than that of Harvard, can we guess that the state connection to Williams was similar to that of Harvard? Or to what extent can we guess that it was different?

A complete list of sources — primary and secondary — in which these "snippets" might appear would be encyclopedic. Almost any book or set of documents touching on the social, economic, religious, intellectual, or political history of any of our states over the hundred-year period could deal with the college-state relation. Similarly, the list could include all works on the men connected with state governments or with the colleges. Someday I would like to be able to compile as thorough a list of sources for public aid to higher education as Merle Curti has done for philanthropic aid, in his *Philanthropy in the Shaping of Higher Education* (New Brunswick, N.J.: Rutgers Press, 1965). For now, I will merely suggest that many paths must be followed to accomplish this task.

Index

Mathews, James, 103*n*
Maxwell, Hugh, 103*n*
Mercantile Library Association, 105
Merrimac Confederation of Congregational Churches (New Hampshire), 176
Merrill, Payson, 214*n*
Methodists, 42, 136
Miami University (Ohio), 49
Michigan General Assembly, 134, 136
Michigan State University, 190
Miner, Dwight C.: on Columbia, 10, 30
Ministers: as college trustees, 13, 16, 39–40, 51, 114, 198–99, 210–11; as fund-raisers, 197
Missouri General Assembly, 134
Moor's Charity School, 15
Morril, David, 80
Morrill, Justin, 179
Morrill Act: passage, 179–80; Daniel Coit Gilman on, 180; social effects, 198; Charles Eliot on, 232. *See also* Land-grant colleges
Morton, Marcus, 118
Motley, John Lothrop, 100, 119–20
Muzzey, Artemas, 201

Nash, Stephen, 220
National Education Association, 231, 234
National university, 49–50, 231–33
Nativism, in Massachusetts, 158
New Connecticut, 33
New Hampshire College of Agriculture, 184
New Hampshire General Court: financial grants to Dartmouth, 35, 239; land grants to Dartmouth, 35, 183–84; alterations in charter of Dartmouth college, 62, 65; reaction to case of *Trustees* v. *Woodward*, 78–80
New Hampshire Literary Fund, 78, 79
New Hampshire Superior Court, 65, 72

New Hampshire University. *See* University of New Hampshire
New York Asylum for Deaf and Dumb, 166
New York City: as a political center, 30; relations with Columbia College, 105–07; philanthropy in, 170
New York Free Academy, 169
New York General Assembly: financial grants to Columbia, 14, 24, 27; reorganizations of Columbia, 21–22; financial grants to common schools, 24–26; financial grants to colleges other than Columbia, 24, 108, 119; land grants to Columbia, 25–26; land grants to colleges other than Columbia, 25, 188–89; stipulations for college charters by, 103; refusals of aid to Columbia, 108, 169; investigation of Columbia Board of Trustees, 161–64
New York Public School Society, 105
New York University. *See* University of the City of New York
Niles, Nathaniel, 54
Nocturnal Stellegeri, 39
North American Review, on *Trustees* v. *Woodward*, 83, 84
Northwest Ordinance of *1787*, 49*n*
Northwest territory: universities in, 49
Norton, William A., 172

Obligation of contracts, 67, 72, 75. *See also* Contracts
Ogden, Gouverneur, 219, 222
Ohio Company of Associates, 49
Ohio University, 49
Olcott, Mills, 77
Origin of American State Universities, The, 85–86
Ovid Agricultural College (New York), 188
Oxford, University of, 69

Parsons, Theophilus, 18
Party politics: effects on colleges, 18–21, 151, 232–33